Exploring the Intersection of Islāmic Spirituality and Psychotherapy

G. Hussein Rassool

Exploring the Intersection of Islāmic Spirituality and Psychotherapy

Healing the Soul

Springer

G. Hussein Rassool
Centre for Islāmic Studies and Civilisations
Charles Sturt University
North Parramatta, NSW, Australia

ISBN 978-3-031-72723-8 ISBN 978-3-031-72724-5 (eBook)
https://doi.org/10.1007/978-3-031-72724-5

This Springer imprint is published by the registered company Springer Nature Switzerland AG
The registered company address is: Gewerbestrasse 11, 6330 Cham, Switzerland

Dedicated to Idrees Khattab Rassool Ibn Adam Ibn Hussein Ibn Hassim Ibn Sahaduth Ibn Rosool Ibn Olee Al Mauritiusy.

Preface

The intersection of Islāmic spirituality and psychotherapy is a rich, yet often under-explored, domain. The purpose of this book is to examine this intersection, examining how Islāmic principles can be integrated into therapeutic practices to foster mental, emotional, and spiritual health. Through a comprehensive exploration of Islāmic teachings and contemporary psychological theories, this book aims to offer valuable insights for both practitioners and students of Islāmic psychotherapy. In **Chap.** 1, the focus is on the convergence of Islāmic spirituality and psychotherapy, setting the stage by discussing the contextual backdrop and defining key terms. We explore the concept of "soulless psychology" and introduce spiritually integrative psychotherapy, offering an Islāmic perspective on spirituality and religiosity. This chapter highlights the importance of a holistic approach that includes spiritual dimensions in psychological practice. **Chapter** 2 focuses on monotheism as the foundation of Islāmic psychotherapy. It identifies the criteria for authentic Islāmic psychotherapy, emphasising alignment with the monotheism and the Six Articles of Faith. This chapter also discusses the sources and integration of knowledge, highlighting the *Tawhîd* paradigm as central to Islāmic therapeutic approaches. Through this foundation, we aim to establish a robust framework for Islāmic psychotherapy. **Chapter** 3 addresses the critical task of decolonising psychological knowledge. It examines the Islāmic awakening and the globalisation of psychological knowledge, advocating for the integration of Islāmic spirituality into psychological practices. This chapter challenges the prevailing Western-centric paradigms and promotes a more inclusive and culturally relevant approach to psychology.

In **Chapter** 4, we examine the anatomy of Islāmic psychotherapy and focus the mental health and spirituality of Muslims, the core elements and characteristics of the Islāmic worldview, and the epistemological, ontological, and axiological underpinnings of Islāmic psychotherapy. By analysing these elements, we aim to provide a comprehensive understanding of the principles and practices that define Islāmic psychotherapy. **Chapter** 5 explores the concept of *fitrah*, the spiritual nature of human behaviour. Through Qur'ânic and *hadīth* explanations, scholars' perspectives, and empirical studies, we examine the characteristics, alienation, corruption, and restoration of the *fitrah*. This chapter emphasises the importance of aligning therapeutic practices with the innate spiritual nature of individuals.

Chapter 6 explores the psychology of the soul, focusing on the *nafs* and the *rûh*. We explore the concept and explanations of the *nafs*, including Al-Ghazālī's perspectives and the different levels of the self. Additionally, we discuss the *rûh* and its relationship with the *nafs*, providing an enlightened understanding of the self in Islāmic psychology. **Chapter** 7 continues the exploration of the self, focusing on the qalb and the *'aql*. Through the perspectives of Ibn Al-Qayyim, Qur'ânic verses, *hadīths*, and scholarly views, we examine the different types of hearts, their trials and tribulations, and the concept of 'aql (intellect). This chapter highlights the interrelationship between the *qalb*, *'aql,* and *nafs*, offering a holistic view of the self in Islāmic psychology.

Chapter 8, we analyse various psychological approaches and their congruence or dissonance with Islāmic spirituality. We provide overviews of psychoanalytic therapy, client-centred therapy, and cognitive-behavioural therapy, discussing their alignment or conflict with Islāmic beliefs. This chapter aims to identify therapeutic approaches that resonate with Islāmic values and principles. **Chapter** 9 focuses on post-modern therapies and their compatibility with Islāmic spirituality. We explore solution-focused brief therapy, narrative therapy, and hope therapy, examining their congruence or dissonance with Islāmic beliefs. This chapter introduces Islāmic adaptations of these therapies, offering culturally and spiritually relevant approaches for Muslim clients. **Chapter** 10 examines the relationship between emotion and mental health from an Islāmic perspective. We discuss the Qur'ânic and *hadīth* views on emotional behaviours and regulation, highlighting the Islāmic foundations of healing. This chapter aims to integrate emotional and spiritual dimensions in therapeutic practices, promoting holistic healing. **Chapter** 11 explores the healing power of compassion (*rahmah*), forgiveness (*istighfar*), gratitude (*shukr*), hope (*raja*), and patience (*sabr*). We discuss Islāmic models and processes for integrating these virtues into psychotherapy, emphasising their therapeutic benefits and alignment with Islāmic teachings. **Chapter** 12 synthesises and consolidates the themes discussed throughout the book. We reflect on the integration of Islāmic spirituality in psychotherapy, providing practical strategies and tools for Islāmic psychotherapists. This final chapter aims to inspire a transformative journey, encouraging practitioners to embrace a spiritually integrated approach to psychological health.

This book is a humble effort to bridge the gap between Islāmic spirituality and psychotherapy, offering insights and guidance for those seeking to integrate these domains. It is my sincere hope that this work will serve as a valuable resource for practitioners, scholars, and students, fostering a deeper understanding and appreciation of Islāmic psychotherapy.

North Parramatta, NSW, Australia G. Hussein Rassool

Acknowledgements

All praise is due to Allāh and may the peace and blessings of Allāh be upon our Prophet Muhammad (ﷺ) his family and his companions.

I extend my heartfelt thanks to Bruno Fiuza, Editor of Behavioural, Health and Social Sciences at Springer, for commissioning this book. I am deeply grateful to the past and current students of the following courses at Al-Balagh Academy: Islāmic Counselling and Psychology (Level 2), Addiction Counselling and Islāmic Psychology, Islāmic Marriage Counselling, and Mental Health, *Jinn* Possession, and Islāmic Psychology. Their dedication to learning and exploring the intricacies of Islāmic psychotherapy and counselling has profoundly shaped my knowledge and skills in this domain.

I owe immense gratitude to my beloved parents, who instilled in me the value of education. Their unwavering love and guidance have been fundamental in shaping who I am today, and I am truly thankful for their wisdom and encouragement. I am deeply grateful for the unwavering love and support of Mariam, Idrees Khattab Ibn Adam Ali Hussein Ibn Hussein Ibn Hassim Ibn Sahaduth Ibn Rosool Al Mauritiusy, Adam Ali Hussein, Nabila Akhrif, Reshad Hasan, Fatima Ezzahra Bennaoui, Yasmin Soraya, Isra Oya, Asiyah Maryam, Nusaybah Burke, Musa Burke, Dr Najmul Hussein, and Mohammed Ali. Their presence in my life is a blessing, and I am forever indebted to them for their love, support, and inspiration.

I also wish to acknowledge the invaluable contributions of my teachers, who have played a crucial role in deepening my understanding of authentic Islām. Through their guidance and teachings, I have been able to follow the Creed of *Ahlus-Sunnah wa'l-Jamaa'ah*. I sincerely pray to Allāh to forgive me and accept my humble effort in writing this book. May He make it a source of benefit and fruitfulness for all those who find it useful and informative. I pray to Allāh to forgive me for any unintentional shortcomings in this book and to make this effort helpful and fruitful to any interested parties. May this book serve as a means of guidance and understanding for those who seek knowledge and insight. Finally, whatever benefits and correctness you find within this book are by the Grace of Allāh alone, and any mistakes are mine alone. May this book serve as a means of guidance and understanding for those who seek knowledge and insight. Finally, whatever benefits and correctness you find within this book are out of the Grace of Allāh, alone, and whatever mistakes you find are mine alone.

مَّآ أَصَابَكَ مِنْ حَسَنَةٍ فَمِنَ ٱللَّهِ ۖ وَمَآ أَصَابَكَ مِن سَيِّئَةٍ فَمِن نَّفْسِكَ

- *Whatever of good befalls you, it is from Allāh; and whatever of ill befalls you, it is from yourself.* (An-Nisā' 4:79, interpretation of the meaning).

بسم الله الرحمن الرحيم

Praise be to Allāh, we seek His help and His forgiveness. We seek refuge with Allāh from the evil of our own souls and from our bad deeds. Whomsoever Allāh guides will never be led astray, and whomsoever Allāh leaves astray, no one can guide. I bear witness that there is no god but Allāh, and I bear witness that Muhammad is His slave and Messenger (*Sunan al-Nasa'i: Kitaab al-Jumu'ah, Baab kayfiyyah al-khutbah*).

- *Fear Allāh as He should be feared and die not except in a state of Islām (as Muslims) with complete submission to Allāh* (Ali-'Imran 3:102, interpretation of the meaning).[1]
- *O mankind! Be dutiful to your Lord, Who created you from a single person, and from him He created his wife, and from them both He created many men and women, and fear Allāh through Whom you demand your mutual (rights), and (do not cut the relations of) the wombs (kinship) Surely, Allāh is Ever an All-Watcher over you* (Al-Nisā' 4:1, interpretation of the meaning).
- *O you who believe! Keep your duty to Allāh and fear Him and speak (always) the truth* (Al-Aĥzāb, interpretation of the meaning 33:70).
- *What comes to you of good is from Allāh, but what comes to you of evil, [O man], is from yourself.* (An-Nisā 4:79, interpretation of the meaning).

The essence of this book is based on the following notions:

- The foundation of Islām as a religion is based on the Oneness of God.
- The source of knowledge is based on the Qur'ān and Hadith (*Ahl as-Sunnah wa'l-Jamā'ah*).

[1] The translations of the meanings of the verses of the Qur'ān in this book have been taken from Saheeh International, The Qur'ān: Arabic Text with corresponding English meanings.

- Empirical knowledge from sense perception is also a source of knowledge through the work of classical and contemporary Islāmic scholars and research.
- Islām takes a holistic approach to health: physical, psychological, social, emotional, and spiritual health cannot be separated.
- Muslims have an Islāmic or Qur'ânic worldview different from the Western-oriented worldview.
- It is a sign of respect that Muslims would utter or repeat the words "Peace and Blessing Be Upon Him" after hearing (or writing) the name of Prophet Muhammad (ﷺ).

Contents

List of Figures

List of Tables

Chapter 1
Navigating the Intersection: Islāmic Spirituality and Psychotherapy

1.1 Introduction and Context

In our contemporary, ever more diverse and interwoven global landscape, mental health practitioners are tasked with delivering care that is culturally responsive to the distinct needs of varied ethnocultural and religious communities. The consequences of civil war, crisis situations, genocide, Islāmophobia, microaggressions, and prejudice can all contribute to an increase in the prevalence of mental health and psycho-spiritual problems among Muslims (El-Khani et al., 2016; Hwang & Goto, 2008; Khan, 2021; Kira et al., 2014; Sue et al., 2007). For instance, Islāmophobia can also contribute to internalised stigma and self-hatred among Muslims, exacerbating mental health issues. Research evidence suggests that experiences of discrimination and life stressors are associated with negative mental-health outcomes for Muslim populations in Western countries (Kathawalla & Syed, 2021); and the marginalisation and "othering" experienced by Muslim Americans have led to a range of adverse psychological symptoms, including feelings of fear, stress, worry, isolation, numbness, desensitisation, and insecurity (Areeza, 2017). Exposure to traumatic events, such as war, conflict, displacement, or natural disasters, can have profound psychological effects on individuals. The traumatic experiences faced by refugee families during war, displacement, and resettlement have significant impacts on child development. Both parents and children are at heightened risk of experiencing mental health issues as a consequence of these traumatic events, manifested as psychopathology and psychosomatic symptoms (Hazer & Gredebäck, 2023). Trauma can lead to conditions such as post-traumatic stress disorder (PTSD), depression, anxiety, and substance use disorder, somatisation with chronic pain, dissociation, psychosocial dysfunctions, and suicidal behaviour (Rozanov et al., 2019). Many Muslims around the world have experienced or been affected by traumatic events, which can have long-lasting effects on their mental health and well-being. Understanding the unique challenges faced by Muslims is essential for mental health professionals seeking to provide effective and culturally competent care (Table 1.1).

G. H. Rassool, *Exploring the Intersection of Islāmic Spirituality and Psychotherapy*,
https://doi.org/10.1007/978-3-031-72724-5_1

The Pew-Templeton Global Religious Future Project (2020) found that over 80% of the world's population identifies with a religion. Spirituality holds profound significance in the lives of many Muslims, providing a framework for understanding the world, finding purpose, and coping with life's challenges. Islāmic teachings emphasise the interconnectedness of the spiritual, psychological, and physical dimensions of human existence, promoting balance and harmony in all aspects of life. In times of adversity, such as facing mental health issues, spirituality often serves as a source of strength and guidance for Muslims. Islāmic practices like prayer (*salah*), recitation of the Qur'ân, supplication (*dua'h*), and remembrance of God (*dhikr*) are not only acts of worship but also means of seeking solace, peace, and healing. These practices instil a sense of connection with the Divine and provide comfort during difficult times. However, despite the intrinsic link between spirituality and mental health, there has historically been a gap in mental health services that adequately integrate spiritual dimensions. Traditional therapeutic approaches may overlook or neglect the spiritual needs of Muslims, leading to a disconnect between their faith and their mental health care. In response to this gap, there has been a growing demand among Muslims for therapy that acknowledges and integrates spirituality into the healing process. This approach recognises that mental health is not solely a medical or psychological issue but also a spiritual one. Integrating spirituality into therapy allows individuals to draw upon their faith as a source of resilience, coping mechanisms, and inner strength. In addition, integrating spirituality into therapy can facilitate a holistic approach to mental health care, addressing the interconnectedness of the mind, body, and spirit. This chapter explores the complex interplay between Islāmic spirituality and psychotherapy,

1.2 Spirituality, Psychology, and Psychotherapy

Spirituality and psychology are two domains often viewed as distinct, with spirituality pertaining to personal beliefs and existential questions, and psychotherapy focusing on mental and emotional health. Historically, organised religion has played a significant role in the development of psychotherapy and counselling. In the Judeo-Christian and Islāmic traditions, spirituality, informal counselling, and guidance shared a common purpose of caring for the souls of individuals. However, the rise of "soulless" psychology in the nineteenth century stemmed from the adoption of the positivist Western scientific paradigm. According to Halmos (1965), religious faith was gradually replaced by a set of beliefs and values termed the "faith of the counsellors". Halmos's assertion that religious faith was gradually replaced by what he terms the "faith of the counsellors" reflects an intriguing perspective on the evolution of psychotherapy and counselling. This suggests a transition from reliance on religious principles and beliefs to a more secular framework within the field of counselling. It implies that therapist may adhere to a distinct set of values and beliefs, possibly influenced by psychological theories and methodologies, rather than traditional religious doctrines. This concept raises questions about the role of spirituality and faith in contemporary counselling practice and highlights the ongoing debate surrounding the integration of spirituality and secular approaches in therapy.

The integration of spirituality and psychotherapy has deep roots in both psychological and spiritual traditions. Early pioneers like Carl Jung highlighted the importance of spirituality in understanding the human psyche. Jung's concept of individuation involves integrating the conscious and unconscious aspects of the self, often incorporating spiritual experiences and symbols. Jung argued that humans possess an innate religious inclination, with the "religious function" being as potent and essential as the instincts for sex or aggression (Ellenberger, 2018; Jung, 2013). Jung believed that religion aids not only in surviving difficult situations but also in personality development and the lifelong process of individuation. Existential psychology, as exemplified by Viktor Frankl (1963) and Rollo May (1983), emphasises the search for meaning as a fundamental human drive. Frankl's logotherapy asserts that finding meaning in suffering is crucial for psychological health, intrinsically recognising the spiritual dimension of human existence. Fromm, a humanistic philosopher and psychologist, had a distinctive perspective on spirituality. Fromm believed in the need to spiritualise psychoanalysis in the mid-twentieth century. This belief stemmed from his recognition of the significant role a person's cultural and spiritual condition plays (Araullo, 2010).

Fromm's attempt to integrate spirituality into psychoanalysis is known as the "Psycho-Spiritual Discourse", focusing on the realisation of humanity within individuals. Fromm's spiritual perspective is rooted in humanistic principles. Fromm (1950) examines the relationship between psychological principles and religious beliefs, exploring how they intersect and influence each other. He offers insights into how spirituality can inform psychological understanding and vice versa, shedding light on the complex interplay between these two domains of human experiences. He sees spirituality as vital for personal transformation, advocating for love, faith, and self-realisation in relationships and individual growth. His approach transcends distinctions between theistic and non-theistic religions, focusing on the interconnectedness of individuals. In contemporary psychotherapy, transpersonal psychology stands out for its explicit integration of spiritual elements. This approach expands beyond the individual self to encompass spiritual experiences and higher states of consciousness as essential aspects of human development. Wilber (2000) discusses the integration of spirituality into psychology, providing insights into transpersonal psychology's perspective on human development and therapy.

A growing body of research and clinical practice demonstrates the potential benefits of integrating spirituality into psychotherapeutic practices Religious involvement has often been linked to improved well-being and mental health outcomes, as supported by various studies (Cornish & Wade, 2010; Cotton et al., 2007; Johnstone et al., 2012; Oman & Syme, 2018; Park et al., 2016). Additionally, in psychotherapeutic practice, spirituality has been recognised as a significant factor influencing client outcomes. Pargament (2011) emphasises how integrating spirituality can lead to better therapeutic outcomes by addressing clients' spiritual needs, thus enhancing resilience and overall mental health. Spiritual practices like prayer, meditation, and religious rituals can offer clients additional coping mechanisms and a deeper sense of purpose. There is evidence to indicate a positive correlation between spirituality and improved mental health outcomes and that religious and spiritual practices are associated with lower levels of depression, anxiety, and addiction (Koenig, 2012). However, there is a noted limitation in understanding how spirituality can be effectively applied in clinical settings to enhance positive psychosocial outcomes for clients (Blando, 2006).

1.3 Soulless Psychology

Freud and Skinner, both influential figures in the development of psychology as a science, had critical views on religion. Freud (1961) saw religion as an illusion, a means for people to cope with the harsh realities of life. He believed that religious beliefs were a way for individuals to avoid confronting their unconscious fears and desires, describing religion as a collective neurosis. Similarly, Skinner (1971) viewed religion through a behaviourist lens, considering it a form of social control that reinforced certain behaviours and discouraged others, without empirical evidence to support its claims. Both formative leaders aimed to establish psychology firmly on solid scientific principles and empirical evidence. In the context of mainstream psychotherapy and counselling, there is widespread dissatisfaction with secular psychology, often labelled as "soulless" psychology or lacking a spiritual dimension (Rassool, 2025). The term "soulless psychology" suggests a critique of modern psychological practices and theories that exclude spiritual dimensions. This criticism is particularly notable given that the term "psychology" historically implies the study of the soul or spirit. Spirituality, religious experiences, and ethical behaviours hold significant importance that go beyond what is typically examined in Western scientific approaches to psychology. This alienation of the spiritual or religious dimensions within the paradigm of "soulless" psychology means that "religious ideas, practice, and organisations lose their influence in the face of scientific and other knowledge" (McLeish, 1995, p. 668).

The established contemporary psychotherapy and counselling have primarily been shaped by Eurocentric and Orientalist perspectives, which favour Western cultures and worldviews. This bias often fails to adequately address the diverse experiences and cultural contexts of individuals from non-Western backgrounds. Such ethnocentric approaches are criticised for stigmatising and marginalising both individuals and entire cultural groups (Charema & Shizha, 2008). The limitations of the Eurocentric and Orientalist approach to psychotherapy are particularly evident when working with Muslim clients. These clients have religious and cultural values, beliefs, and practices that significantly shape their perceptions of mental health. Ignoring these aspects can undermine the effectiveness and relevance of traditional therapy for spiritually oriented clients. The traditional secular psychotherapeutic approach may be limiting, as it often fails to fully grasp the complexity of human behaviours and experiences. Individuals with strong religious beliefs, such as

Muslims, often encounter a disconnection between their worldview and the secular methods used in mainstream psychotherapy. This dissonance highlights the need for a psychologically informed approach that integrates Islāmic traditions and principles, leading to the revival of *Ilm an-nafs* (the knowledge of the self) (Rassool, 2025).

Pargament (2011) observed that individuals are not just psychological, social, and physical beings but also spiritual beings. When seeking therapy, people bring their spiritual beliefs, practices, experiences, values, relationships, and struggles with them into the therapeutic process. These spiritual factors implicitly or explicitly influence the course of psychotherapy. This statement highlights the holistic dimension of human beings and the importance of recognising spirituality in the therapeutic process. It acknowledges that individuals bring their spiritual dimensions into therapy, which can profoundly influence their experiences, values, and struggles. By acknowledging and addressing these spiritual aspects, therapists can provide more comprehensive and effective care, attending to the whole person rather than just isolated and disconnected aspects of their being. This approach promotes greater understanding, validation, and integration of spirituality within the therapeutic context, ultimately fostering deeper healing and growth for clients.

1.4 Spiritually Integrative Psychotherapy

Spiritually Integrated Psychotherapy is an approach that embeds spiritual dimensions into the therapeutic process, recognising the significant role spirituality can play in an individual's mental health. This method acknowledges the intrinsic human need for meaning, connection, and transcendence, and integrates these elements into conventional psychotherapeutic practices. Sperry (2013) offers a valuable perspective on spiritually integrative therapy, stating that

> Spiritually integrated psychotherapy is a term that broadly characterises a variety of psychotherapeutic approaches that are sensitive to the spiritual dimension. These approaches range from non-Christian approaches and transpersonal psychotherapies . . . to theistic . . . and various Christian approaches . . . and evidence-based religious accommodative forms of psychotherapy. . . . Individuals seeking explicitly spiritually integrated psychotherapy range from relatively healthy spiritual seekers to disordered clients presenting with symptomatic distress or impairment in one or more areas of life functioning . . . spiritually integrated psychotherapy is distinct from pastoral counselling and spiritual direction in its emphasis and treatment focus. It draws on spiritual resources in addressing spiritual issues and struggles to resolve psychological and relational problems. Although it can also foster spiritual change and growth, spiritually integrated psychotherapy accomplishes this as a by-product that accompanies psychological change. (p. 227)

Sperry (2013) provides a comprehensive definition of spiritually integrated psychotherapy, describing it as a broad term that encompasses various psychotherapeutic approaches attuned to the spiritual dimension. These approaches can include non-Christian and transpersonal psychotherapies, theistic methods, and diverse Christian approaches, as well as evidence-based religious accommodative forms of psychotherapy. The approach is designed to address a broad audience, from healthy spiritual seekers to individuals experiencing significant psychological distress. It distinguishes itself from pastoral counselling and spiritual direction by focusing primarily on resolving psychological and relational problems through the incorporation of spiritual resources. Sperry's definition of spiritually integrative therapy highlights the valuable role that spiritual resources can play in the therapeutic process, promoting not only psychological and relational healing but also facilitating spiritual growth as a by-product of effective therapy. This integrative approach ensures that therapy addresses the whole person, acknowledging the interplay between psychological, relational, and spiritual dimensions of well-being.

Spiritually integrative psychotherapy has been incorporated into various mainstream therapeutic traditions, offering a holistic approach that acknowledges and incorporates the spiritual dimension of human experience. In spiritually integrated CBT, therapists may include spiritual beliefs and practices as part of cognitive restructuring and behavioural interventions (Richards & Bergin, 2005, 2014). This can involve using spiritual texts or principles to challenge irrational beliefs and incorporating spiritual rituals to reinforce positive behaviours. Gestalt therapy's focus on present-moment awareness and personal responsibility can be enriched with spiritual practices like mindfulness and meditation (Sperry & Shafranske, 2005). This enables clients to achieve greater self-awareness and inner peace through spiritual reflection. Spiritually integrated interpersonal therapy might explore the role of spirituality in clients' relationships and social interactions, addressing how spiritual beliefs influence their communication patterns and relational dynamics (Richards & Bergin, 2014). The humanistic therapy emphasises personal growth and self-actualisation, which can incorporate spiritual exploration as a pathway to achieving a deeper sense of meaning and purpose in life, often involving practices that enhance spiritual awareness and connection (Richards & Bergin, 2005, 2014). Jungian therapy, with its inherent interest in the collective unconscious and archetypes, naturally aligns with spiritual themes (Sperry & Shafranske, 2005). Therapists may engage with clients' spiritual symbols and dreams to facilitate deeper understanding and integration of the self.

In multicultural therapy, recognising and respecting clients' diverse spiritual backgrounds and practices are critical (Richards & Bergin, 2005, 2014).Therapists integrate spirituality by being culturally competent and sensitive to the spiritual traditions that influence clients' worldviews and experiences. Spiritually integrated psychodynamic therapy may involve exploring the spiritual dimensions of the unconscious mind, examining how spiritual beliefs and experiences shape clients' internal conflicts, defences, and overall psychological development (Sperry & Shafranske, 2005). In Rational-Emotive Behaviour Therapy (REBT), therapists might incorporate spiritual beliefs as part of disputing irrational beliefs, helping clients to use their spiritual values to challenge and replace dysfunctional thoughts and behaviours with more constructive and spiritually aligned ones (Richards & Bergin, 2005, 2014). Transpersonal therapy includes spiritual and transcendent experiences as central to the therapeutic process (Richards & Bergin, 2005, 2014). Techniques may involve meditation, guided visualisation, and other spiritual practices aimed at facilitating higher states of consciousness and personal transformation. Narrative therapy, a post-modern approach, posits that people understand their lives through the stories they create. For spiritually oriented individuals, couples, and families, spirituality plays an active role in shaping these life stories, contributing to their understanding of life (Akbulut, 2020). Patient-centred mindfulness involves the use of mindfulness and other meditation methods that are based on the patient's own faith tradition, rather than applying Eastern forms of mindfulness (Koenig, 2023). Koenig claims these are a secular approach appropriate for everyone regardless of religious beliefs, even if those beliefs are not consistent with the Buddhist religious or philosophical approach.

These approaches have been applied to diverse client populations and clinical issues and used with adherents of major world religions such as Buddhism, Christianity, Islām, and Judaism (Richards & Bergin, 2014; Richards et al., 2023; Sperry & Shafranske, 2005). By integrating spirituality into these various therapeutic frameworks, therapists can provide more holistic and culturally sensitive care (Alexander et al., 2021) that respects and utilises clients' spiritual resources for healing and growth. It is important to note that the integration of spirituality into psychotherapy does not involve preaching or steering clients towards or away from specific religious or spiritual beliefs, which would be unethical (Richards et al., 2023). Instead, it emphasises respecting the client's spiritual orientation and supporting their right to make informed decisions about psychospiritual matters.

1.5 Spirituality and Religiosity: An Islāmic Perspective

There has been a longstanding dichotomy between religion and mental health. Unexplained religious phenomena, such as spiritual experiences and possession syndrome, have often been labelled as psychotic disorders (Rassool, 2019). Freud (1907) even described religion as a "universal obsessional neurosis" (p. 25). The concept of spirituality and religiosity for individuals of different cultures, races, and communities often carries many interpretations. From a secular tradition, these concepts are not interchangeable words and have been a perennial source of controversy Research exploring the beliefs and practices of cultural groups and individuals often reveals fluid boundaries between religiosity, spirituality, and secularism (Jensen, 2021). This highlights the complexity of human beliefs and behaviours regarding religion, spirituality, and secularism. Rather than existing as distinct and rigid categories, these concepts often overlap and interact in dynamic ways within individual belief systems and cultural contexts. For instance, individuals may identify with a specific religious tradition but also engage in practices or hold beliefs that are considered more spiritual or secular in nature. Likewise, someone may identify as secular but still incorporate elements of spirituality into their worldview or practices. This plasticity suggests that simplistic categorisations may not fully capture the richness and diversity of human beliefs and experiences, involved in understanding how individuals and communities navigate the realms of religion, spirituality, and secularism.

Jensen (2021) suggested that religiosity involves a positive connection to one or more organised religions, characterised by adherence to shared doctrinal beliefs and communal practices. In contrast, spirituality applies to an individual's quest for or perception of connection with the sacred, supernatural, or ultimate reality. Koenig et al. (2024) define spirituality as a personal quest to comprehend the meaning and purpose of life, which may or may not involve the adoption of religious rituals. They acknowledge that spiritual enlightenment can be achieved independently of religious affiliation, emphasising that religious participation is not a prerequisite for spiritual fulfilment. However, they also recognise that for some individuals, spirituality is intertwined with religious engagement, suggesting that religious practices can serve as a tool for spiritual experiences and understanding. For example, spirituality is "expressed in an individual's search for ultimate meaning through participation in religion and/or belief in God, family, naturalism, rationalism, humanism, and the arts. All of these factors can influence how patients and health care professionals perceive health and illness and how they interact with one another" (AAMC, 1999, pp. 25–26). According to The Royal College of Psychiatrists (2018), spirituality is universally accessible, offering meaning, purpose, hope, and healing during times of suffering and loss. It also promotes positive relationships with oneself, others, and beyond. In the West, many perceive religion and spirituality as distinct concepts. Religion is seen as a structured system of beliefs, practices, rituals, and symbols aimed at fostering closeness to a God (Koenig et al., 2024). Therefore, religion is considered more exclusive than spirituality, encompassing the belief in spiritual reality and God.

From an Islāmic perspective, religion and spirituality are inseparable. The typical characteristics of religiosity, such as frequency of service attendance and belief in God, do not fully capture the comprehensive concept of "deen" for Muslims (Islām & Umarji, 2022). The concept of "*deen*" in Islām refers to the comprehensive and all-encompassing way of life guided by the principles and teachings of Islām. It goes beyond the narrow definitions of religion that focus solely on rituals and beliefs. Instead, *deen* integrates every aspect of a Muslim's existence, including faith and belief (*iman*), worship and rituals (*ibadah*), ethical conduct (*'akhlaq*), legal framework (*shar'iah*), social relations, and personal development. Religion encompasses spirituality, with religious thoughts and practices providing the spiritual path for salvation and a way of life. There is no concept of spirituality without religion in Islām (Rassool, 2000). According to Rassool (2016), "Muslims embrace the acceptance of the Divine, and they seek meaning, purpose and happiness in worldly life and the hereafter. This is achieved through the belief in the 'Oneness of God (*tawhîd*),' without any partner, and the understanding and application of Qur'anic practices and the guidance of the Prophet (ﷺ)" (p. 27). This unicity of God is "the very foundation of Islām on which all the other pillars and principles depend. If one's *Tawhîd* is not sound, the rest of one's Islām becomes, in effect, a series of pagan rituals. In this model, Allah's unity must be maintained" (Philips, 1994 p. vii). In Islām, spirituality and religion are deeply intertwined and inseparable which encompasses a holistic approach to life where religious beliefs and practices permeate every aspect of existence. Spiritual growth and religious observance are seen as mutually reinforcing aspects of a Muslim's life. The practices prescribed by Islām are designed to nurture both the spiritual and moral dimensions of a person. The domains of Islāmic Integrated psychology and psychotherapy are presented in Table 1.1

Table 1.1 The domains of Islāmic Integrated psychology and psychotherapy

Domain	Islāmic psychology and psychotherapy	Authors
Educational	Advancing Islāmic Psychology Education: Knowledge Integration, Model, and Application	Rassool (2023a, b)
	Islāmic Psychology: The Basics	Rassool (2023a, b)
	Alcohol-The Forbidden Nectar: An Islāmic Perspective	Rassool (2022)
	Mother of all Evils: Addictive Behaviours from an Islāmic Perspective.	Rassool (2021)
	The Science of the Soul (*Ilm an Nafs*): Themes in Islāmic Psychology.	Rassool (2021)
	Islāmic Psychology: Human Behaviour and Experience From an Islāmic Perspective	Rassool (2021)
	Health and Psychology: An Islāmic Perspective. Volume 1 & 2	Rassool (2020)
	Sexuality Education from an Islāmic Perspective.	Khan et al. (2020)
Educational Historical	Maristans and Islāmic Psychology: A Historical Model for Modern Implementation	Awaad and Demir (2025)
	Foundations of Islāmic Psychology: Classical Scholars to Contemporary Thinkers.	Rassool and Luckman (2022).
Research	Integrated Research Methodologies in Islāmic Psychology	Rassool (2023)
Clinical	Islāmically Integrated Psychotherapy With Domestic Abuse	Haque (2025)
	Spiritual Integration in Islāmic Psychotherapy: Unveiling the Therapist's Soul	Rassool (2025a)
	Islāmic Counselling & Psychotherapy: From Theory to Practice	Rassool (2025b)
	Working With Crisis and Trauma: An Islāmic Perspective	Ismail et al. (2025)
	Tazkiya Therapy in Islāmic Psychotherapy	Riyono (2024)
	Treating Addictive Behaviours from an Islāmic Perspective	Rassool (2025c)
	Islāmically Modified Cognitive Behavioural Therapy	Qasqas (2024)
	Integrating Spiritual Interventions in Islāmic Psychology: A Practical Guide	Latif et al. (2024a)
	Integrating Acceptance and Commitment Therapy with Islāmic Psychotherapy for Managing Chronic Pain	Bhatti-Ali (2023)
	Applying Islāmic Principles to Clinical Mental Health Care: Introducing Traditional Islāmic ally Integrated Psychotherapy,. (TIIP)	Keshavarzi et al. (2021)
	Islāmic ally Integrated Psychotherapy: Uniting Faith and Professional Practice.	Al-Karam (2018)
	Islāmic Counselling: From Theory to Practice	Rassool (2016)
Ethics	Islāmic Ethics in Islāmic Psychology	Fahm (2025)
Public Health	Contemporary Islāmic Perspectives in Public Health	Aboul-Enein et al. (2025)

1.6 Conclusion

The exploration of spirituality, psychology, and psychotherapy reveals a profound interconnectedness that significantly enhances the healing process. Traditional psychology often overlooks the spiritual dimension of human existence, leading to what can be termed "soulless psychology". This approach tends to focus solely on the cognitive and emotional aspects of well-being, neglecting the spiritual needs that many individuals consider central to their identity and purpose. By integrating spirituality into psychotherapy, a more holistic form of healing emerges, addressing not only the psyche and emotions but also the soul. Spiritually integrative psychotherapy acknowledges the importance of faith, meaning, and connection to a higher power, offering a more comprehensive framework for understanding and treating psychological distress.

From an Islāmic perspective, spirituality and religiosity are inseparable components of a believer's life, deeply influencing their psychological health. Islāmic teachings provide a robust foundation for integrating spirituality into therapeutic practices, emphasising principles such as *tawhîd* (Oneness of God), patience (*sabr*), gratitude (*shukr*), and trust in divine wisdom (*tawakkul*), repentance (*tawbah*), and forgiveness. These principles offer valuable insights and practical tools for fostering emotional resilience, mental clarity, and overall well-being. By incorporating these spiritual elements, therapy can resonate more deeply with Muslim clients, ensuring that their religious and spiritual values are respected and utilised as strengths in the healing process. This approach not only enriches the therapeutic experience but also aligns it with the holistic view of human nature that is central to Islāmic tradition.

References

Aboul-Enein, B. H., Rassool, G. H., Benajiba, N., Bernstein, J., & Mo'ez Al-Islam, E. F. (2025). *Contemporary Islāmic perspectives in public health*. Cambridge University Press.

Akbulut, Z. (2020). The use of spirituality in narrative couples and family therapy. *Spiritual Psychology and Counseling, 5*(1), 113–130. https://doi.org/10.37898/spc.2020.5.1.0

Alexander, M.-A., Mosqueiro, B. P., & Bhugra, D. (Eds.). (2021). *Spirituality and mental health across cultures*. Oxford Cultural Psychiatry; online edn, Oxford Academic. https://doi.org/10.1093/med/9780198846833.001.0001

Al-Karam, C. Y. (Ed.). (2018). *Islāmically integrated psychotherapy: Uniting faith and professional practice. Abstract*. Templeton Press.

Araullo, A. (2010). Erich Fromm's psycho-spiritual discourse. *Fromm Forum* (English Edition). Tuebingen (Selbstverlag) (pp. 52–56).

Areeza, A. (2017). *The impact of Islāmophobia on the Muslim American community: Accounts of psychological suffering, identity negotiation, and collective trauma*. Masters thesis, Smith College. https://scholarworks.smith.edu/theses/1879. Accessed 15 May 2024.

Association of American Medical Colleges (AAMC). (1999). *Report III: Contemporary issues in medicine: Communication in medicine, medical school objectives project*. Association of American Medical Colleges.

Awaad, R., & Nursoy-Demir, M. (2025). *Maristans and Islāmic psychology: A historical model for modern implementation* (Focus Series on *Islā*mic Psychology and Psychotherapy) (1st ed.). Routledge.

Bhatti-Ali, R. (2023). *Integrating acceptance and commitment therapy with Islāmic psychotherapy for managing chronic pain*. Taylor & Francis.

Blando, J. A. (2006). Spirituality, religion, and counseling. *Counseling and Human Development, 39*(2), 1–14.

Charema, J., & Shizha, E. (2008). Counselling indigenous Shona people in Zimbabwe: Traditional practices versus Western Eurocentric perspectives. *AlterNative: An International Journal of Indigenous Peoples, 4*(2), 123–139. https://doi.org/10.1177/117718010800400209

Cornish, M. A., & Wade, N. G. (2010). Spirituality and religion in group counselling: A literature review with practice guidelines. *Professional Psychology: Research and Practice, 41*(5), 398–404.

Cotton, S., Grossoehme, D. H., & Tsevat, J. (2007). Religion/spirituality and health in adolescents. In T. G. Plante & C. E. Thoresen (Eds.), *Spirit, science, and health: How the spiritual mind fuels physical wellness* (pp. 143–156). Praeger Publishers/Greenwood Publishing Group.

El-Khani, A., Ulph, F., Peters, S., & Calam, R. (2016). Syria: The challenges of parenting in refugee situations of immediate displacement. *Intervention: Journal of Mental Health and Psychosocial Support in Conflict Affected Areas, 14*(2), 99–113. https://doi.org/10.1097/WTF.0000000000000118

Ellenberger, H. F. (2018). *The discovery of the unconscious: The history and evolution of dynamic psychiatry*. Basic books.

Fahm, A. G. (2025). *Islāmic ethics in Islāmic psychology* (Focus Series on Islāmic Psychology and Psychotherapy) (1st ed.). Routledge.

Frankl, V. E. (1963). *Man's search for meaning: An introduction to Logotherapy*. Beacon Press.

Freud, S. (1907). *Obsessive acts, religious practices*. Reprinted (1953–1974) in the Standard Edition of the Complete Psychological Works of Sigmund Freud (J. Strachey, Trans. and Ed., vol. 7). Hogarth Press.

Freud, S. (1961/1927). *The future of an illusion* (James Strachey, Trans.). W. W. Norton.

Fromm, E. (1950). *Psychoanalysis & religion*. Yale University Press.

Halmos, P. (1965). *The faith of the counsellors*. Constable.

Haque, K. (2025). *Islāmically integrated psychotherapy with domestic abuse* (Focus Series on Islāmic Psychology and Psychotherapy) (1st ed.). Routledge.

Hassem, Z., Ismail, S., Vad Walla, N., & Rassool, G. H. (2025). *Working with Crisis and Trauma from an Islamic Perspective* (Focus Series on Islāmic Psychology and Psychotherapy) (1st ed.). Routledge.

Hazer, L., & Gredebäck, G. (2023). The effects of war, displacement, and trauma on child development. *Humanities and Social Sciences Communications, 10*, 909. https://doi.org/10.1057/s41599-023-02438-8

Hussein, R. G. (2022). *Alcohol: A forbidden nectar: An Islamic perspective*. Islamic Psychology Publication (IIP) & Institute of Islamic Psychology Research (RIIPR). Amazon/Kindle.

Hussein, R. G., & Luckman, M. (2022). *Foundations of Islāmic Psychology: From classical scholars to contemporary thinkers*. Routledge.

Hwang, W. C., & Goto, S. (2008). The impact of perceived racial discrimination on the mental health of Asian American and Latino college students. *Cultural Diversity & Ethnic Minority Psychology, 14*(4), 326–335. https://doi.org/10.1037/1099-9809.14.4.326

Islām, F., & Umarji, O. (2022). *Faith in mind: Islām's role in mental health*. Yaqeen Institute. https://yaqeeninstitute.org/read/paper/faith-in-mind-Islāms-role-in-mental-health. Accessed 19 May 2024.

Jensen, L. A. (2021). The cultural psychology of religiosity, spirituality, and secularism in adolescence. *Adolescent Research Review, 6*(3), 277–288. https://doi.org/10.1007/s40894-020-00143-0

Johnstone, B., Yoon, D. P., Cohen, D., Schopp, L. H., McCormack, G., Campbell, J., & Smith, M. (2012). Relationships among spirituality, religious practices, personality factors, and health for five different faith traditions. *Journal of Religion and Health, 51*(4), 1017–1041. https://doi.org/10.1007/s10943-012-9615-8

Jung, C. G. (2013). *Psychology and religion*. Yale University Press.

Kathawalla, U.-K., & Syed, M. (2021). Discrimination, life stress, and mental health among muslims: A preregistered systematic review and meta-analysis. *Collabra: Psychology, 7*(1), 28248. https://doi.org/10.1525/collabra.28248

Keshavarzi, H., Khan, F., Ali, B., & Awaad, R. (Eds.). (2021). *Applying Islāmic principles to clinical mental health care: Introducing traditional Islāmically integrated psychotherapy*. Routledge.

Khan, Z. (2021). *The impact of Islāmophobia on the mental health of Muslim post-secondary students* (Major Research Paper). York University. https://ys.library.yorku.ca/server/api/core/bitstreams/06b0c377-94e4-4e2a-85a9-c16779984cd9/content. Accessed 15 May 2024.

Khan, A., Rassool, G. H., Mabud, S., & Ahsan, M. (2020). *Sexuality education from an Islāmic perspective*. Cambridge Scholars Ltd.

Khan, F., Keshavarzi, H., & Rothman, A. (2021). The role of the TIIP, Therapist scope of practice and proposed competencies, in H.

Kira, I. A., Lewandowski, L., Ashby, J. S., Templin, T., Ramaswamy, V., & Mohanesh, J. (2014). The Traumatogenic dynamics of internalized stigma of mental illness among Arab American, Muslim, and refugee clients. *Journal of the American Psychiatric Nurses Association, 20*(4), 250–266. https://doi.org/10.1177/1078390314542873

Koenig, H. G. (2012). Religion, spirituality, and health: The research and clinical implications. *ISRN Psychiatry, 2012*, 278730. https://doi.org/10.5402/2012/278730

Koenig, H. G. (2023). Person-centered mindfulness: A culturally and spiritually sensitive approach to clinical practice. *Journal of Religion and Health, 62*(3), 1884–1896. https://doi.org/10.1007/s10943-023-01768-w

Koenig, H. G., VanderWeele, T., & Peteet, J. R. (2024). *Handbook of religion and health* (3rd ed.). Oxford University Press. (Online edn, Oxford Academic, 23 November 2023). https://doi.org/10.1093/oso/9780190088859.001.0001

Latif, J., Shaakirah Dockrat, G., & Rassool, H. (2024a). *Integrating spiritual interventions in Islāmic psychology: A practical guide*. Taylor & Francis.

Latif, J., Dockrat, S., & Rassool, G. H. (2024b). In 1 (Ed.), *Integrating spiritual interventions in Islāmic psychology: A practical guide* (Focus Series on Islāmic Psychology and Psychotherapy). Routledge.

May, R. (1983). *The discovery of being: Writings in existential psychology*. Norton.

McCrae, N., & Whitley, R. (2014). Exaltation in temporal lobe epilepsy: Neuropsychiatric symptom or portal to the divine? *The Journal of Medical Humanities, 35*(3), 241–255. https://doi.org/10.1007/s10912-014-9294-4

McLeish, K. (1995). *Key ideas in human thought*. Prima Publishing.

Moreira-Almeida, A., Mosqueiro, B. P., & Bhugra, D. (Eds.). (2021). *Spirituality and mental health across cultures*. Oxford University Press. https://doi.org/10.1093/med/9780198846833.001.0001

Oman, D., & Syme, S. L. (2018). Social and community-level factors in health effects from religion/spirituality. In D. Oman (Ed.), *Why religion and spirituality matter for public health. Religion, spirituality and health: A social scientific approach* (Vol. 2). Springer. https://doi.org/10.1007/978-3-319-73966-3_5

Pargament, K. I. (2011). *Spiritually integrated psychotherapy: Understanding and addressing the sacred*. Guilford Press.

Park, C. L., Currier, J. M., Harris, J. I., & Slattery, J. M. (2016). *Trauma, meaning, and spirituality. Translating research into clinical practice*. American Psychological Association.

Philips, A. A. B. (1994). *The fundamentals of Tawheed (Islāmic monotheism)*. International Islāmic Publishing House.

Qasqas, M. (2024). *Islāmically modified cognitive behavioural therapy*. Taylor & Francis.
Rassool, G. H. (2016). *Islāmic counselling. An introduction to theory and practice*. Routledge.
Rassool, G. H. (2019). *Evil eye, jinn possession and mental health issues: An Islāmic perspective*. Routledge.
Rassool, G. H. (2000). The crescent and Islām: Healing, nursing and spiritual dimension: Some considerations towards an understanding of the Islāmic perspectives of caring. *Journal of Advanced Nursing, 32*(6), 1476–1484.
Rassool, G. H. (2021). Re-examining the anatomy of Islāmic psychotherapy and counselling: Envisioned and enacted practices. *Islāmic Guidance and Counseling Journal, 4*(2). 10.25217/.
Rassool, G. H. (2023a). *Integrated research methodologies in Islāmic Psychology*. Taylor & Francis.
Rassool, G. H. (2023b). *Advancing Islāmic psychology education: Knowledge integration, model, and application*. Taylor & Francis.
Rassool, G. H. (2025a). *Islāmīc counselling and psychotherapy: From theory to practice* (2nd ed.). Routledge.
Rassool, G. H. (2025b). *Islāmic counselling & psychotherapy* (2nd ed.). Routledge.
Rassool, G. H. (2025c). *Treating addictive behaviours from an Islāmic perspective* (Focus Series on Islāmic Psychology & Psychotherapy) (1st ed.). Routledge.
Richards, P. S., & Bergin, A. E. (2005). *A spiritual strategy for counseling and psychotherapy* (2nd ed.). American Psychological Association. https://doi.org/10.1037/11214-000
Richards, P. S., & Bergin, A. E. (Eds.). (2014). *Handbook of psychotherapy and religious diversity* (2nd ed.). American Psychological Association. https://doi.org/10.1037/14371-000
Richards, P. S., Pargament, K. I., Exline, J. J., & Kawika Allen, G. E. (2023). Introduction: Bringing spiritually integrated psychotherapies into the health care mainstream. In P. Scott, G. E. Richards, K. Allen, & D. K. Judd (Eds.), *Handbook of spiritually integrated psychotherapies* (pp. 3–29). American Psychological Association. https://doi.org/10.1037/0000338-000
Riyono, B. (2024). *Tazkiya Therapy in Islāmic Psychotherapy*. Taylor & Francis.
Rozanov, V., Frančišković, T., Marinić, I., et al. (2019). Mental health consequences of war conflicts. In A. Javed & K. Fountoulakis (Eds.), *Advances in psychiatry* (pp. 281–304). Springer. https://doi.org/10.1007/978-3-319-70554-5_17
Sadiq, N. R. (2019). *Understanding Muslim women clients of counselling: An interpretive phenomenological analysis*. A thesis submitted in partial fulfilment of the requirements of the University of the West of England, Bristol for the degree of Professional Doctorate in Counselling Psychology Faculty of Health and Social Sciences, University of the West of England. https://www.semanticscholar.org/paper/Understanding-Muslim-women-clients-of-counselling%3ASadiq/7fe0f7d2f83bd0c53106d73ad636058a261431d2. Accessed 20 May 2024.
Skinner, B. F. (1971). *Beyond freedom and dignity*. Penguin Books Ltd.
Sperry, L. (2013). Distinctive approaches to religion and spirituality: Pastoral counseling, spiritual direction, and spiritually integrated psychotherapy. In K. I. Pargament, A. Mahoney, & E. P. Shafranske (Eds.), *APA handbook of psychology, religion, and spirituality: Vol. 2. An applied psychology of religion and spirituality* (pp. 223–238). American Psychological Association. https://doi.org/10.1037/14046-011
Sperry, L., & Shafranske, E. P. (Eds.). (2005). *Spiritually integrated psychotherapy*. American Psychological Association. https://doi.org/10.1037/10886-000
Sue, D. W., Capodilupo, C. M., Torino, G. C., Bucceri, J. M., Holder, A. M., Nadal, K. L., & Esquilin, M. (2007). Racial microaggressions in everyday life: Implications for clinical practice. *The American Psychologist, 62*(4), 271–286. https://doi.org/10.1037/0003-066X.62.4.271
Tsui, P., & Schultz, G. L. (1985). Failure of rapport: Why psychotherapeutic engagement fails in the treatment of Asian clients. *The American Journal of Orthopsychiatry, 55*(4), 561–569. https://doi.org/10.1111/j.1939-0025.1985.tb02706.x
Wilber, K. (2000). *Integral psychology: Consciousness, spirit, psychology, therapy*. Shambhala Publications.

Chapter 2
Monotheism as the Foundation of Islāmic Psychotherapy

2.1 Introduction

Monotheism, the belief in a single, all-powerful deity, serves as the cornerstone of Islāmic psychotherapy. This approach integrates the spiritual, metaphysical, psychological, and physical aspects of human well-being, drawing on the rich tradition of Islāmic teachings to address mental and emotional distress. In contrast, contemporary psychology, particularly as it has developed within the Judeo-Christian tradition, has historically maintained a complex relationship with spirituality and religion. While Judeo-Christian values have influenced the moral and ethical frameworks of Western psychology, the discipline has often separated spiritual considerations from clinical practice. This separation has led to a more secular and sometimes "soulless" approach to mental health, focusing primarily on cognitive and behavioural aspects. In recent years, there has been a growing recognition of the importance of spirituality in psychological healing within the Judeo-Christian tradition. This has led to the development of spiritually integrative psychotherapy, which seeks to incorporate clients' religious and spiritual beliefs into therapeutic practice. This movement acknowledges that for many individuals, faith is a central component of their identity and resilience. As we explore the foundations of Islāmic psychotherapy, it is essential to understand how monotheism shapes this approach and contrasts with the Judeo-Christian influenced psychological practices, highlighting the unique contributions of each tradition to the field of mental health. This chapter focuses on Islāmic monotheism as the foundation of Islāmic psychotherapy.

G. H. Rassool, *Exploring the Intersection of Islāmic Spirituality and Psychotherapy*,
https://doi.org/10.1007/978-3-031-72724-5_2

2.2 Islāmic Monotheism as the Foundation of Islāmic Psychology

The concept of monotheism, known as *tawhîd* in Arabic, is the most important concept in Islām and forms the foundation of Islāmic psychology. *Tawhîd*, derived from the verb "Wahad", means "making one" or "asserting oneness" (Cowan & Wehr, 1976, p. 1055). It signifies that God is a singular, indivisible unity, not composed of parts. This unicity or oneness of God underpins all aspects of Islām. Every act of worship or ritual, whether inwards or outwards, holds no meaning or value if the concept of *tawhîd* is compromised in any way. The Oneness of God in Islāmic theology is divided into three distinct categories: *Tawhîd ar-Ruboobeeyah*, *Tawhîd al-'Ibādah*, and *Tawhîd al-Asmaa was-Sifaat*. The ***Tawhîd ar-Ruboobeeyah*** **(Oneness of God in His Lordship)** asserts that Allāh has complete mastery over the universe and is solely responsible for its creation and maintenance. He caused all things to exist from nothing and governs all events. According to Philips (2005), since God is the only real power in existence, everything that occurs in creation is by His will and permission. No one shares in His dominion; He is the sole Creator and sustainer of the universe, without any partners. ***Tawhîd al-'Ibādah*** **(Devotion of All Worship to God Alone)** emphasises that all acts of worship and devotion should be directed exclusively to Allāh. Worshiping anything or anyone besides Him compromises this principle and nullifies the essence of *Tawhîd*. ***Tawhîd al-Asmaa was-Sifaat*** **(Oneness of God in His Names and Attributes)**: This affirms that God's names and attributes are unique and unparalleled. Allāh's names and attributes are not shared or comparable to any other being. These categories collectively affirm the comprehensive nature of God's oneness, encompassing His lordship, the exclusive devotion due to Him, and His unique attributes.

The maintenance of the unity of Allāh's worship, known as *Tawhîd al-'Ibādah*, is the most important aspect of *Tawhîd*. It dictates that all forms of worship must be directed solely to Allāh, as He alone has the power to grant benefits to humanity through worship. There is no need for any intercessor or intermediary between man and God in devotion and supplications. Allāh emphasises the importance of exclusive worship in the Qur'ān, highlighting that the essence and purpose of man's creation, as well as the core message of all prophets, is to direct worship to Him alone. This central theme is echoed in the following verse of the Qur'ān.

وَلَقَدْ بَعَثْنَا فِى كُلِّ أُمَّةٍ رَّسُولًا أَنِ ٱعْبُدُوا۟ ٱللَّهَ.

- *And we certainly sent into every nation a messenger [saying], 'Worship Allāh. and avoid false objects of worship (false Gods).* (An-Nahl, 16:36, interpretation of the meaning).

This verse captures the essence of Islāmic monotheism, emphasising that the core purpose of human creation and prophetic missions is to establish and maintain the worship of Allāh alone, free from any form of association with false deities. Philips (2005) asserts that affirming *Tawhîd al-'Ibādah* requires the rejection of all forms of intercession or association of partners with Allāh, emphasising that worship should be directed to Allāh alone. Worshiping anyone other than Allāh is considered the greatest possible sin in Islām. The oneness of Allāh in His names and attributes (*Tawhîd al-Asmaa was-Sifaat*) means that Allāh's attributes are unique and perfect, and He does not share these attributes with any created beings, nor do they share in His attributes. Assigning divine attributes to created beings or vice versa constitutes polytheism. Associating Allāh with other partners is a grave sin in Islām, as it compromises the fundamental belief in the oneness of Allāh.

2.3 Criteria for Authentic Islāmic Psychotherapy: Alignment with the Six Articles of Faith

To be genuinely considered Islāmic, any psychological framework must adhere to the six axioms of the Articles of Faith *(imān)*, known as *Arkān al-Imān.* As Iakhin (2022) emphasises, ignoring any of these foundational beliefs disqualifies a psychological approach from being truly Islāmic. These six core principles are integral to ensuring that the psychological practices align with Islāmic theology and values.

- Belief in one God (*Tawhîd*): This means having absolute faith in the oneness of God that He is Unique in His Names and Attributes; and to whom worship is due. This belief is the core of Islāmic theology and underpins all other articles of faith.
- Belief in His Angels (*Malaikah*): Angels are honourable slaves of Allāh; they obey Him and execute His Commands.
- Belief in His Books (*Kutub*): Muslims believe in the divine scriptures revealed to various prophets, including the Torah revealed to Prophet Moses (Musa); the Psalm revealed to Prophet David (Dawud); and the Gospel revealed to Prophet Jesus (Eesa), which have been superseded by the Qur'ān, the final revelation. This belief highlights the continuity and culmination of divine guidance through these sacred texts.
- Belief in the Prophets (*Nubuwwah*). Prophet Muhammad (ﷺ) being the last of the Prophets and Messengers. All Prophets and Messengers were human beings with no Divine qualities and had no access to the unseen world.
- Belief in the Last Day and the Afterlife (*Akhirah*): All Muslims believe that this life is made of trials and tribulations. Both the Last Day and the Afterlife are important dimension in the Islāmic worldview. The belief is that, after death, there is the continued existence of the soul and a transformed physical existence. All humankind will be divided between those destined to Paradise or Hell.
- Belief in Predestination (*Al Qadr*): This article of faith means believing that Allāh has created everything and has predestined everything that will happen both in the universe and in the lives of individuals as part of the divine masterplan.

For a psychological framework to be genuinely Islāmic, it must incorporate these six axioms, ensuring that therapeutic practices and psychological theories are rooted in these foundational beliefs. This integration means that Islāmic psychotherapy addresses not only the mental and emotional aspects of human experience but also the spiritual and metaphysical dimensions, offering a holistic approach to healing and spiritual purification. By aligning with the Articles of Faith, Islāmic psychotherapy ensures that its practices resonate with the religious and spiritual values of Muslim clients, fostering an environment where psychological and spiritual growth are intertwined. Through this integration, Islāmic psychotherapy offers a comprehensive approach to healing that addresses the cognitive, emotional, and spiritual dimensions of human experience.

2.4 Sources of Knowledge

In Islāmic tradition, knowledge is derived from two primary sources: the Qur'ān and the *Sunnah* (teachings and practices of the Prophet Muhammad (ﷺ) *(Ilm naqli)*, and from rational knowledge based on human intellect (*'aql*), observation and empirical evidence (*Ilm 'aqli*). Malkawi (2014) suggested that the foundation of knowledge is the Qur'ān "is viewed as the springhead of all knowledge and all sciences, not because it contains the knowledge itself but, rather, because it inspires the Muslim to develop a distinctive vision of the unity among the various spheres of knowledge. The notion of this unity arises out of an awareness of the unity of the Divine and its applications to the various spheres of human knowledge" (p. 20). The notion that the Qur'ān serves as the foundation of knowledge in Islām stems from the belief that it is a divine revelation from Allāh, the source of all truth and wisdom. The Qur'ān inspires Muslims to develop a holistic vision of knowledge that recognises the interconnectedness and unity among various fields of study. This unity arises from the acknowledgment of the Divine as the ultimate source of knowledge and the realisation that all branches of knowledge ultimately lead back to Allāh. The Qur'ān is considered the ultimate source of divine guidance, and it provides Muslims with spiritual, moral, and practical guidance. It covers a wide range of topics, including monotheism, morality, human nature, and social justice "The Qur'ân deals with the human psych[e] and exemplifies the challenges to behavioural change and character development through its narratives, analogies and direct guidance" (Hussain, 2011, p. 14). In Islāmic psychotherapy, the Qur'ān serves as a source of wisdom and inspiration, offering insights into human behaviour, mental health, and personal development.

The *Sunnah* consists of the teachings, actions, approvals, and disapprovals of the Prophet Muhammad (ﷺ), as recorded in *hadīth* collections. It provides practical examples of how to implement Qur'ānic principles in daily life. It is divine revelation from Allāh and the *Sunnah* of Prophet Muhammad (ﷺ) that become one of the primary and most fundamental sources of knowledge. In Islāmic psychotherapy, the *Sunnah* serves as a model for ethical behaviour, interpersonal relationships, and emotional regulation. Virtues related to mental health, such as the importance of patience (*sabr*), gratitude (*shukr*), **forgiveness** (*maghfirah*), **hope (*raja*),**

contentment (*qana'ah*), optimism (*al-tumā'ninah*), compassion (*raḥmah*), resilience (*sumūd*), and self-compassion (*al-raḥmah ʿalā al-nafs*) are particularly relevant in therapy.

Utz (2011) suggested that "It is only through revelation that we can comprehend the true nature of the soul and the unseen world and ascertain the methods for purifying the soul and developing it to its fullest potential. Allāh is the only One with authentic and complete knowledge of the unseen world, so we turn only to Him for this understanding. Human beings, especially Muslims, must not speculate or guess in relation to this domain" (pp. 39–40). Utz's statement underlines the Islāmic belief in the primacy of revelation as the source of authentic knowledge, particularly regarding the nature of the soul and the unseen world. According to Islāmic teachings, Allāh possesses complete and perfect knowledge of the unseen realm, including the intricacies of the human soul. Therefore, seeking understanding and guidance in matters pertaining to the soul and the unseen world necessitates turning to Allāh and His revelations. Furthermore, the statement reflects the Islāmic perspective on knowledge acquisition, highlighting the centrality of revelation in understanding profound spiritual realities and cautioning against relying solely on human speculation in matters beyond the physical realm. This highlights the importance of adhering to the teachings of Islām and following the guidance provided in the Qur'ān and the *Sunnah*. Through these sources, psychotherapists are provided with clear instructions and methods for purifying the soul and nurturing its development towards its fullest potential.

Knowledge acquisition involves a diverse set of processes that encompass sense perception, rationalisation, observation, experimentation, and intuition. Sensory perception enables us to gather information about our environment and perceive objects and events. Intuition, though less tangible, aids in problem-solving and decision-making. Observation is essential for gathering empirical evidence and identifying trends, especially in scientific inquiry. Rationalisation involves logical analysis to make sense of experiences and formulate hypotheses. Experimentation, a cornerstone of the scientific method, allows for the manipulation of variables to draw conclusions based on empirical evidence. Together, these methods contribute to our understanding of the world and help refine existing theories while uncovering new knowledge. By integrating these different approaches, we can develop a more comprehensive understanding of reality.

Knowledge gained from sense perception, rationalisation, observation, experimentation, and intuition should not be neglected. The integration of Divine revelation and empirical knowledge in Islāmic psychotherapy highlights the complementary nature of these two sources of knowledge. While revelation, derived from the Qur'ân and *Sunnah*, serves as the primary source of guidance and ethical considerations, empirical knowledge obtained through science, observation, and reason is also valued. However, it is essential to recognise that scientific evidence should be evaluated within the framework of divine revelation. Muslim psychologists are encouraged to prioritise Islāmic ethical principles over rationality and empirical evidence, considering them as secondary to the primary sources of revelation (Rassool, 2021). This approach ensures that psychological theories and practices align with Islāmic values and principles. Nevertheless, there is no inherent contradiction between divine knowledge from revelation and rational, empirical knowledge, as both emanate from the same source—God, the Almighty (Rassool, 2021).

In Islām, the pursuit of knowledge through inquiry and probing is not only permissible but encouraged. "Enquiring or probing is permissible in Islām so as to arrive at the truth" (Leaman, 2006, p. 571). Muslims are encouraged to seek truth and understanding through reasoned inquiry, observation, and experimentation. This is reflected in the following verse:

وَإِذْ قَالَ إِبْرَٰهِـۧمُ رَبِّ أَرِنِى كَيْفَ تُحْىِ ٱلْمَوْتَىٰ ۖ قَالَ أَوَلَمْ تُؤْمِن ۖ قَالَ بَلَىٰ وَلَـٰكِن لِّيَطْمَئِنَّ قَلْبِى ۖ قَالَ فَخُذْ أَرْبَعَةً مِّنَ ٱلطَّيْرِ
فَصُرْهُنَّ إِلَيْكَ ثُمَّ ٱجْعَلْ عَلَىٰ كُلِّ جَبَلٍ مِّنْهُنَّ جُزْءًا ثُمَّ ٱدْعُهُنَّ يَأْتِينَكَ سَعْيًا ۚ وَٱعْلَمْ أَنَّ ٱللَّهَ عَزِيزٌ حَكِيمٌ

- *And [mention] when Abraham said, "My Lord, show me how You give life to the dead." [Allāh] said, "Have you not believed?" He said, "Yes, but [I ask] only that my heart may be satisfied." [Allāh] said, "Take four birds and commit them to yourself. Then [after slaughtering them] put on each hill a portion of them; then call them – they will come [flying] to you in haste. And know that Allāh is Exalted in Might and Wise*." (Al-Baqarah 2:260, interpretation of the meaning).

From the verse shown above, it has been suggested that it is evident that Allāh entertained the query [from Prophet Abraham] (Leeman, 2006, p. 572). This passage recounts the dialogue between the Prophet Abraham (Ibrahim) and Allāh offers profound insights into the nature of faith, inquiry, and the demonstration of divine power. Abraham's request to witness the resurrection of the dead reflects his deep faith in Allāh's ability to perform miracles, yet he seeks further reassurance to satisfy his heart. This passage emphasises the compatibility of faith and inquiry in Islām, encouraging believers to seek knowledge and understanding while maintaining trust in Allāh's wisdom and power.

2.5 Knowledge Integration

Knowledge in Islām is seen as interconnected, despite the existence of various schools of thought within the religion. The schools of thought, including different theological (e.g. Ash'ari, Maturidi), jurisprudential (e.g. Hanafi, Shafi'i, Maliki, Hanbali), and philosophical traditions (e.g. Sufi mysticism, Islāmic philosophy). Each school offers unique perspectives but generally agrees on the fundamental tenets of Islām The diversity of interpretations and methodologies enriches Islāmic scholarship and reflects the dynamic and comprehensive nature of Islāmic knowledge. Malkawi (2014) suggested that the classical Muslim scholars, despite their different schools of thought, agreed that "knowledge should be interconnected, complementary, and organically linked to the knowledge of God. In the view of these scholars, the fact that all sciences originate from a single divine source is the foundation for the ultimate integration and unity of knowledge" (p. 12). Malkawi (2014) also maintained that the Islāmic principle of divine oneness, i.e. *Tawhīd,* is the foundation in both the unity of knowledge and epistemological integration (p. 6).This constitutes a frame of reference and foundation for a monotheistic Islāmic psychotherapy. This interconnected and integrated perspective emphasises that all forms of knowledge, whether derived from religious texts, empirical observation, rational inquiry, or intuition, ultimately converge towards a unified understanding of truth.

Islāmic thought encourages the integration of divine revelation (the Qur'ân and *Sunnah*) with rational and empirical knowledge. Islāmic scholars, like Al-Ghazālī and Ibn Rushd (Averroes), have historically emphasised that reason and faith are not in opposition but rather support each other in understanding the divine and the natural world. This integration is evident in Islāmic philosophy, theology, and jurisprudence. Both Al-Ghazālī, and Ibn Rushd have made significant contributions to the discourse on the relationship between reason and faith in Islāmic thought. Al-Ghazālī, (2000), in "The Incoherence of the Philosophers" (*Tahafut al-Falasifa*) critiques the philosophers of his time for their reliance on reason alone while defending the compatibility of reason and revelation. He argues that while philosophy can be useful, it must not contradict divine revelation. Al-Ghazālī's position is that reason has its limits and should ultimately be guided by faith. Al-Ghazālī (1999) emphasises that true knowledge and certainty are achieved through a combination of reason and divine revelation. Ibn Rushd (2012), in "The Incoherence of the Incoherence" (*Tahafut al-Tahafut*), responds to Al-Ghazali's critiques by defending the use of Aristotelian philosophy and arguing that there is no contradiction between philosophy and Islāmic teachings. He asserts that philosophy, grounded in reason, can lead to a deeper understanding of the divine. Ibn Rushd (2001) addresses the relationship between religion and philosophy. He argues that both reason and revelation come from the same divine source and therefore cannot be in true conflict. He advocates for the use of reason to interpret and understand revelation, suggesting that apparent contradictions arise from misinterpretations. These works provide a rich context for understanding how these prominent Islāmic scholars viewed the interplay between reason and faith. Their contributions continue to influence contemporary Islāmic thought, highlighting the complementary roles of rational inquiry and religious belief in the pursuit of knowledge.

The synthesis of revelation and empirical knowledge in Islāmic psychotherapy reflects a holistic approach that values both spiritual insights and scientific inquiry. By harmonising these two sources of knowledge, Islāmic psychologists and therapist can develop culturally sensitive and ethically grounded interventions that address the holistic needs of individuals and communities. This systematic integration of the sources and means of knowledge into a synthesised approach is known as epistemological [relating to theory of knowledge] integration (*al-takamul al-ma'arifi*), enriching the understanding of psychological phenomena and human behaviour.

2.6 The *Tawhîd* Paradigm

The *Tawhîd* paradigm of Islāmic psychotherapy is a holistic approach based on the principle of *Tawhîd*, emphasising the oneness of God as the sole creator, sustainer, and ruler of the universe. The principles of the *Tawhîd* paradigm in Islāmic psychotherapy is presented in Fig. 2.1. All aspects of life, including mental health, are interconnected and should be understood within the framework of *Tawhîd*, emphasising unity and coherence in a person's spiritual, metaphysical, psychological, and social life. It recognises that human beings are interconnected with God and that a balanced and healthy relationship with God is essential for psychological health and purification of the soul. The approach highlights the interconnectedness of mind, body, and spirit, offering resilience through faith and trust in Allāh. In Islāmic psychotherapy, the *Tawhîd* paradigm emphasises the understanding that the ultimate source of healing and well-being is from God. The *Tawhîd* paradigm advocates for the integration of faith and spirituality into therapy sessions. It encourages therapists to help clients explore their beliefs, values, and spiritual practices as a way to find meaning, purpose, and strength in their lives. This includes incorporating

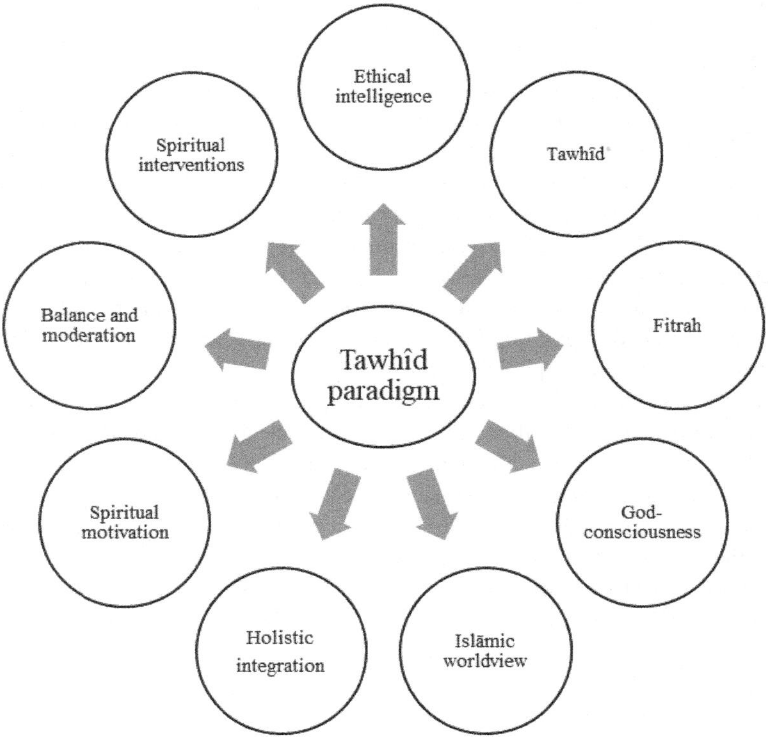

Fig. 2.1 *Tawhîd* paradigm in Islāmic psychotherapy

Islāmic teachings, such as the Qur'anic verses and Prophetic traditions, into the therapeutic process.

In Islāmic theology, "*fitrah*" is understood as the inherent nature or innate disposition of humans to recognise and submit to the existence of Allāh. This concept suggests that every human being is born with an intrinsic awareness of and inclination towards the divine. This natural predisposition towards recognising the oneness of Allāh and adhering to moral and ethical conduct is seen as a foundational aspect of human nature. Islāmic psychotherapy acknowledges the role of *fitrah* in shaping human behaviour, emotions, and beliefs. Therapists recognise that individuals may experience distress or dissatisfaction when they deviate from their *fitrah* or when their spiritual needs are not adequately addressed. Therefore, therapy approaches often integrate principles that align with *fitrah*, aiming to restore individuals' spiritual well-being and align their behaviours with their innate disposition towards spirituality. The relationship between *fitrah* and spiritual motivation is deeply intertwined. Fitrah serves as the natural inclination towards spirituality, acting as an internal compass that directs individuals towards spiritual awareness and moral goodness. Because the *fitrah* is inherent, it provides a continuous and underlying motivation for individuals to seek a deeper connection with Allāh and live in accordance with His guidance. *Fitrah* as the spiritual nature of human behaviour is examined in Chap. 5.

Spiritual motivation, defined as a psychospiritual drive arising from an individual's spiritual or religious beliefs, values, and worldviews, plays a crucial role in Islāmic psychotherapy (Rassool, 2025). According to Rassool (2025), this motivation is central to understanding how individuals find meaning and purpose in their lives through their connection to God and their faith. Utz (2011) further elaborates that spiritual motivation is an inherent aspect of human nature, driving individuals to reflect on God, contemplate their life's purpose, and consider their final destiny. This inner drive encourages individuals to acknowledge a higher power, express gratitude for their blessings, and engage in acts of worship. In the context of Islāmic psychotherapy, spiritual motivation is highly relevant as it forms the foundation of the therapeutic process. It aligns with the *Tawhîd* paradigm and encourages patients to align their thoughts, emotions, and behaviours with Islāmic teachings and values. Spiritual motivation is integral to Islāmic psychotherapy as it taps into the core of an individual's faith and beliefs, guiding them towards personal growth, ethical behaviour, and psychological resilience. It helps clients develop a holistic sense of well-being by integrating their spiritual and psychological dimensions, leading to a more balanced and fulfilling life.

Taqwa, meaning "God-consciousness" or "piety", is a fundamental concept in the *Tawhîd* paradigm. It encompasses a heightened awareness of one's actions and intentions, driven by a profound reverence for God. This manifests as a continuous contemplation that influences every aspect of a believer's life, guiding them towards a path of sincerity, honesty, and righteousness. *Taqwa* is a comprehensive concept that permeates all facets of a Muslim's life, guiding them towards a holistic adherence to Islāmic principles and fostering a harmonious relationship with God, oneself, and others. In practical terms, *taqwa* influences how an Islāmic therapist interacts with others, their approach to work, their pursuit of knowledge, and their engagement in community and social responsibilities. It motivates them to perform acts of kindness, charity, and service, contributing to the well-being of society. This *Tawhîd* paradigm integrates Islāmic rules, theology, and spirituality to guide therapeutic practices, promoting goodness (*'amr bil ma'aruf*) and preventing what is wrong (*nahi al-munkar*). Ethical intelligence, being a component of the *Tawhîd* paradigm, involves the ability to recognise, understand, and navigate moral and ethical issues effectively (Rassool, 2025). It includes assessing the moral implications of actions, making ethical decisions, and behaving in accordance with ethical principles and values. Ethically intelligent psychotherapists are aware of when and how to act ethically to pursue moral good, which goes beyond knowing what is permissible or wrong to include the capability and willingness to perform morally right actions.

The Islāmic worldview is an integral component of the *Tawhîd* paradigm. This worldview encompasses a comprehensive understanding of existence, human nature, ethics, and purpose, all within the framework of *tawhîd*. At the core of the Islāmic worldview is the belief in the unity and sovereignty of Allāh, who is the Creator and Sustainer of the universe. This belief shapes how Muslims perceive the world around them, as everything is seen as interconnected and dependent on the will of Allāh. From this perspective, the universe and all its phenomena are considered signs (*Ayat*) of Allāh's existence and attributes, inviting contemplation and submission to His divine will. Human beings are viewed as the vicegerents of Allāh on earth, entrusted with the responsibility of stewardship (*khilafah*) over creation. This entails upholding moral and ethical principles, promoting justice, and striving for the betterment of society, all in accordance with the guidance provided in the Qur'ân and *Sunnah*. Additionally, the Islāmic worldview recognises the innate dignity and worth of every human being, regardless of race, ethnicity, or social status, as all are equal before Allāh. Ethics and morality are central to the Islāmic worldview and the pursuit of ethical conduct is seen as a means of drawing closer to Allāh and fulfilling one's purpose in life. The Islāmic worldview will be examined in Chap. 4.

Within the *Tawhîd* paradigm, holistic healing is recognised as important addressing the interconnected physical, psychological, and spiritual and metaphysical dimensions of individuals. Islāmic psychotherapists operating within this framework strive to create therapeutic environments that adhere to Islāmic values and principles, fostering culturally sensitive and spiritually nourishing experiences for clients. This approach encourages clients to explore and address their psychological and psychospiritual difficulties while also seeking guidance and support from their faith in Allāh. By integrating psychological interventions with spiritual practices such as prayer, reflection, and seeking forgiveness, therapists aim to facilitate comprehensive healing that encompasses all aspects of the individual's well-being. Through this holistic approach, clients are empowered to navigate life's challenges with resilience, faith, and a deeper sense of spiritual fulfilment. Balance and moderation (*wasatiyyah*) are essential elements within the *Tawhîd* paradigm. *Wasatiyyah* refers to the principle of maintaining a middle path, avoiding extremes and excesses in all aspects of life. This concept is deeply rooted in Islāmic teachings and serves as a guiding principle for personal conduct, social interactions, and societal governance. *Wasatiyyah* is a fundamental element within the *Tawhîd* paradigm, emphasising the importance of balance, moderation, and fairness in all aspects of life. It serves as a guiding principle for personal conduct, social interactions, and governance, fostering harmony, justice, and well-being within Muslim communities and societies.

2.7 Conclusion

In the exploration of Islāmic psychotherapy, the role of monotheism stands as a key foundation. Monotheism, captured in the concept of *tawhîd*, highlights the unity and sovereignty of Allāh, providing a framework for understanding the interconnectedness of all aspects of life. This belief in the oneness of God permeates Islāmic psychotherapy, guiding both therapists and clients towards healing that acknowledges the spiritual dimension of existence. Furthermore, the criteria for authentic Islāmic psychotherapy, as delineated by alignment with the six Articles of Faith, ensure that therapeutic interventions remain rooted in the foundational tenets of Islām, fostering a holistic approach to mental health that respects the core beliefs of the faith.

Furthermore, the integration of knowledge from various sources, including the Qur'ân, *Sunnah*, and empirical research, enriches the practice of Islāmic psychotherapy. This knowledge integration fosters a comprehensive understanding of human psychology and spirituality, allowing therapists to address mental health concerns from a multidimensional perspective. Within the *Tawhîd* paradigm, this integration serves to uphold the principle of holistic healing, recognising the interconnectedness of the physical, psychological, and spiritual and metaphysical aspects of individuals. By embracing monotheism, adhering to the criteria of authentic Islāmic psychotherapy, and integrating diverse sources of knowledge, Islāmic psychotherapists are equipped to provide effective and culturally sensitive care that promotes healing and well-being in accordance with Islāmic principles.

References

Al-Ghazālī. (1999). *Deliverance from error (Al-Munqidh min al-Dalal)* (R. J. McCarthy, Trans.). Fons Vitae.

Al-Ghazālī. (2000). *The incoherence of the philosophers (Tahāfut al-Falāsifah): A parallel English-Arabic Text. Marmura, Michael E. Utah.* Brigham Young University Press.

Cowan, J. M., & Wehr, H. (Eds.). (1976). *A dictionary of modern written Arabic* (3rd ed.). Spoken Language Service.
Hussain, F. A. (2011). *Therapy from the Qur'ân and Ahādīth. A reference guide for character development.* Maktaba Dar-Us-Salam.
Ibn Rushd (Averroes). (2001). *The decisive treatise (Fasl al-Maqal)* (Charles E. Butterworth, Trans.). Brigham Young University Press.
Ibn Rushd (Averroes). (2012). *The incoherence of the incoherence (Tahafut al-Tahafut)* (Simon Van Den Bergh, Trans., Vols. 1 & 2). Oxbow Books.
Leaman, O. (Ed.). (2006). *The Qur'ân: An encyclopedia.* Routledge.
Malkawi, F. H. (2014). *Epistemological integration: Essentials of an Islāmic methodology.* The International Institute of Islāmic Thought.
Philips, A. A. B. (2005). *The fundamentals of Tawheed (Islāmic monotheism).* International Islāmic Publishing House.
Rassool, G. H. (2021). *Islāmic psychology: Human behaviour and experience from an Islāmic perspective.* Routledge.
Rassool, G. H. (2025). *Spiritual integration in Islāmic psychotherapy: Unveiling the therapist's soul.* Focus Series. Islāmic Psychology and Psychotherapy). Routledge.
Utz, A. (2011). *Psychology from an Islāmic perspective.* International Islāmic Publishing House.

Chapter 3
Shifting the Paradigm: Decolonising Psychology Knowledge

3.1 Introduction

The evolution of Islāmic psychotherapy and counselling in Western countries is driven by several factors. One primary reason is the growing Muslim population in these regions, which creates a demand for culturally and religiously sensitive mental health services. Western societies are increasingly recognising the importance of integrating spiritual and cultural contexts into therapeutic practices to enhance their effectiveness for diverse populations. Additionally, the rising awareness of mental health issues within Muslim communities, coupled with the stigma often associated with seeking help, has prompted the development of tailored approaches that align with Islāmic values and teachings. These culturally competent services aim to bridge the gap between traditional religious guidance and contemporary psychological practices, fostering a more holistic approach to mental health care that resonates with Muslim clients. Furthermore, the collaboration between Western-trained mental health professionals and Islāmic scholars helps in creating frameworks that respect religious beliefs while addressing psychological needs, thereby enriching the field of psychotherapy with diverse perspectives and methodologies. This chapter examines the Islāmic awakening in decolonising psychology knowledge and the rationale or an Islāmic psychotherapy and counselling.

3.2 The Islāmic Awakening

The Islāmic awakening is referred to as *tajdid* in Arabic. *Tajdid* means renewal or revival, and it is often used in the context of renewing Islāmic thought, practices, or revival of Islāmic principles. The Islāmic reformers of the nineteenth to twenty-first centuries actively resisted the colonisation of knowledge through various means,

G. H. Rassool, *Exploring the Intersection of Islāmic Spirituality and Psychotherapy*,
https://doi.org/10.1007/978-3-031-72724-5_3

including the revitalisation of Islāmic intellectual traditions, the promotion of education, the critique of Western imperialism, and the development of indigenous knowledge systems. Some of the key Islāmic reformers of the Islāmic awakening, including Shah Wali Allah, Muhammad Abduh, Rashid Rida, Jamal al-Din al-Afghani, Muhammad Iqbal, Hasan al-Banna, Sayyid Qutb, Mohammed Qutb, Abul, Ismail Raji al-Faruqi, Syed Muhammad Naquib al-Attas, and Fazlur Rahman. These reformers have significantly contributed to Islāmic thought, education, and socio-political movements. The collective contributions of Islāmic reformers have significantly shaped the Islāmic awakening by emphasising a return to the Qur'ân and *Sunnah*, advocating for independent reasoning (*ijtihad*), and integrating modern sciences with Islāmic teachings to reform educational curricula. These reformers challenged the intellectual hegemony of Western colonial powers by revitalising Islāmic scholarship, promoting education, and encouraging critical engagement with both Islāmic and Western thought. They highlighted the moral and spiritual shortcomings of Western ideologies, advocating for Islāmic alternatives, and engaged in political activism to promote Islāmic governance and social justice, influencing various Islāmic movements and political parties. Additionally, they developed Islāmic metaphysics and epistemology to counter secular thought and promote a holistic Islāmic worldview. Their works continue to inspire contemporary Islāmic thought and movements, playing a crucial role in the ongoing process of Islāmic revival and reform.

The concept of the Islāmisation of Knowledge refers to an intellectual movement aimed at integrating Islāmic principles and values with contemporary knowledge and sciences. Key figures such as Ismail Raji al-Faruqi and Syed Muhammad Naquib al-Attas played pivotal roles in this movement. Al-Faruqi (1982) and Al-Attas (2014) laid the philosophical groundwork for integrating Islāmic principles with various disciplines, including psychology. Their works emphasised the importance of embedding ethical and spiritual dimensions into scientific knowledge. Al-Faruqi is one of the most prominent figures in the Islāmisation of Knowledge movement. He argued that the secularisation of knowledge had led to a disconnection between science and ethics, resulting in moral and social crises. He proposed the integration of Islāmic principles into all fields of knowledge. Al-Faruqi wrote extensively on the need for an Islāmic approach to knowledge. His works, such as "Islāmisation of Knowledge: General Principles and Work Plan" (Abū:Sulayman, 1997), provide a comprehensive framework for integrating Islāmic values into contemporary education and research. Al-Attas is another major proponent of the Islāmisation of Knowledge. He emphasises the importance of recognising the metaphysical and epistemological foundations of Islāmic knowledge. He believes that modern knowledge must be reoriented to align with Islāmic worldviews. Al-Attas introduced the concept of *adab* (etiquette) in education, which involves the inculcation of good manners, ethics, and proper understanding of one's role in society. He argues that education should produce individuals who are morally and intellectually sound.

There are other scholars that must be credited, directly or indirectly for their demands in the decolonisation of knowledge and for the *tajdid* (awakening) of the Muslim *Ummah* in relation to the revival of Islāmic education Some of the scholars include Ashraf Ali Thanvi, Syed Abul A'la Maududi, and Seyyed Hossein Nasr. For A'la Mawdudi, the Islāmisation of Knowledge focused on a "critical analysis of western humanities and sciences to recast them in accordance with the teachings of Islām" (Moten, 2004, p. 257). He asserted that Islām is not merely a religion in the traditional sense but a comprehensive system encompassing all aspects of life, including politics, economics, legislation, science, humanism, health, psychology, and sociology. Islām makes no discrimination based on race, colour, language, or other external categories and aims to appeal to and reach the heart of every human being. Seyyed Hossein Nasr is a prominent contemporary Islāmic scholar who has made significant contributions to the Islāmisation of knowledge. Nasr emphasises the importance of integrating Islāmic principles with modern knowledge, advocating for a holistic approach that respects both traditional Islāmic teachings and contemporary scientific advancements. Nasr believes that the crisis in modern education stems from its disconnection from spiritual and moral values, which can be addressed by reintroducing an Islāmic perspective that harmonises science and spirituality. In "The Need for a Sacred Science" (Nasr, 1989), he calls for a science that acknowledges the sacred and integrates metaphysical principles, contrasting it with the secular, reductionist approach of modern science. Nasr's has fostered a deeper appreciation of Islāmic contributions to global knowledge and encouraged a revival of Islāmic intellectual traditions in the modern world.

3.3 Globalising Psychology Knowledge

Since the colonial period, psychology's epistemologies and knowledge systems have remained largely unchanged, still rooted in Western-centric and Eurocentric views. This perpetuates white dominance, stereotypes, and prejudices against non-white cultures. The influence of globalised-Eurocentric psychology, rooted in Judeo-Christian traditions, has deeply permeated colonised countries and remains institutionalised in many post-colonial nations. This Westernised psychological paradigm continues to spread rapidly due to the momentum of globalisation. The impact of globalisation is evident in the shifting attitudes, values, and behaviours of indigenous populations, leading to a dilution of religious and cultural beliefs that shape cultural identity and collective obligations. The colonial impact is particularly noticeable in the widespread adoption and expansion of hegemonic psychology in undergraduate and postgraduate courses in post-colonial Muslim countries (Rassool & Luqman, 2023).

There are concerns that globalisation and Americanisation of psychology (both academic and clinical) perpetuate colonial and neo-colonial traditions. The "White curriculum" in psychology, as described by Peters (2018) and Picower (2009, p. 198), is based on "Whiteness" as an ideology that sustains White supremacy. This curriculum, prevalent in both Western and Muslim-majority countries, impacts students by promoting Eurocentric psychology knowledge and clinical practice. Bhatia (2017) noted that this curriculum is often presented as race-neutral and universal, while Gillborn (2021) asserted that White practices are portrayed as the correct practices and the legitimate producers of knowledge (Johnson & Joseph-Salisbury, 2018). The colonial impact is evident in the expansion of hegemonic psychology in undergraduate and postgraduate courses in post-colonial Muslim countries. Moghaddam and Harre (1995) observed that power inequalities between and within nations remain a crucial factor shaping psychology, posing ethical issues. They argued that "Third World" psychologists are trained in the US and other Western countries without considering the appropriateness of their training, thus continuing exploitative traditions established through colonialism (1995). Watters (2010) highlighted the problematic influences of globalisation on cross-cultural psychological practices, stating, "We are engaged in the grand project of Americanising the world's understanding of the human mind" (p. 1). He suggested that America leads in creating new mental health treatments and theories, exporting psychopharmaceuticals and categorising disorders in a way that defines global perceptions of mental illness and health, often without regard for cultural appropriateness (APA, 2021). Bulhan (1985) highlighted that European colonisation extended beyond land occupation and resource appropriation to the occupation of the mind.

This psychological colonisation has led Muslim psychologists to follow Western theories of personality, motivation, and behaviour, which often contradict Islāmic principles (Badri, 2016). Badri argued that these theories, presented as scientific, lead many Muslim psychologists to accept and apply them uncritically, despite their unsuitability for Muslim contexts. Rassool and Luqmam (2023) termed this phenomenon "psychological *taqlid*", referring to the blind following of secular psychology by Muslim psychologists (pp. 2–3).The blind imitation of Western psychology by Muslim psychologists leads to the inappropriate export of Western theories to non-Western contexts, causing several negative consequences. It marginalises indigenous psychology knowledge systems, devalues local psychological and psychospiritual practices, and fosters cultural homogenisation, where diverse identities are suppressed in favour of a dominant Western paradigm. This approach undermines the cultural relevance and effectiveness of psychological interventions, perpetuates intellectual and cultural dependency, and echoes colonial exploitation. Ignoring indigenous knowledge systems leads to a lack of culturally sensitive mental health care, limiting the potential for truly inclusive and diversified global psychological practice.

3.4 Decolonising Psychology Knowledge

There has been a propagation of the literature focusing on the decolonisation of psychological science (Adams et al., 2015; Adams et al., 2018; Dudgeon & Walker, 2015; Gómez-Ordóñez et al., 2021; Rassool, 2020, 2023). Despite the momentum for an Islāmic psychology paradigm shift in the 1980s to replace mainstream psychology, the decolonisation of psychology knowledge and the "White curriculum" remain prevalent in most universities in Muslim countries. In the context of Islāmic psychology decolonisation of psychology knowledge is

> the process of embedding an Islāmic epistemologies, knowledge systems, theories, research and clinical practices in empirical psychology disciplines. In other words, it is about balancing the secular psychology narratives with Islāmic psychology, ethics and sciences while both evidenced-based psychological knowledge and Islāmic intellectual tradition are maintained. (Rassool, 2021, p. 583)

Decolonisation of psychological knowledge entails challenging and undoing Orientalist and Eurocentric worldviews in psychology, freeing minds from colonial ideology and supremacy. It involves shifting from secular and Western paradigms to psychological knowledge rooted in Indigenous religio-cultural worldviews. Decolonising psychology and psychotherapy involve critically examining and integrating non-Western perspectives and approaches to mental health, historically marginalised or dismissed. The argument suggests that a more integrated psychology in the twenty-first century should prioritise ethics and human values, recognising them as essential aspects of psychological inquiry. Reber (2006) contends that issues such as ethics, human values, aesthetics, and the nature of life are inherently linked to psychology, emphasising the importance of incorporating philosophical and religious perspectives into psychological discourse.

Rassool (2023) suggested that "In order to dismantle Eurocentric-US psychology knowledge in institutions, some of the approaches of reclaiming psychology include diversification of knowledge, indigenisation of knowledge and knowledge integration. Diversification of psychology knowledge means addressing the impact and importance of race and diversity to understand human behaviour and experiences; otherwise, it can be argued that psychology is incomplete" (p. 15). In the context of Islāmic psychology, diversifying psychology knowledge is a preliminary step, but it does not address the perceived "soullessness" of Western psychology. Badri (2016) emphasised the absence of consideration for the spiritual aspects of humanity within Western psychology, which can only find relevance in materialistic societies. Indigenisation of knowledge, another approach, aims to reflect local cultural contexts and wisdom within the psychological disciplines, thereby challenging the hegemony of Western psychology and contributing to the decolonisation process.

Attempts to indigenise psychology, whether from within or from without, face inherent challenges. Long (2014) argues that indigenisation from without is paradoxical because Western psychology, rooted in a secular metatheory, cannot accommodate the Islāmic worldview, resulting in revisions that may essentially replicate the original framework. On the other hand, indigenisation from within, led by individuals without professional training in psychology who focus solely on Islāmic spirituality, may prioritise spiritual advocacy over the integration of Islāmic principles into psychology itself (Long, 2014). Rassool (2021) likens these challenges to navigating between *Scylla* and *Charybdis*,[1] suggesting that attempts to indigenise psychology encounter formidable obstacles regardless of the approach.

[1] is an idiom deriving from Greek mythology, which has been associated with "to choose the lesser of two evils"?

3.5 Knowledge Integration: Islāmic Spirituality and Psychology

Badri (2013) emphasised the integration of Islāmic teachings into psychological practice, advocating for a holistic approach that prioritises spiritual well-being as central to mental health. His efforts in establishing Islāmic psychology as a discipline have fostered a new generation of psychologists trained to incorporate Islāmic principles in their practice. Rassool (2021, 2023) has significantly advanced Islāmic psychology and psychotherapy by integrating Islāmic concepts with contemporary practices. He promotes a holistic approach to mental health that includes spiritual, metaphysical, psychological and physical dimensions, highlighting their interconnectedness for overall well-being. Through undergraduate and postgraduate courses, training programmes, workshops, and seminars, Rassool educates mental health professionals on incorporating Islāmic principles into their practice, spreading knowledge and best practices internationally. Both Badri and Rassool highlight the necessity of crafting psychological theories grounded in Islāmic epistemology, which appreciates the integral role of spiritual and moral dimensions in human experience. By critiquing the limitations of Western-centric paradigms, they advocate for a more holistic understanding of mental health that aligns with Islāmic teachings. Their efforts have been instrumental in establishing educational programmes that integrate Islāmic values with psychological sciences. These programmes provide students with a framework that is not only academically rigorous but also culturally and religiously pertinent, enabling future psychologists to offer more relevant and effective mental health care to Muslim communities. Through these initiatives, Badri and Rassool contribute to a more inclusive and diversified field of psychology that respects and incorporates the rich spiritual heritage of Islām.

Knowledge integration in psychology involves combining Islāmic sciences, ethics, and worldview with classical and contemporary psychological knowledge. This approach maintains both evidence-based psychological knowledge and Islāmic traditions derived from the Qur'ān and *Sunnah* in the curriculum. Despite differences in sources and methodologies, Islāmic theology and psychology share common concerns such as humanity, purpose, meaning, spirituality, suffering, morality, and human potential. The Qur'ān and *Sunnah* provide insights that enhance the understanding of human behaviours and experiences. Rassool (2022, 2023) has created a model for integrating knowledge in psychology, which includes six key components: (1) planning, (2) mastering, (3) deconstructing, (4) curriculum mapping, (5) scope/level of integration with Islāmic studies/psychology, and (6) knowledge transfer. These mechanisms function systematically to develop psychology knowledge within an Islāmic framework.

3.6 Conclusion

For Islāmic psychology to become a significant force in majority Muslim countries, educationalists and clinicians must focus on decolonising psychology curricula. This initial step is crucial for the broader decolonisation of clinical assessment and therapeutic interventions. The pervasive influence of European colonisation, as highlighted by Bulhan (1985), has led Muslim psychologists to adopt theories of personality, motivation, and behaviour that often contradict Islāmic principles, as noted by Badri (2016). Badri criticises these theories for being misleadingly presented as scientific, which causes many Muslim psychologists to uncritically accept and apply them, even when they are unsuitable for Muslim contexts. To successfully integrate Islāmic psychology and ethical values into psychology curricula, it is essential to assess and manage the readiness of both individuals and institutions. This preparation is crucial before implementing changes in educational programmes. The ultimate goal is to equip clinicians with the most effective approaches to address the psychosocial and spiritual issues faced by the Muslim *Ummah* (community). By doing so, Islāmic psychology can offer culturally and spiritually relevant solutions, enhancing the well-being of Muslim populations.

References

Abū:Sulayman, 'AbdulHamid. (1997). *Islāmization of knowledge: General principles and work plan* (3rd ed.). International Institute of Islāmic Thought (IIIT).

Adams, G., Dobles, I., Gómez, L., Kurtiş, T., & Molina, L. E. (2015). Decolonizing psychological science: Introduction to the special thematic session. *Journal of Social and Political Psychology, 3*(1), 213–238.

Adams, G., Estrada-Villalta, S., & Gómez Ordóñez, L. H. (2018). The modernity/coloniality of being: Hegemonic psychology as intercultural relations. *International Journal of Intercultural Relations, 62*(4), 13–22.

Al-Attas, S. M. N. (2014). *Prolegomena to the metaphysics of Islām: An exposition of the fundamental elements of the worldview of Islām*. Penerbit UTM Press.

Al-Faruqi, I. R. (1982). *Islāmization of knowledge: General principles and work plan*. International Institute of Islāmic Thought (IIIT).

American Psychiatric Association. (2021). *Abstract. Crazy like us: The globalization of the American psyche*. https://psycnet.apa.org/record/2010-00036-000. Accessed 2 June 2024.

Badri, M. (2013). *Contemplation: An Islāmic psychospiritual study*. International Institute of Islāmic Thought (IIIT).

Badri, M. (2016). *The dilemma of Muslim psychologists*. Islāmic Book Trust.

Bhatia, S. (2017). *Decolonizing psychology: Globalization, social justice, and Indian youth identities*. Oxford University Press.

Bulhan, H. A. (1985). *Frantz fanon and the psychology of oppression*. Plenum Press.

Dudgeon, P., & Walker, R. (2015). Decolonising Australian psychology: Discourse, strategies, and practice. *Journal of Social and Political Psychology, 3*(1), 276–297. https://doi.org/10.5964/jspp.v3i1.126

Gillborn, S., Woolnough, H., Jankowski, G., & Sandle, R. (2021). 'Intensely white': Psychology curricula and the (re) production of racism. *Educational Review*. https://doi.org/10.1080/00131911.2021.1978402

Gómez-Ordóñez, L., Adams, G., Ratele, K., Suffla, S., Stevens, G., & Reddy, G.(2021). Decolonising psychological science: encounters and cartographies of resistance. *The Psychologist*, September, 54–57.

Johnson, A., & Joseph-Salisbury, R. (2018). 'Are you supposed to be in here?' Racial microaggressions and knowledge production in higher education. In J. Arday & H. S. Mirza (Eds.), *Dismantling race in higher education* (pp. 143–160). Palgrave Macmillan.

Long, W. (2014). Critical reflections on the Islamicisation of psychology. *Revelation and Science, 4*(1), 10.31436/revival.v4i1.104.

Moghaddam, F. M., & Harre, R. (1995). The Islāmization of psychology: Its "why", its "what", its "how" and its "who". *International Journal of Islāmic Psychology, 3*(1), 22–33. Cited in Badri, M. (2020).

Moten, A. R. (2004). Islāmization of knowledge in theory and practice. *Islāmic Studies, 43*(2), 247–272.

Nasr, S. H. *1989, Knowledge and the sacred*. State University of New York Press. Digitized 2011.

Peters, M. A. (2018). Why is my curriculum white? A brief genealogy of resistance. In J. Arday & H. Mirza (Eds.), *Dismantling race in higher education*. Palgrave Macmillan. https://doi.org/10.1007/978-3-319-60261-5_14

Picower, B. (2009). The unexamined whiteness of teaching: How white teachers maintain and enact dominant racial ideologies. *Race Ethnicity and Education, 12*(2), 197–215.

Rassool, G. H. (2020). Cognitive restructuring of psychology: The case for a vertical and horizontal integrated, embedded curriculum model for Islāmic psychology. *Islāmic Studies, 59*(4), 477–494.

Rassool, G. H. (2021). Decolonising psychology and its (dis) contents. In G. H. Rassool (Ed.), *Islāmic psychology: Human behaviour and experiences from an Islāmic perspective* (pp. 583–601). Routledge.

Rassool, G. H. (2022). *Mechanism of knowledge integration and process-driven model of curriculum integration*. (Unpublished Paper).

Rassool, G. H. (2023). *Advancing Islāmic psychology education: Model, application, and implementation* (Focus Series on Islāmic Psychology and Psychotherapy). Routledge.

Rassool, G. H., & Luckman, M. (2023). *Foundations of Islāmic psychology: From classical scholars to contemporary thinkers*. Routledge.

Reber, J. (2006). Secular psychology: What's the problem? *Journal of Psychology and Theology, 34*(3), 193–204. https://doi.org/10.1177/009164710603400302

Watters, E. (2010). *Crazy like us: The globalization of the American psyche*. Free Press.

Chapter 4
The Anatomy of Islāmic Psychotherapy

4.1 Introduction

Psychotherapy, a discipline traditionally rooted in Western psychological paradigms, focuses on the treatment of mental health issues through various psychological techniques. However, the universality of psychological experiences necessitates a broader perspective that encompasses diverse cultural and religious contexts. Islāmic psychotherapy emerges as a distinctive approach that integrates principles of Islām with contemporary psychotherapeutic practices. This fusion aims to address the psychological needs of Muslim clients in a manner that is both culturally relevant and spiritually enriching. Islāmic psychotherapy is not merely a subset of religious therapy but a comprehensive therapeutic framework that considers the spiritual, psychological, and social dimensions of the individual. At its core, it acknowledges the profound impact of faith and spirituality on mental well-being. Central to this approach is the Qur'ânic view of the human psyche, which encompasses the *nafs* (self), *qalb* (heart), *rûh* (spirit), and *'aql* (intellect). These concepts are integral to understanding the holistic nature of human existence in Islāmic thought.

The practice of Islāmic psychotherapy involves utilising therapeutic techniques that are congruent with Islāmic teachings and values; and Islāmic healing. Additionally, it incorporates the rich tradition of Islāmic ethical and moral guidance, which provides a framework for addressing issues of guilt, shame, and forgiveness. The therapist's role extends beyond the clinical setting, encompassing a duty to guide the client towards spiritual and moral rectitude in line with Islāmic principles (Rassool, 2016, 2025a, b).In contemporary times, the relevance of Islāmic psychotherapy is highlighted by the growing Muslim populations in Western societies and the increasing recognition of the importance of culturally competent mental health care. Resources indicate that the number of Muslims around the world is projected to increase rapidly in the decades ahead, growing from about 1.6 billion

G. H. Rassool, *Exploring the Intersection of Islāmic Spirituality and Psychotherapy*,
https://doi.org/10.1007/978-3-031-72724-5_4

in 2010 to nearly 2.8 billion in 2050 (Pew Research Center, 2015). Muslim clients often face unique challenges, such as Islāmophobia, cultural dislocation, and identity conflicts, which can exacerbate mental health issues. By aligning therapeutic practices with Islāmic beliefs, Islāmic psychotherapy offers a supportive and validating environment that respects the client's cultural and religious identity. This integration of Islāmic spirituality and psychotherapy not only provides a culturally sensitive approach to treatment but also contributes to the broader field of psychotherapy by introducing alternative perspectives and methodologies. In this exploration of the anatomy of Islāmic psychotherapy, the focus of the chapter is to provide a comprehensive rationale for the development of Islāmic psychology and psychotherapy, addressing the unique mental health needs and challenges faced by Muslim clients. It will explore the epistemological, ontological, and axiological foundations of Islāmic psychotherapy, detailing how knowledge, the nature of being, and ethical values are derived from Islāmic teachings. The chapter will also review the Islāmic worldview and identify the paradigm of Islāmic psychotherapy,

4.2 Muslim: Mental Health and Spirituality

Globally, Muslims encounter numerous psychosocial challenges and the myriad conflicts in Middle Eastern countries have led to high rates of Post Traumatic Syndrome Disorder, depression, anxiety, and stress among Muslims (Rassool, 2019). Globally, Muslims encounter numerous psychosocial challenges across these domains: within the larger community, within their local communities, interpersonally, and intrapersonally (Tanhan & Young, 2022). In some religious communities and among religious individuals, possession is often used as an explanatory model for illnesses such as epilepsy, panic, and depression (Littlewood, 2004; McRae & Whitley, 2014; Rassool, 2019). Mental health problems among Muslims can be attributed to three main factors: spiritual causes (such as the evil eye (*hasad or nathla*), demon possession (*Jinn*), and magic influences (*sihr*) (Rassool, 2019), internal factors (including genetic predispositions, brain disorders, and personal conflicts), and external psychosocial factors (encompassing social and environmental influences like discrimination, stigma, societal pressures, and traumatic events). The supernatural belief, common among both indigenous Muslims and those in the West, contributes to the stigma surrounding mental health. This stigma hinders individuals and families from seeking help and leads to social rejection and discrimination, impacting marriage, socialisation, and business relationships. This has severe implications for mental health, psychosocial, and spiritual issues. Clinicians will likely provide care for a Muslim some time in their careers and, depending on the location of their practice, may deliver care to a relatively large and diverse group of Muslims.

Spirituality plays a significant role in the lives of many Muslims, serving as a source of strength, guidance, and resilience in times of adversity. Many clients have a desire to discuss spirituality or religion in psychotherapy or counselling. There is evidence to suggest a growing acceptance in the psychotherapeutic world that the spiritual dimension is very important to many clients. Though religion and spirituality are important issues for clients from a faith background, they may not always feel comfortable bringing their religious beleifs and values into counselling due to fear, shame, and guilt (Rose et al., 2008; Mayers et al., 2007; Warwick, 2002). Some researchers advocate incorporating religion into mainstream therapeutic approaches for Muslim clients, arguing that this alignment with their belief systems can enhance the effectiveness of the therapy (Hodge & Nadir, 2008; Meer & Mir, 2014). Clients felt that discussing religious concerns in therapy was appropriate and preferred to talk about spiritual and religious issues during their sessions (Rose et al., 2008; Sadiq, 2019). The most significant factor influencing this preference was the clients' own spiritual experiences (Rose et al., 2008).

However, various therapeutic approaches, such as psychoanalytic, person-centred, cognitive, and integrative therapies, have been described and developed primarily within the context of Western therapy, which are based on Eurocentric and Orientalist assumptions. These approaches are grounded in Western philosophical and cultural norms, emphasising individualism, personal autonomy, and self-actualisation. These Eurocentric foundations mean that the therapeutic models and their evaluations (Reavey et al., 2006) are often aligned with values that prioritise individual achievement and personal responsibility, which may not resonate with Muslim clients from collectivist cultures. These principles can clash with the collectivist values prevalent in many Muslim communities, where the focus is on family, community, and interdependence. Muslim clients may prioritise collective well-being, social harmony, and religious obligations over individual achievements. This cultural disconnection can lead to misunderstandings and reduced effectiveness of therapy, as the therapeutic goals and methods may not resonate with the clients' values and lived experiences. In addition, Eurocentric assumptions inherent in elements of Western therapy can trigger internal and interpersonal conflict for clients from collectivist cultures (Owusu-Bempah & Howitt, 2000). As a result, these Western-developed therapies might not fully address the cultural and spiritual dimensions that are integral to the identity and well-being of clients from diverse backgrounds. This misalignment can lead to misunderstandings, reduced therapeutic efficacy, and the need for culturally adapted therapeutic practices that better align with the clients' worldviews and values.

For Muslims, there is a need to apply a faith-based therapeutic approach in dealing with mental and psychosocial problems. This necessity arises from the fact that mainstream therapeutic approaches, primarily developed within Western contexts, often do not align with the cultural and religious values integral to Muslim clients. Several researchers and practitioners have highlighted the importance of incorporating Islāmic principles into therapeutic practices to enhance their relevance and effectiveness for Muslim clients (Ahmed & Amer, 2012; Hodge & Nadir, 2008; Ibrahim & Mojab, 2022; Meer & Mir 2014; Podikunju-Hussain, n.d.; Rassool, 2015, 2016, 2025a, b). For instance, Hodge and Nadir (2008) emphasise that integrating religious beliefs into therapy can help Muslim clients feel more understood and respected, fostering a therapeutic environment that is congruent with their faith.

They argue that this alignment can enhance the therapeutic alliance and increase the likelihood of positive outcomes. Similarly, Meer and Mir (2014) discuss how culturally sensitive counselling that incorporates Islāmic teachings can better address the spiritual and psychological needs of Muslim clients, providing a holistic approach that considers both their mental health and spiritual well-being. Moreover, some Muslims believe that establishing a spiritual connection with the Creator can aid in overcoming mental health challenges (Ibrahim & Mojab, 2022). In effect, matching client with therapist for Muslim clients is likely to result in better understanding, particularly regarding cultural references and religious metaphors (Meer & Mir, 2014). However, for Muslim clients trust, empathy, warmth, respect and care, and therapist' cultural awareness and understanding of Islāmic values were considered in the therapeutic process (Meer & Mir, 2014; Shafi, 1998).

Muslim clients often bring cultural expectations and preferences to the therapy room where there may be a greater emphasis on hierarchy and authority figures, including in therapeutic relationships. As a result, these clients may feel more comfortable and reassured when the therapist takes a more active and directive role in the therapy process in resolving problems (Mir et al., 2015; Rassool, 2016, 2025a, b, c) This preference for directive therapy approaches can also stem from cultural norms regarding communication styles, problem-solving strategies, and high-context communication (Adair et al., 2024). High-context communication means that much of the information is conveyed through the context, including body language, tone of voice, and the surrounding social environment, rather than through explicit words. This reliance on non-verbal cues requires a shared understanding of cultural norms and values, allowing individuals to communicate effectively without direct statements. Therapists working with Muslim clients may need to adopt an approach to align with these communication preferences. This might involve being more proactive in providing guidance and interventions early on in therapy, as well as adopting communication styles that are direct and clear. By recognising and respecting these cultural nuances, therapists can enhance the therapeutic alliance and improve the effectiveness of therapy.

The above factors have provided significant impetus for reverting to Islāmic psychology and psychotherapy, emphasising the need to develop therapeutic practices that are culturally and spiritually aligned with the holistic needs of Muslim clients. The field of Islāmic psychology has gained momentum as scholars and practitioners recognise the importance of integrating Islāmic principles with conventional therapeutic methods. This integration seeks to address the unique cultural and spiritual needs of Muslim clients. Islāmic psychotherapy promotes a holistic view of health, addressing the interconnectedness of mind, body, and spirit. This approach resonates with the holistic health paradigm found in Islāmic teachings. Islāmic psychotherapy is a unique and distinct approach to psychological interventions that incorporates the principles, values, and teachings of Islām into the therapeutic process. Over the past two decades, a substantial body of literature has emerged in the field of education, research, and clinical domains in Islāmic psychology and psychotherapy.

4.3 Islāmic Worldview: Core Elements and Characteristics

The Islāmic worldview (*Tasawur or Ru'yah al-Islām li al-Wujud*) or the Qur'ānic worldview

is integral to the epistemology, ontology, and axiology of Islāmic psychotherapy, providing a comprehensive framework that shapes the understanding and practice of therapy. The Islāmic worldview is rooted in the Qurʾān, *Sunnah,* and Islāmic civilisation. The Islāmic worldview, as described by various scholars, encompasses a comprehensive and holistic vision of reality and truth, integrating all aspects of life and existence.

Syed Naquib Al-Attas (1995) defines it as a vision that encompasses both the visible and invisible worlds, presenting a metaphysical survey of existence (*wujud*) and its ontological aspects. Sayyid Qutb (1983) describes it as "*al-Tashawwur al-Islami*" a vision that brings Muslims closer to the essence of the world, life, and their surroundings, fostering a profound connection with all elements of existence. Hassan (1994) expands on this by portraying the Islāmic worldview as a comprehensive conception of Allāh, humanity, and the universe, highlighting their interrelationships from an Islāmic perspective. Malkawi (2014) adds that this worldview is an expression of the belief-based conceptualisation rooted in Islāmic doctrine, embodying the overall Islāmic belief system. Akhmetova (2021) defines worldview as a comprehensive set of positions, attitudes, values, stories, and expectations that shape our understanding of the world and influence all our thoughts and actions. The Islāmic worldview provides a coherent and integrated framework for understanding reality, guiding individuals in their perception of life, existence, and their place within the cosmos according to Islāmic teachings. This worldview acts as a set of parameters encompassing a wide range of fundamental matters, including philosophy, themes, values, emotions, ethics, language, culture, and religion. It shapes a subjective way of thinking, offering a vision for interacting with the world that aligns with Islāmic principles and perspectives, thereby influencing every thought and action of believers.

Islāmic worldview, based principally on a system of values and principles, derived from the Qurʾān, inherently ethical and monotheistic, centred on the belief in one God and encompassing both visible and the unseen world (*ghayb*). The Islāmic worldview based on the *Tawhîdic* paradigm covers all aspects of life for its adherents. It is "based on three fundamental principles which are: *Tawhîd* (Theism), *Khilâfah* (Vicegerency), and *'Adâlah* (Justice). These principles not only frame the Islāmic worldview, but they also constitute the fountainhead of the objectives (*Maqasid*) and the strategy of Man's life in this world" (Abdullah & Nadvi, 2011, p. 271). The Islāmic worldview, beyond the concept of *tawhîd* incorporates an extensive ethical dimension known as *akhlāq*, or morality. This moral framework emphasises profound respect for humanity and the pursuit of social justice, promoting equality, inclusive relationships, and moral courage to uphold the truth. It advocates for the acceptance of diversity with tolerance, practicing restraint and forgiveness in times of provocation, and leading a disciplined life. Additionally, there is a strong commitment to charity, reverence for human life, and the use of reason and intellect in making decisions. Central to *akhlāq* is the accountability for one's actions and the paramount importance of justice (*'adl*) for both individuals and society. These principles form the foundation of a moral society where fairness, responsibility, and compassion are prioritised. By adhering to these ethical guidelines, individuals contribute to a just and harmonious community, reflecting the core values of Islām (Alwee, 2005).

The ethical aspect of Islāmic worldview is reflected in the following verse. Allāh says:

لَّيْسَ ٱلْبِرَّ أَن تُوَلُّوا۟ وُجُوهَكُمْ قِبَلَ ٱلْمَشْرِقِ وَٱلْمَغْرِبِ وَلَـٰكِنَّ ٱلْبِرَّ مَنْ ءَامَنَ بِٱللَّهِ وَٱلْيَوْمِ ٱلْـَٔاخِرِ وَٱلْمَلَـٰٓئِكَةِ وَٱلْكِتَـٰبِ وَٱلنَّبِيِّـۧنَ
وَءَاتَى ٱلْمَالَ عَلَىٰ حُبِّهِۦ ذَوِى ٱلْقُرْبَىٰ وَٱلْيَتَـٰمَىٰ وَٱلْمَسَـٰكِينَ وَٱبْنَ ٱلسَّبِيلِ وَٱلسَّآئِلِينَ وَفِى ٱلرِّقَابِ وَأَقَامَ ٱلصَّلَوٰةَ وَءَاتَى ٱلزَّكَوٰةَ
وَٱلْمُوفُونَ بِعَهْدِهِمْ إِذَا عَـٰهَدُوا۟ ۖ وَٱلصَّـٰبِرِينَ فِى ٱلْبَأْسَآءِ وَٱلضَّرَّآءِ وَحِينَ ٱلْبَأْسِ ۗ أُو۟لَـٰٓئِكَ ٱلَّذِينَ صَدَقُوا۟ ۖ وَأُو۟لَـٰٓئِكَ هُمُ ٱلْمُتَّقُونَ

- *Righteousness is not in turning your faces towards the east or the west. Rather, the righteous are those who believe in Allāh, the Last Day, the angels, the Books, and the prophets; who give charity out of their cherished wealth to relatives, orphans, the poor, 'needy' travellers, beggars, and for freeing captives; who establish prayer, pay alms-tax, and keep the pledges they make; and who are patient in times of suffering, adversity, and in 'the heat of' battle. It is they who are true 'in faith', and it is they who are mindful 'of Allāh'* (Al-Baqarah 2:177, interpretation of the meaning).

This verse captures the essence of being true in faith of Allāh, suggesting that genuine piety and righteousness are characterised by a combination of faith, moral integrity, social responsibility, and resilience in the face of challenges. The fundamental elements of ethical and moral values in Islām serve as integrating principles, organising standards of behaviour and values into a unified system that forms the Islāmic worldview. This comprehensive framework shapes how Muslims perceive and interact with the world, reflecting a coherent order grounded in Islāmic teachings. Additionally, the Islāmic worldview encompasses both an epistemological system, which outlines the nature and scope of knowledge, and a methodology, guiding the processes and practices of acquiring and applying that knowledge. The characteristics of an Islāmic worldview are presented in Fig. 4.1.

The Islāmic worldview is fundamentally derived from God and based on the *Tawhîdic* paradigm, which emphasises monotheism and the belief in Allāh's existence as understood through His revelations to the Prophet Muhammad (ﷺ). Central to this worldview is the *Shari'ah*, which represents the divine law revealed by Allāh. This comprehensive framework encompasses various aspects of existence, including God, humanity, the universe, and the Hereafter, providing a holistic understanding of life and its purpose. This worldview balances the understanding of divine values with human aspects, promoting a harmonious relationship between God, humans, the universe, and the Hereafter. It encourages a positive and

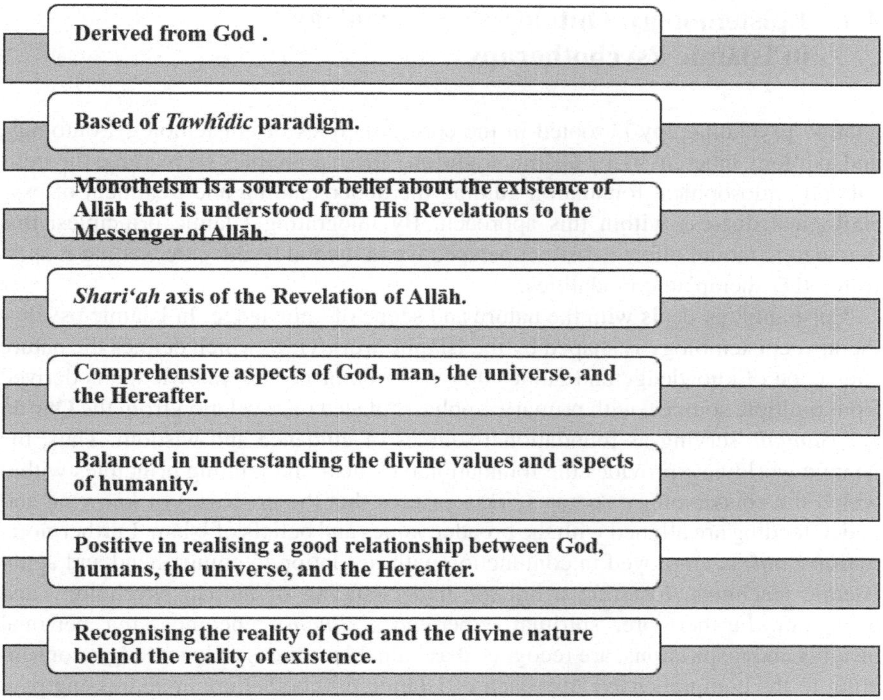

Fig. 4.1 Characteristics of Islāmic worldview

interconnected approach to existence, recognising the reality of God and the divine nature that underlies all aspects of life. Through this lens, Muslims interact with the world, guided by a coherent system of beliefs and values that integrate both spiritual and temporal dimensions. Islāmic psychotherapy is deeply influenced by the Islāmic worldview, which shapes how therapists understand concepts such as human suffering, resilience, and well-being. This worldview, rooted in principles derived from the Qur'ân and *hadīth*, emphasises a holistic understanding of human existence that integrates spiritual, psychological, and physical dimensions. Therapists practicing Islāmic psychotherapy consider the impact of spiritual beliefs and religious practices on mental health, recognising that faith and spirituality play important roles in an individual's coping mechanisms and overall well-being. By drawing on the rich tradition of Islāmic teachings, therapists can provide insights into the nature of human suffering, encouraging clients to find meaning and strength through their faith. By integrating the Islāmic worldview into their practice, therapists offer clients a culturally sensitive and faith-based approach that aligns with their religious beliefs and values, enhancing the effectiveness of therapy.

4.4 Epistemology, Ontology, and Axiology in Islāmic Psychotherapy

Islāmic psychotherapy is rooted in the core principles of epistemology, ontology, and axiology inherent in the Islāmic tradition. These principles serve as the theoretical and philosophical foundation guiding the understanding and treatment of psychological distress within this approach. By integrating Islāmic principles, this therapeutic model offers a distinct perspective in mental health care, setting it apart from other therapeutic modalities.

Epistemology deals with the nature and scope of knowledge. In Islāmic psychotherapy, epistemology is shaped by the Islāmic worldview, which defines the nature and scope of knowledge and guides how it is obtained. True knowledge is derived from multiple sources, with primary emphasis placed on revelation from the Qur'ân and *Sunnah*, serving as foundational sources of guidance and wisdom. Thus, the Islāmic worldview provides the foundational context and guiding principles within which the epistemology operates. This ensures that the processes of knowing and understanding are aligned with the broader values and beliefs of Islām. Furthermore, reason (*'aql*) is employed in conjunction with revelation to comprehend and apply Islāmic teachings, fostering a holistic understanding of human psychology and behaviour. Furthermore, spiritual experiences (*ilham*), encompassing personal insights and inspirations, are recognised as valuable sources of knowledge, contributing to the comprehensive approach of Islāmic psychotherapy in addressing psychological distress and promoting mental health. Islāmic scholarship recognises multiple sources of true knowledge: divine revelation, intuition, empirical observation, and rational inquiry. Islāmic epistemology values rational knowledge derived from human intellect, observation, and empirical evidence, leading to a systematic integration of these sources known as epistemological integration. Malkawi (2014) emphasises that the Islāmic principle of *tawhîd* (divine oneness) underpins the unity of knowledge and epistemological integration. This principle provides a cohesive framework for integrating diverse sources of knowledge, which is essential for a monotheistic Islāmic psychotherapy. In Islāmic psychotherapy, epistemology is linked to both scholarly consensus (*ijma*) and reasoning, within Islāmic doctrines. Although divine knowledge is supreme, Islāmic scholarship places significant emphasis on individual reasoning (*ijtihad*) within Islāmic principles. It stresses that all knowledge should be interconnected and complementary, ultimately deepening the understanding of God.

Ontology, which addresses questions of existence and reality, at a philosophical level, plays a pivotal role in shaping the foundation of Islāmic psychotherapy. Islāmic ontology acknowledges the dualistic nature of humans, comprising both physical and metaphysical aspects, including the self, intellect, soul, emotion, and heart. This perspective highlights the interconnectedness of the *nafs* (self), *'aql* (intellect), *rûh* (soul), *ihsas* (emotion), and *qalb* (heart). It highlights that achieving psychological well-being involves more than just addressing external factors, emphasising the holistic integration of these elements. It acknowledges that to achieve healing and growth a more thorough examination of their complex life—physical, social, psychological, and spiritual is necessary, with an emphasis on bringing these facets into line with the ideals and principles of Islām. Consequently, Islāmic psychotherapy offers a robust framework that takes into account the holistic dimension of a person, their mind, body, and spirit, in the pursuit for holistic psychospiritual health. Ontologically, in Islāmic psychotherapy the concept of *fitrah* holds a significant role in understanding human nature and spirituality. Therapists emphasise reconnecting individuals with their *fitrah* as a crucial pathway for spiritual healing and self-exploration. In Islāmic psychotherapy, belief in the afterlife (*akhirah*) profoundly influences the understanding of the soul's purpose and journey, providing a comprehensive ontological framework for human existence and therapeutic practice. This belief instils a sense of accountability and ultimate purpose, guiding individuals to align their actions and thoughts with spiritual and moral principles. It encourages a deeper exploration of existential questions and the meaning of life, framing psychological and spiritual well-being in the context of an eternal journey.

Axiology, the study of values, is integral to Islāmic psychotherapy, which relies on Islāmic teachings to comprehend and apply moral values, virtues, and ethical conduct. This approach recognises that ethical behaviour and moral conduct are essential for psychological and spiritual health. Therapists incorporate Islāmic ethics into their therapeutic practices, emphasising that aligning actions and attitudes with Islāmic value, such as justice, kindness, gratitude, forgiveness, hope, integrity, and honesty, fosters a harmonious and balanced life. By adhering to these values, individuals can navigate their lives with a sense of moral clarity and purpose, which is essential for overcoming psychological distress and achieving inner peace. This alignment with Islāmic values is known as *Tazkiyah an-nafs*, or the purification of the soul, and it involves a process of personal growth, emotional healing, and spiritual development. Therapists guide individuals to integrate these values into their daily lives, helping them achieve fulfilment and a deeper sense of purpose. This holistic approach not only addresses psychological issues but also enhances spiritual health, promoting a comprehensive model of health that is both psychologically and spiritually enriching. By embedding these core values into therapy, Islāmic psychotherapy provides a pathway to enhanced psychological resilience, emotional stability, and spiritual satisfaction, leading to a more meaningful and satisfying life.

4.5 The Anatomy of Islāmic Psychotherapy

The anatomy of Islāmic psychotherapy comprises several interconnected components that work together to provide a holistic approach to mental health care rooted in Islāmic spirituality. At the core of Islāmic psychotherapy lies the Islāmic worldview, which shapes the understanding of human existence, purpose, and well-being. This worldview emphasises the oneness of God (*tawhîd*) and the interconnectedness of physical, psychological, and spiritual dimensions of life. It provides the overarching framework within which therapy operates, guiding therapists and clients alike in their understanding of mental health issues and their solutions. Islāmic psychotherapy draws upon Islāmic epistemology, which outlines the sources and methods of acquiring knowledge within the Islāmic tradition. In the anatomy of Islāmic psychotherapy, ontology acknowledges the dualistic nature of humans, considering both physical and metaphysical aspects of existence. Axiology is important with therapists integrating Islāmic ethics into therapy to promote moral conduct and spiritual growth. This holistic approach emphasises the interconnectedness of psychological, spiritual, and cultural dimensions in addressing mental health issues.

Islāmic psychotherapy utilises various therapeutic techniques and interventions grounded in Islāmic principles, such as Islāmically cognitive-behavioural techniques, Islāmic contemplative and reflective practices, spiritual counselling, and the incorporation of Islāmic spiritual interventions like remembrance of Allāh, rituals, and prayers. These aim to address psychological distress while fostering spiritual growth and resilience. Central to Islāmic psychotherapy is the emphasis on aligning actions with Islāmic moral values like justice, kindness, gratitude, integrity, and honesty, promoting personal growth, emotional healing, and spiritual development. Moreover, cultural sensitivity is prioritised, acknowledging the diverse backgrounds and experiences of clients within the Muslim community, and therapists strive to create a safe and inclusive environment supportive of clients' mental health. Overall, the anatomy of Islāmic psychotherapy encompasses a holistic approach to mental health care that integrates Islāmic principles, epistemology, therapeutic techniques, ethics, and cultural sensitivity. By addressing the psychological, spiritual, and cultural needs of clients, Islāmic psychotherapy offers a comprehensive pathway to healing and growth within the framework of Islāmic teachings and values. A summary of the anatomy of Islāmic psychotherapy is presented in Table 4.1.

Table 4.1 Anatomy of Islāmic psychotherapy

Category	Summary
Islāmic worldview	Emphasises *tawhîd* (oneness of God) and the interconnectedness of physical, psychological, and spiritual dimensions, guiding therapy approaches
Islāmic epistemology	Draws from divine revelation, reason, empirical observation, and spiritual experiences to inform therapeutic interventions and gain insights into psychological well-being
Ontology	Acknowledges the dualistic nature of humans, viewing individuals as both physical and spiritual entities, enabling therapists to address mental health holistically
Axiology	Integrates Islāmic ethics and values, emphasising ethical behaviour aligned with Islāmic principles for promoting psychological and spiritual well-being
Integration of Islāmic ethics	Centralises Islāmic moral values like justice, kindness, gratitude, integrity, and honesty within therapy sessions to promote personal, emotional, and spiritual development
Cultural sensitivity	Prioritises creating a safe, inclusive environment that respects the diverse backgrounds and experiences of Muslim clients, supporting their mental health journey

4.6 Paradigm of Islāmic Psychotherapy

The paradigm of Islāmic psychotherapy underlines the interconnectedness of various dimensions of human existence, encompassing the physical, social, psychological, environmental, and spiritual aspects. Although there is no universally accepted paradigm, key elements commonly included in Islāmic psychotherapy comprise beliefs in monotheism (*tawhîd*), divine revelation, adherence to ethical values, following Prophet Muhammad (ﷺ) as a role model, recognition of metaphysical components of the soul, principles of Islāmic anthropology, integration of faith with psychology, cultural competence, and the holistic approach to mental health. These elements collectively form the framework guiding Islāmic psychotherapy practices, emphasising the holistic well-being of individuals within the Islāmic context. Table 4.2 provides a summary of the key elements of Islāmic psychotherapy:

Table 4.2 Summary of the key elements of Islāmic psychotherapy

Key elements of Islāmic psychotherapy	Description
Belief in monotheism or *tawhîd*	Emphasises the belief in the oneness of God, central to Islāmic faith
Belief in divine revelation	Recognises divine revelation, such as the Qur'ân and *hadīth*, as sources of knowledge about Allāh, the hidden world, and the purpose of life
Belief in religious characteristics	Acknowledges the connection with the supernatural and invisible world, integral to Islāmic spirituality
Adoption of Prophet Muhammad as a role model	Considers Prophet Muhammad (ﷺ) as an exemplary figure with outstanding character (*khuluqyl 'adhiym*) to emulate
Belief in metaphysical components of the self	Recognises the spiritual entities of *qalb* (heart), *rûh* (soul), *nafs* (self, desire-nature), and *'aql* (intellect, reason) as integral to human existence
Belief in fundamentals of Islāmic anthropology	Includes the concept of *fitrah*, the innate disposition towards Islām, as well as other Islāmic anthropological principles.
Belief in Islāmic ethical and moral values	Emphasises adherence to Islāmic ethical and moral values, guiding behaviour and decision-making
Belief in Qur'ânic and prophetic guidance	Relies on guidance from the Qur'ân and teachings of prophet Muhammad (ﷺ) in addressing psychological issues
Belief in integration of faith and psychology	Recognises the importance of integrating Islāmic faith with psychological principles in therapy
Belief in knowledge integration and integrated research	Emphasises the integration of Islāmic knowledge and research methodologies in the field of Islāmic psychology
Belief in cultural competence and sensitivity	Values cultural competence and sensitivity in therapy, recognising the diverse backgrounds and experiences of clients
Belief in the holistic dimension of Islāmic	Considers the holistic approach to mental health, addressing physical, social, psychological, environmental, and spiritual dimensions of human existence

Source: Adapted from Rassool (Rassool, 2025a, b)

4.7 Islāmic Psychotherapy: Spiritually Integrated Therapy

To grasp the essence of Islāmic psychotherapy, it is essential to examine the definition of Islāmic psychology. This field of study seeks to comprehend human behaviour, cognition, and emotions through the lens of Islāmic beliefs and teachings. Islāmic psychology is defined as "the study of the science of the soul, mental processes, and behaviour according to the principles of empirical psychology, rationality and divine revelation from the Qur'ān and Sunnah" (Rassool, 2023, p.52). This definition underlines the integration of both scientific inquiry and religious principles in understanding human psychology. By combining empirical methods with insights from Islāmic scripture and tradition, Islāmic psychology aims to provide a comprehensive understanding of human nature and behaviour. This approach acknowledges the importance of both empirical evidence and spiritual guidance in addressing mental health challenges and promoting well-being within an Islāmic framework. Islāmic counselling or psychotherapy has been defined as "A form of counselling [or psychotherapy] which incorporates spirituality into the therapeutic process and has a faith-based perspective." (Rassool, 2016, p. 193). This form of counselling or psychotherapy, often referred to as spiritually integrated therapy or faith-based therapy, integrates spirituality into the therapeutic process and adopts a faith-based perspective. By acknowledging the significance of spirituality in individuals' lives, therapists incorporate religious beliefs, practices, and values into the therapeutic sessions. This approach aims to address not only psychological and emotional issues but also spiritual concerns, fostering a deeper sense of meaning, purpose, and connection with one's faith.

The past few decades have seen significant progress in the development and application of integrated Islāmic therapies, reflecting a growing recognition of the importance of addressing mental health within the context of religious identities. The literature includes: Islāmic Counselling: (Rassool, 2016); Islāmically Integrated Psychotherapy (Al-Karam, 2018); Traditional Islāmically Integrated Psychotherapy (TIIP) (Keshavarzi et al., 2021); Acceptance and Commitment Therapy with Islāmic Psychotherapy (Bhatti-Ali, 2023); Integrating Spiritual Interventions in Islāmic Psychology (Latif et al., 2024); Islāmic Counselling & Psychotherapy (Rassool 2025); Tazkiya Therapy in Islāmic Psychotherapy (Riyono, 2024); Treating Addictive Behaviours from an Islāmic Perspective (Rassool,2025a, b); Islāmically Modified Cognitive Behavioural Therapy (Qasqas, 2024); Crisis and Trauma: An Islāmic Perspective (Hassem et al., 2024); Spiritual Integration in Islāmic Psychotherapy (Rassool, 2025a, b) Islāmically Integrated Psychotherapy With Domestic Abuse (Haque, 2025).

Despite the increasing demand for Islāmic psychotherapy services among Muslim clients, the availability of such services has not kept pace. Notable centres like the Khalil Centre in the USA and Canada, and the Ihsan Centre, Al Nour in the UK, exemplify successful integration of Islāmic spirituality into therapeutic care. However, these initiatives are relatively isolated and do not represent a widespread trend. In the absence of widespread institutional support, many Islāmic psychotherapists and clinicians have taken to private practice. These professionals offer individualised care that integrates Islāmic principles, providing essential services to their clients. Private practice allows for flexibility and personalised approaches but may not reach as many people as larger, more established centres.

Rassool (2021) has pointed out significant distinctions between Islāmic psychotherapy and Western-oriented psychotherapeutic approaches. These distinctions encompass The rejection of certain fundamental philosophical principles regarding human nature and personality development, the emphasis on collectivistic values, the cultivation of ethical standards, and the incorporation of Islāmic beliefs and practices. Islāmic psychotherapy, firmly rooted in Islāmic traditions, recognises the significance of integrating religious teachings, ethics, and spirituality into the therapeutic process. It offers a unique approach that acknowledges the multidimensional nature of human beings and emphasises the interconnectedness between the mind, body, and soul. By incorporating Islāmic principles and values, Islāmic psychotherapy provides individuals with the opportunity to address their mental health concerns in a manner that resonates with their religious beliefs and aligns with their quest for meaning and purpose. This integration aims to offer a holistic approach to mental health that takes into account the physical, social, psychological, and spiritual dimensions of individuals' lives.

4.8 Conclusion

The exploration of Islāmic psychotherapy reveals a rich tapestry of interconnected elements that form its anatomy. From the foundational understanding of Muslim mental health, spirituality, and therapy to the core elements of the Islāmic worldview, this holistic approach emphasises the integration of faith, culture, and psychology. Epistemology, ontology, and axiology play pivotal roles in shaping the therapeutic process, providing a framework for understanding knowledge, existence, and values within an Islāmic context. As we explore deeper into the paradigm of Islāmic psychotherapy, it becomes evident that spirituality is interwoven with psychological well-being, and therapy is imbued with cultural sensitivity and a commitment to holistic healing.

Furthermore, the anatomy of Islāmic psychotherapy highlights the significance of spiritually integrated therapy, where Islāmic principles and values are integrated into therapeutic practices. This spiritually integrated approach acknowledges the interconnectedness of physical, social, psychological, metaphysical, environmental, and spiritual dimensions of human existence, offering a comprehensive pathway to mental health and well-being. By embracing the paradigm of Islāmic psychotherapy, therapists are equipped to provide culturally sensitive and faith-based interventions that resonate with the beliefs, values, and experiences of Muslim clients, fostering personal growth, emotional healing, and spiritual development.

References

Abdullah, M., & Nadvi, M. J. (2011). Understanding the principles of Islāmic worldview. *The Dialogue, 4*(3), 268–289.

Adair, W. L., Buchan, N. R., Chen, X. P., & Liu, L. A. (2024). Listening and speaking without words: Effective communication in multicultural teams. In *What isn't being said. Springer series in emerging cultural perspectives in work, organizational, and personnel studies.* Springer. https://doi.org/10.1007/978-3-031-53645-8_4

Ahmed, S., & Amer, M. M. (2012). *Counseling Muslim: Handbook of mental health issues and interventions*. Routledge.

Akhmetova, E. (2021). *Cited in methodology of scientific research and concept analysis* (ITKI 60001). Week 3 Worldviews. Institute of Knowledge Integration. http://ikiacademy.org

Akhmetova, E., & Rafikov, I. (2021). *Course on methodology of scientific research and concept formation* (ITKI 6001). Institute of Integrated Knowledge. http://ikiacademy.org.

Al-Karam, C. Y. (Ed.). (2018). *Islāmically integrated psychotherapy: Uniting faith and professional practice*. Templeton Press.

Alwee, A. I. (2005). *Ethical dimension of Islām* (Young AMP's Focus Group Discussion Series No. 1). National University of Singapore. http://thereadinggroup.sg/Articles/Ethical%20Dimension%20of%20Islām.pdf. Accessed 21 May 2024.

Bhatti-Ali, R. (2023). *Integrating acceptance and commitment therapy with Islāmic psychotherapy for managing chronic pain* (Focus Series on Islāmic Psychology and Psychotherapy). Routledge.

Haque, K. (2025). *islāmically integrated psychotherapy with domestic abuse* (Focus Series on Islāmic Psychology and Psychotherapy). Routledge.

Hassan, K. M. (1994). *The Islamic Worldview' in Abdul Monir Yaacob and Ahmad Faiz Abdul Rahman, 'Towards a Positive Islamic World-View: Malaysian and American Perceptions* (pp. 11–33). Institute of Islamic Understanding Malaysia.

Hassem, Z., Ismail, S., Walla, N. V., & Rassool, G. H. (2025a). *Working with crisis and trauma: An islāmic perspective* (Focus Series on Islāmic Psychology and Psychotherapy). Routledge.

Hassem, Z., Ismail, S., Vad Walla, N., & Rassool, G. H. (2025b). *Working with Crisis and Trauma from an Islamic Perspective* (Focus Series on Islāmic Psychology and Psychotherapy) (1st ed.). Routledge.

Hodge, D. R., & Nadir, A. (2008). Moving toward culturally competent practice with Muslims: Modifying cognitive therapy with Islāmic tenets. *Social Work, 53*(1), 31–41. https://doi.org/10.1093/sw/53.1.31

Ibrahim, M., & Mojab, F. (2022). Healing through faith: The role of spiritual healers. In providing psychosocial support to Canadian Muslims. *Journal of Muslim Mental Health, 17*(1), 72–79.

Keshavarzi, H., Khan, F., Ali, B., & Awaad, R. (2021). *Applying Islāmic principles to clinical mental health care: Introducing traditional Islāmically integrated psychotherapy*. Routledge.

Latif, J., Dockrat, S., & Rassool, G. H. (2024). *Integrating spiritual interventions in Islāmic psychology: A practical guide* (Focus Series on Islāmic Psychology and Psychotherapy). Routledge.

Littlewood, R. (2004). Possession states. *Psychiatry, 3*(8), 8–10.

Malkawi, F. H. (2014). *Epistemological integration: Essentials of an Islāmic methodology*. The International Institute of Islāmic Thought.
May, R. (1983). *The discovery of being: Writings in existential psychology*. Norton.
Mayers, C., Leavey, G., Vallianatou, C., & Barker, C. (2007). How clients with religious or spiritual beliefs experience psychological help-seeking and therapy: A qualitative study. *Clinical Psychology & Psychotherapy, 14*(4), 317–327.
McCrae, N., & Whitley, R. (2014). Exaltation in temporal lobe epilepsy: Neuropsychiatric symptom or portal to the divine? *The Journal of Medical Humanities, 35*(3), 241–255. https://doi.org/10.1007/s10912-014-9294-4
McLeish, K. (1995). *Key ideas in human thought*. Prima Publishing.
Meer, S., & Mir, G. (2014). Muslims and depression: The role of religious beliefs in therapy. *Journal of Integrative Psychology and Therapeutics, 2*(1), 1–8.
Mir, G., Meer, S., Cottrell, D., McMillan, D., House, A., & Kanter, J. W. (2015). Adapted behavioural activation for the treatment of depression in Muslims. *Journal of Affective Disorders, 180*, 190–199. https://doi.org/10.1016/j.jad.2015.03.060
Owusu-Bempah, K., & Howitt, D. (2000). *Psychology beyond Western perspectives*. Wiley-Blackwell.
Philips, A. A. B. (1994). *The fundamentals of Tawheed (Islāmic monotheism)*. International Islāmic Publishing House.
Podikunju-Hussain, S. (n.d.). Working with Muslims: Perspectives and suggestions for counseling. *Vistas Online, American Counseling Association, 22*, 103–106. https://www.counseling.org/docs/defaultsource/vistas/working-with-muslims-perspectivesand-suggestions-for-counseling.pdf?sfvrsn=4. Accessed 2 May 2024.
Qasqas, M. (2024). *Islāmically modified cognitive behavioural therapy* (Focus Series on Islāmic Psychology and Psychotherapy). Routledge.
Rassool, G. H. (2015). Cultural competence in counselling the Muslim patient: Implications for mental health. *Archives of Psychiatric Nursing, 29*, 321–325.
Rassool, G. H. (2016). *Islāmic counselling: From theory to practice*. Routledge.
Rassool, G. H. (2019). *Evil eye, jinn possession and mental health issues: An Islāmic perspective*. Routledge.
Rassool, G. H. (2021). *Islāmic psychology: Human behaviour and experience from an Islāmic perspective*. Routledge.
Rassool, G. H. (2023). *Islāmic Psychology: The Basics*. Routledge.
Rassool, G. H. (2025a). *Spiritual integration in Islāmic psychotherapy: Unveiling the therapist's soul* (Focus Series on Islāmic Psychology and Psychotherapy). Routledge.
Rassool, G. H. (2025b). *Treating addictive behaviours from an Islāmic perspective* (Focus Series on Islāmic Psychology and Psychotherapy). Routledge.
Rassool, G. H. (2025c). *Islāmic counselling and psychotherapy: From theory to practice* (2nd ed.). Routledge.
Reavey, P., Ahmed, B., & Majumdar, A. (2006). How can we help when she won't tell us what's wrong? Professionals working with south Asian women who have experienced sexual abuse. *Journal of Community & Applied Social Psychology, 16*(3), 171–188.
Riyono, B. (2024). *Tazkiya therapy in Islāmic psychotherapy* (Focus Series on Islāmic Psychology and Psychotherapy). Routledge.
Rose, E. M., Westefeld, J. S., & Ansley, T. N. (2008). Spiritual issues in counseling: Clients' beliefs and preferences. *Psychology of Religion and Spirituality, S*(1), 18–33. https://doi.org/10.1037/1941-1022.S.1.18
Sadiq, N. R. (2019). *Understanding Muslim women clients of counselling: An interpretive phenomenological analysis*. A thesis submitted in partial fulfilment of the requirements of the University of the West of England, Bristol for the degree of Professional Doctorate in Counselling Psychology Faculty of Health and Social Sciences, University of the West of England, Bristol.

Shafi, S. (1998). A study of Muslim Asian women's experiences of counselling and the necessity for a racially similar counsellor. *Counselling Psychology Quarterly, 11*(3), 301–314.
Tanhan, A., & Young, J. S. (2022). Muslims and mental health services: A concept map and a theoretical framework. *Journal of Religion and Health, 61*(1), 23–63. https://doi.org/10.1007/s10943-021-01324-4
Taqiyuddin, M. (2020). In search of Islāmic definition of worldview: Elements, and its characters. *Zawiyah: Jurnal Pemikiran Islam, 6*(2), 206–222.
Warwick, L. L. (2002). Self-in-relation theory and women's religious identity in therapy. *Women & Therapy, 24*(3–4), 121–131.

Chapter 5
The *Fitrah*: Spiritual Nature of Human Behaviour

5.1 Introduction

The concept of *fitrah* holds a profound significance in understanding the spiritual nature of human behaviour. *Fitrah* refers to the innate disposition or primordial nature ingrained within every individual. It is considered the pure, natural state of the human soul, untouched by external influences or societal conditioning. It inclines individuals towards moral goodness, ethical conduct, and a deeper awareness of the divine presence in their lives. This innate inclination towards spirituality and moral righteousness is inherent in every human being from birth, irrespective of cultural or societal backgrounds. It inspires a quest for spiritual fulfilment, leading individuals to reflect on their relationship with Allāh, their purpose in life, and their ultimate destiny. Moreover, *fitrah* plays a crucial role in shaping moral decision-making and ethical behaviour. *Fitrah* serves as a foundational aspect of human psychology, shaping beliefs, attitudes, and behaviours in alignment with one's inherent nature and the divine order.

In Islāmic psychotherapy, the focus is to guide clients towards returning to their *fitrah*, the innate state of purity and spiritual alignment with God. This process entails addressing and overcoming negative influences, psychological and psycho-spiritual disturbances that have led individuals astray from their original state. Therapeutic interventions within this framework involve fostering self-awareness, introspection, and spiritual reflection to reconnect individuals with their intrinsic nature and divine purpose. Through cognitive restructuring, positive reframing, behavioural modification, and spiritual guidance rooted in Islāmic principles, individuals are supported in overcoming psychological barriers and reclaiming their *fitrah*. By restoring the balance between the spiritual, psychological, and emotional dimensions of the self, Islāmic psychotherapy facilitates the journey towards spiritual renewal and inner peace, enabling individuals to realign with their innate disposition towards truth, goodness, and psychospiritual health. This chapter examines

G. H. Rassool, *Exploring the Intersection of Islāmic Spirituality and Psychotherapy*,
https://doi.org/10.1007/978-3-031-72724-5_5

the concept, characteristics, role, alienation, and relationship of *fitrah* with human behaviour, exposing its profound significance in shaping spiritual identity, moral decision-making, and ethical conduct.

5.2 Qur'ân and *Hadīth* Explanations of *Fitrah*

The concept of *fitrah*, derived from sources such as the Qur'ân, *hadīth* literature, Islāmic jurisprudence, and scholarly discourse spanning classical to postmodern perspectives, encompasses linguistic, religious, and pre-existential dimensions (Haque, n.d.). Linguistically, *fitrah* denotes the innate nature inherent in all humans, unalterable and similar to one's disposition. In religious terms, it signifies the natural inclination towards accepting the Oneness of God (*tawhîd*) or innate awareness of the divine. Pre-existentially, *fitrah* is viewed as existing prior to human creation, with God instilling it to facilitate acknowledgment of His Oneness. Mohamed (1996) further elaborates on *fitrah*, exploring linguistic, religious, predestinarian, positive, neutral, and modern interpretations, providing comprehensive insights into its multifaceted understanding and significance.

The Qur'ān uses the concept of *fitrah* in the following way:

أقِمِ وَجْهكَ لِلدِيّنِ حَنيِفاً ج فطِرَتَ أَللِ التَّي فطرَ النـاَّسَ عليَـهْاَ ج لَ تبَدْيِل لـخَلق أَلل ج ذٰلَكِ الدِيّنُ القْيَمِّ وَلكِٰنَّ أكَثْرََ النـاَّسِ لَ يعَلْمُوُنَ

- *So, direct your face toward the religion, inclining to truth. [Adhere to] the Fitrah of Allāh upon which He has created [all] people. No change should there be in the creation of Allāh. That is the correct religion, but most of the people do not know* (Ar-Rum 30:30, interpretation of the meaning).

The verse emphasises the natural disposition (*fitrah*) instilled by Allāh in all human beings and calls for adherence to the true religion, Islām, which aligns with this innate nature. This concept implies that every person is born with an intrinsic understanding of and inclination towards monotheism and morality. According to the exegesis of Ibn Kathir (2000), the above verse is the command to adhere to *tawhîd*. Allāh commands believers to remain steadfast in the prescribed religion, which entails worshiping Him alone. This is the faith of Ibrahim (Abraham), perfectly guided and completed by Allāh. By adhering to this religion, believers maintain the natural disposition (*fitrah*) with which Allāh created humanity. This *fitrah* inherently recognises and understands the oneness of Allāh (*tawhîd*), affirming that there is no God but Him. It is worth noting that natural inclination towards the affirmation of *tawhîd* is part of the *fitrah*. This covenant of monotheism is inscribed on every soul by Allāh, as mentioned in the following verse. Allāh mentions the covenant in the following verse:

وَإِذْ أَخَذَ رَبُّكَ مِنْ بَنِي آدَمَ مِنْ ظُهُورِهِمْ ذُرِّيَّتَهُمْ وَأَشْهَدَهُمْ عَلَىٰ أَنْفُسِهِمْ أَلَسْتُ بِرَبِّكُمْ ۖ قَالُوا بَلَىٰ ۛ شَهِدْنَا ۛ أَنْ تَقُولُوا يَوْمَ الْقِيَامَةِ إِنَّا كُنَّا عَنْ هَٰذَا غَافِلِينَ

- *And (mention) when your Lord took from the children of Adam-from their loins-their descendants and made them testify of themselves, (saying to them): Am I not your Lord? They said: Yes, we have testified. (This) lest you should say on the*

Day of Resurrection, Indeed, we were of this unaware (Al-A'raf 7:172, interpretation of the meaning).

According to Ibn Kathir (2000), Allāh brought forth the descendants of Adam, who testified to Allāh's Lordship and sovereignty, affirming their creation on this *fitrah*, as mentioned in Ar-Rum 30:30.

The religious meaning of *fitrah* is found in the following *hadīth*. It is narrated by Abu Hurayrah (may Allāh' be pleased with him) that Allāh's Messenger (ﷺ) said, "Every child is born with a true faith of Islām (i.e., to worship none but Allāh Alone) but his parents convert him to Judaism, Christianity or Magainism, as an animal delivers a perfect baby animal. Do you find it mutilated?" (Bukhârî, n.d.-a). On the authority of al-Bara' b. 'Azib that Allāh's Messenger (ﷺ) said to a person: "O, so and so, as you go to your bed; the rest of the *hadīth* is the same but with this variation of wording that he said:" Thine Apostle whom Thou sent." If you die that night you would die on *fitrah* [nature] and if you get up in the morning you would get up with a bliss" (Muslim, n.d.-a). Allāh's Messenger (ﷺ) informed us that every child is born with the *fitrah*, meaning the child naturally submits to Allāh's laws and holds correct beliefs. However, through their parents and socialisation, children adopt the religion and beliefs of those around them. The Messenger of Allāh (ﷺ) said: "Allāh created people as believers in pure monotheism (*haneefs*), but the devil misled them, causing them to stray from their religion, forbid what Allāh permitted, and associate others with Allāh. This means that every child is born ready to choose Islām when reaching discretion. They naturally prefer Islām unless influenced by desires, tribalism, or pride, which can lead them to falsehood for personal gain or to follow their ancestors (Islam Q&A, 2009).

5.3 Scholar's Perspectives on *Fitrah*

Abû Haytham, referencing the *hadīth* of Allāh's Messenger (ﷺ), explained that if a child's parents are Jews, Christians, or Magians, they will raise the child in their respective religions regarding their worldly matters like inheritance. The child follows the parents' religion until he can speak for himself. If the child dies before reaching sexual maturity, he remains in the natural state (*fitrah*) he was created with in his mother's womb" (Ibn Manzûr, 1988). Ibn Qutayba al-Daynuri stated that Islāmic theology teaches children are born not as Muslims, but with an inherent spiritual and intellectual inclination towards God and goodness. This inclination stems from a primordial covenant with God (Al-A'raf 7:172). Every child possesses a natural constitution that helps them understand reality, and this tendency is supported and enhanced by the guidance provided through Islām. Ibn Taymīyyah (2000) explained that the Prophet's *hadīth* indicates that God created humans with the inherent nature of Islām. This essential nature was affirmed when God addressed humankind, asking, "Am I not your Lord?" and they responded, "Yes, You are" (Al-A'raf 7:172). Ibn Taymīyyah (2000) stated that "God created man with a particular nature, *fitrah*. The beliefs, values and the principles of Islāmic life and society have their roots in this *fitrah*. Islām is the religion of *fitrah*. And the whole purpose of Islām is the perfection of man on the lines of his *fitrah*. Reason is part of *fitrah*" (p. xxxiii). Islām is also called *Dîn al-fitrah*, the religion of human nature and the natural religion for humankind to believe in and submit to One Creator.

An overview of the *fitrah*, as understood by various scholars, encompasses several key concepts related to human nature and spirituality. Imam Al-Ghazālī (1982) explains the *fitrah* as the original purity of the human being, which inclines him towards recognising his Creator and fulfilling His commands. Al-Tabari describes *fitrah* as the innate religion or natural disposition towards Allāh's guidance. Abû Haytham explains *fitrah* as the state of being born either spiritually prosperous or unprosperous. Abu Ishaaq az-Zajjaaj refers to the *hadīth* stating that Allāh created humans with an inclination to believe in Him, affirming this as part of *fitrah*. Abul-Lait as-Samarqandi emphasises that humans and *jinn* are created with *fitrah* and are obligated to follow God's law. Al-Sayyuti defines *fitrah* as the way of the prophets in alignment with revealed laws, responding to natural inclinations as identified in the Qur'ân. Ibnu Ashur equates *fitrah* with the rational faculty or sound moral judgment inherent in the human soul, affirming moral laws. Imâm Nawawî describes *fitrah* as an unconfirmed state until the individual consciously acknowledges their belief. These perspectives collectively highlight *fitrah* as an innate aspect of human nature that inclines towards belief in Allāh and adherence to moral and spiritual principles, as affirmed in Islāmic teachings. A summary of the explanation of the fitrah by classical, contemporary scholars and thinkers is presented in Table 5.1.

Fitrah, as described by various contemporary scholars and thinkers, encompasses several key aspects related to human nature and spirituality. These perspectives collectively highlight *fitrah* as the inherent inclination within humans towards recognising their Creator, adhering to moral values, and acknowledging divine guidance.

5.4 Evidence of *Fitrah* from Islāmic Theology and Empirical Studies

Islāmic theology and empirical studies both provide evidence for the existence of the *fitrah*. The Qur'ân explicitly mentions the concept of *fitrah* in Surah Ar-Rum (30:30, interpretation of the meaning), stating "So direct your face toward the religion, inclining to truth. [Adhere to] the *fitrah* of Allāh upon which He has created [all] people. No change should there be in the creation of Allāh". The *hadīth* of Prophet Muhammad (ﷺ) who said that "Every child is born upon the fitrah". This hadith suggests that all humans are born with a natural disposition towards monotheism and the worship of Allāh, which can be altered by external influences. Ibn Taymīyyah (1991) argues what is necessitated by the *fitrah* "requires no proof, because it is the most firmly-rooted of epistemologies, the most established of all

Table 5.1 Classical, contemporary scholars and thinkers' perspectives on the *fitrah*

Scholars	Definition of explanation of *fitrah*
Al-Tabari	*Fitrah*: the *deen* (way or religion) of Allāh
Abû Haytham	*Fitrah* means to be born either prosperous or unprosperous [in relation to the soul]
Abu Ishaaq az-Zajjaaj	"Allah, may He be glorified and exalted, created people with the inclination to believe in Him according to what is mentioned in the hadith. Allah, may He be exalted, took from the loins of Adam his progeny like tiny particles, and made them testify concerning themselves that He was their Creator. [al-A'raaf 7:172, interpretation of the meaning]." (Islam Q&A, 2017)
Abul-Lait as-Samarqandi	Humans and *Jinn* are created with *fitrah*, and thus obligated *(taklīf)* to follow God's lawn (p. 243)
Ibn Qutaybah	Every newborn is born in a state of fitrah "refers to the covenant that Allah took from them when they were in the loins of their father Adam, 'and made them testify concerning themselves (saying): "Am I not your Lord?" They said: "Yes"' [al-A'raaf 7:172, interpretation of the meaning]." (Islam Q&A, 2017)
Al-Sayyuti	"The best explanation of *fitrah* is that it is the Sunnah (way) of all of the Prophets which is in agreement with (all of) the revealed Laws, indicating that it is a response to naturally created inclinations. In the Holy Qur'an, Almighty God, the Most High and Exalted, has identified the pure *fitrah* with which He created mankind" (Cited in www.missionislam.com)
Ibnu Ashur	Equated fitrah with rational faculty or sound moral judgement, which is engraved in the human soul, that affirms moral laws (Ibnu Ashur, 2009, p. 62)
Imâm Nawawî	*Fitrah* as the unconfirmed state which exists until the individual consciously acknowledges his belief (cited in Mohamed, 1966)
Al-Faruqi	The *fitrah* or innate common sense is a faculty where people understand the quality dimension of reality. This is the faculty of for people granted the knowledge to know Allāh (Al-Faruqi, 1980)
Al-Attas	"When we say that such a man is fulfilling the purpose for his creation and existence, it is obvious that that man's obligation to serve God is felt by him as normal because it comes as a natural inclination on the man's part to do so. This natural tendency in man to serve and worship God is also referred to as *Dîn*...here in the religious context it has a more specific signification of the natural state of being called 'Fitrah'. In fact, *Dîn* also means 'Fitrah'. It is the pattern according to which God has created all things" (Al-Attas, 1985, pp. 57–58)
Badawi & Haleem	*Fitrah* as "the genesis of creation, the original unadulterated nature of things or in other words the unassailable natural disposition" (Badawi & Haleem, 2008, p. 717)
Haque	*Al-fitrah* "human beings are innately good" (Haque, n.d.)
Langgulung	*Fitrah* can be viewed from two perspectives: Human potential (the nurture of the virtuous attributes of God in oneself) and Divine revelations (*wahy*) to His Prophets and Messengers in the form of Islam and *Tawhid*. This means that the religion revealed by Allāh to His messengers through His Revelations is suited to the basic potential or *fitrah* (nature) of mankind" (cited in Bhat, 2016, p. 167)

(continued)

Table 5.1 (continued)

Scholars	Definition of explanation of *fitrah*
Mohamed	*Fitrah* may be defined as a natural predisposition for good and for submission to the One God (Mohamed, 1996)
Rassool	The *fitrah* "embodies the notion that humans begin life not with blank moral slates (tabula rasa) but are hardwired with an innate sense of morality and truth" (Rassool, 2023, p.v98).
Utz	*Fitrah* as "the pristine nature within humans that leads them to acknowledge the truth of God's existence and to follow His guidance" (Utz, 2011, p.v47)

Source: Adapted from Rassool (2023)

knowledges, and the foundation of all foundations" (p. 72). According to the Islāmic theology, the belief in God is built in human soul of the *fitrah*.

Research indicates a strong global inclination towards religious belief, supported by demographic trends and cognitive studies. It is estimated that 84% of the world's population identifies with a religious group. This demographic tends to be younger and has higher birth rates compared to those without religious affiliation, suggesting an increase in global religiosity (Sherwood, 2018). That is why an overwhelming majority of humanity in the world believe in God in one form or another. A survey from the Pew Research Center shows that 62% of people say that religion plays an important role in their lives, while 61% agree that God plays an important role in their lives (Tamir et al., 2020). Studies by the University of Oxford (2011) suggest that children under five naturally find it easier to believe in superhuman properties and often continue to believe in all-seeing, all-knowing supernatural agents, such as Gods.

Neuroscience suggests that the brain is inherently primed to believe in the supernatural, including God (Azar, 2010). Neuroscientific studies have explored how religious experiences and beliefs are processed in the brain. Research using neuroimaging techniques, such as functional MRI, has identified brain regions associated with religious experiences, including the prefrontal cortex and the temporal lobes. For example, the finding of a study showed that religious practices like prayer and meditation activate specific brain regions involved in self-reflection and emotional regulation, providing a neurological basis for the subjective experience of religiosity (Newberg et al., 2001; Newberg & D'Aquili 2008). The development of theory of mind, which is the ability to attribute mental states to oneself and others, is linked to religious belief. This cognitive ability helps in conceptualising Gods and spirits as entities with intentions and desires. Bering's (2011) research shows that humans naturally infer purposeful causality and design in the world, contributing to the formation and persistence of religious beliefs. It has also been suggested that children naturally develop their belief in God because their mental mechanisms have properties that favour learning about God (Barrett, 2012). In an earlier publication, Barrett (2008) claims that young people have a predisposition to believe in a supreme being and that children are more likely to believe in creationism rather than evolution, despite what they may be told by parents or teachers. He added that anthropologists have found that in some cultures children believe in God even when religious teachings are withheld from them. Cross-cultural studies reveal that religious belief is a universal phenomenon, though with variations in the form and intensity of practice. Anthropological research demonstrates that every human society has developed some form of religious belief or spiritual practice, suggesting a deep-rooted aspect of human nature (Boyer, 2001).

Kelemen (2004) demonstrates that children have a tendency towards teleological thinking, which leads them to infer purposeful design in the natural world, aligning with the concept of a Creator. Rottman and Kelemen (2012) argue that religiosity originates primarily from within individuals due to evolved components of the human mind, which predispose people towards religious beliefs early in life. They assert that cognitive science, anthropology, and psychology provide strong evidence that young children can be inherently religious. Additionally, research by Bloom (2013) indicates that humans possess an innate moral sense, with babies demonstrating empathy, compassion, and rudimentary justice. The God gene hypothesis, proposed by Hamer (2004) and supported by Asadi et al. (2016), suggests that human spirituality is influenced by heredity, with the VMAT2 gene predisposing individuals to spiritual experiences.

Islāmic theology, through scholars like Ibn Taymīyyah and foundational texts such as the Qur'ân and *hadīth*, asserts that *fitrah* is an innate human disposition towards recognising and worshipping Allāh. This is supported by empirical studies in cognitive science and developmental psychology and cross-cultural research, which show that humans, especially children, have natural inclinations towards belief in supernatural agents and purposeful creation.

5.5 Characteristics of *Fitrah*

Fitrah encompasses both spiritual and physical elements. Ibn Ashour categorised *fitrah* into two types: physical, which includes sensory characteristics, and mental, which involves the ability to understand divine laws. The determination of what aligns with *fitrah* is based on heavenly laws; what these laws endorse is *fitrah*, and what they forbid is against it (cited in Oziev, 2022). The spiritual element of *fitrah* is the natural inclination to worship God alone and follow divine guidance. It includes adherence to the revealed Laws (*shar'iah*) and the *Sunnah* of Allāh's Messenger (ﷺ). *Fitrah* acts as a natural compass for distinguishing good from evil and identifying behaviours as *halāl* (allowed) or *harām* (forbidden). The Qur'ân identifies this pure *fitrah* with which God created mankind (Ar-Rum 30:30). In the verse (Ar-Rum 30:30), Allāh, the Almighty identifies the pure *fitrah* with which He created mankind and for mankind to adhere to pure monotheism. It has been suggested that "Believing in Oneness of God, concept of healthy family (male and female only) etc .are the only correct *fitrah* (innate nature)" (Oziev, 2022). Table 5.2 presents the characteristics of the *fitrah*.

Table 5.2 Characteristics of the *fitrah*

Characteristics	Explanations
Innate knowledge of God	An innate awareness and acknowledgment of a higher authority, prompting an instinctual belief in the existence of God.
Spiritual connection	Profound bridge spiritually connecting human beings to Allāh, the Creator
Natural inclination to worship	An inherent tendency to worship God alone and seek a relationship with the divine.
Moral compass	An intrinsic sense of good and evil, guiding individuals to distinguish between *halāl* and *harām* behaviours.
Source of spiritual fulfilment and growth	Nurturing *fitrah* is essential for spiritual growth, with practical tips aiding individuals in deepening their spiritual journey.
Sense of purity	A natural inclination towards purity and cleanliness, both physically and spiritually
Compliance with divine laws	An inclination to adhere to the divine laws (*Shar'iah*) and the teachings of prophets.
Desire for truth	A fundamental drive to seek and accept truth, and a resistance to falsehood.
Innate compassion	A natural tendency towards empathy, compassion, and kindness towards others.
Rationality and intellect	The capacity for reason, critical thinking, and understanding, which aligns with divine guidance.
Inclination to good deeds	A natural tendency to perform good deeds and avoid harmful actions. Enjoin what is good and forbid what is wrong.
Impact on ethical behaviour	Facilitates the development of personal ethics, fostering virtuous conduct aligned with innate nature
Resilience of the *fitrah*	Despite various external influences and changes in belief systems, the core of fitrah remains resilient. It cannot be eliminated or destroyed
Deviation of the *fitrah*	Straying from *fitrah* leads to behaviours that contradict innate righteousness, resulting in moral decay and deviant behaviours.
Seeking alignment with the *fitrah*	Seek alignment with the *fitrah* by engaging in regular spiritual practices like prayer and reflection, and by living ethically Maintain physical and mental well-being, and nurture positive relationships and environmental stewardship.

It is obligatory on Muslims to following the commands of the Prophet Muhammad (ﷺ) as mentioned in the following verse from the Qurʾān. Allāh says:

وَمَآ ءَاتَىٰكُمُ ٱلرَّسُولُ فَخُذُوهُ وَمَا نَهَىٰكُمْ عَنْهُ فَٱنتَهُوا۟ وَٱتَّقُوا۟ ٱللَّهَ إِنَّ ٱللَّهَ شَدِيدُ ٱلْعِقَابِ

- *Whatever the Messenger has given you, take it. And whatever he has forbidden you –refrain from. And fear Allāh. Indeed, Allāh is severe in penalty* (Al-Hashr 59:7, interpretation of the meaning).

According to the exegesis of Ibn Kathir (2000), this verse means, "whatever the Messenger commands you, then do it and whatever he forbids you, then avoid it. Surely, He only commands righteousness and forbids evil". This statement clearly states that all Muslims should fulfil with and maintain the characteristics of *fitrah*. This verse calls for complete obedience to the Prophet Muhammad's instructions as a reflection of one's faith and fear of Allāh, emphasising the serious consequences of neglecting this duty.

The *fitrah* encompasses an intrinsic moral compass that guides individuals to distinguish between good and evil, and *halāl* (acceptable) and *harām* (forbidden) behaviours. It serves as a source of spiritual fulfilment and growth, encouraging practices that deepen one's spiritual journey. This innate nature includes a natural inclination towards physical and spiritual purity, adherence to Divine laws (*shar'iah*), and the teachings of prophets. The *fitrah* also drives a fundamental desire for truth and a resistance to falsehood, coupled with an innate compassion that promotes empathy and kindness towards others. Moreover, the *fitrah* aligns rationality and intellect with divine guidance, fostering critical thinking and understanding. It includes a natural tendency to perform good deeds and avoid harmful actions, promoting virtuous conduct. Despite external influences, the *fitrah*'s core remains resilient and indestructible. Deviation from the *fitrah* leads to moral decay and deviant behaviours, while alignment with it is achieved through spiritual practices, ethical living, maintaining physical and mental well-being, and nurturing positive relationships and environmental stewardship.

It would be valuable to reflect on the statements made by Ibn Sina on the meaning and characteristics of the *fitrah*. He stated that "The meaning of *fitrah* is that a person imagines himself having happened in this world at once while he is sane, but he did not hear an opinion, did not believe a certain path, did not associate with a nation, did not know politics, but he witnessed the sensibilities and took them. Then he exposes a thing to his mind and doubts it. And if his doubt prevails, then *fitrah* does not support it. And if his doubt did not prevail, then it is required by *fitrah*" (Cited in Oziev, 2022). What this statement implies is that the *fitrah* is an inherent guide to truth and natural law, unclouded by societal or cultural conditioning.

5.6 Alienation of the *Fitrah*

Trials and tribulations serve as tests from Allāh, aimed at enabling individuals to break through the clouded *fitrah* obscured by layers of false beliefs accumulated over time. Strong psychosocial influences and acculturation of values incongruent with Islāmic beliefs may lead individuals away from their innate nature. Consequently, they become alienated from their *fitrah*, prioritising purposes and meanings of life other than serving Allāh. Despite this alienation, in moments of trauma and intense suffering, some individuals turn towards the Divine for help and support, seeking clarity and solace in their innate connection with Allāh. Utz (2011) suggested that "Times of crisis are particularly likely to awaken our spiritual side and to uncover the *fitrah* that has been buried by false beliefs, principles, ideals and behaviours. During these times, we are likely to call upon Allāh to save us from hardship and suffering" (p. 193). This is reflected in the following verse of the Qurʾān:

وَإِذَا مَسَّ ٱلْإِنسَٰنَ ٱلضُّرُّ دَعَانَا لِجَنۢبِهِۦٓ أَوْ قَاعِدًا أَوْ قَآئِمًا فَلَمَّا كَشَفْنَا عَنْهُ ضُرَّهُۥ مَرَّ كَأَن لَّمْ يَدْعُنَآ إِلَىٰ ضُرٍّ مَّسَّهُۥ كَذَٰلِكَ زُيِّنَ
لِلْمُسْرِفِينَ مَا كَانُوا۟ يَعْمَلُونَ.

- *And when affliction touches man, he calls upon Us, whether lying on his side, sitting, or standing; but when We remove from him his affliction, he continues [in disobedience] as if he had never called upon Us to [remove] an affliction that touched him. Thus, is made pleasing to the transgressors that which they have been doing* (Yunus 10:12, interpretation of the meaning).

This verse emphasises the common human response to adversity by turning to Allāh for help, yet it also warns against the inconsistency of devotion and gratitude once the hardship is alleviated. It highlights the transient nature of human faith and the consequences of persistent disobedience despite experiencing Allāh's mercy.

In times of trials, tribulations, and prosperity, individuals may become alienated from their *fitrah* when their purpose and meaning of life diverge from serving Allāh. Despite this, moments of trauma and intense suffering often lead some to turn towards the Divine for help and support, seeking clarity and solace. Muslims are reminded that Allāh decrees only what is ultimately beneficial for their worldly and spiritual well-being, fostering trust and reliance on His wisdom and guidance in all circumstances. Suhaib reported that Allāh's Messenger (ﷺ) said: "Strange are the ways of a believer for there is good in every affair of his and this is not the case with anyone else except in the case of a believer for if he has an occasion to feel delight, he thanks (Allāh), thus there is a good for him in it, and if he gets into trouble and shows resignation (and endures it patiently), there is a good for him in it" (Muslim, n.d.-b).

However, the concept of *fitrah* encompasses an inherent duality, reflecting both intrinsic goodness and the potential for evil within human nature (Al-Qarni, 2003). This duality suggests that individuals possess the capacity, intellect, and free will to discern between what is right and lawful, as endowed by Allāh. However, due to psychosocial conditioning and external influences, the *fitrah* can become corrupted, leading individuals towards evil and deviation from Islāmic teachings. Haque (2018) suggested that this dualistic dimension of *fitrah* implies an ongoing struggle between the tendencies towards good and evil. These tendencies are dynamic and possess the potential to elevate individuals to higher spiritual levels in alignment with their pre-existing *fitrah*, or to lower levels that compromise the inherent purity of their original nature. Negative thinking and societal influences play a significant role in this process, shaping individuals' behaviours and beliefs.

How to distinguish between the moral good and wrong? On the authority of an-Nawas bin Sam'an (may Allāh be pleased with him), that the Prophet (ﷺ) said: "Righteousness is in good character, and wrongdoing is that which wavers in your soul, and which you dislike people finding out about" [Muslim]. And on the authority of Wabisah bin Ma'bad (may Allāh be pleased with him) who said: I came to the Messenger of Allāh (ﷺ) said, "You have come to ask about righteousness". I said, "Yes". He (ﷺ) said, "Consult your heart. Righteousness is that about which the soul feels at ease and the heart feels tranquil. And wrongdoing is that which wavers in the soul and causes uneasiness in the breast, even though people have repeatedly given their legal opinion [in its favour]"(An-Nawawi, n.d.). This *hadīth* highlights the innate sense of morality ingrained within each individual, known as f*itrah*. This natural disposition inclines us towards recognising what is right and wrong. However, throughout life, various factors such as societal influences, personal desires, and environmental pressures can obscure or distort this innate guidance, leading to a sense of alienation from our *fitrah.*

To overcome this alienation and fully realise our spiritual potential, the *hadīth* emphasises the importance of reconnecting with our *fitrah* through spiritual means. This involves seeking Divine guidance, which provides a framework for understanding and aligning our actions with what is morally upright. Additionally, following the *Sunnah*, or the teachings and practices of the Prophet Muhammad (ﷺ), serves as a practical manifestation of Divine guidance in both spiritual and worldly matters. By adhering to Divine guidance and the *Sunnah* in all aspects of life, including material pursuits, individuals can harmonise their inner moral compass with their external actions. This alignment fosters a sense of coherence and integrity within oneself, leading to a more balanced and fulfilling existence. It enables individuals to navigate life's challenges with clarity and purpose, striving towards spiritual growth and closeness to the Divine. In essence, reconnecting with our *fitrah* through spiritual guidance facilitates a holistic approach to living, where inner and outer realities are in harmony, nurturing a sense of peace, contentment, and fulfilment.

5.7 The Corruption of the *Fitrah*

The corruption of the *fitrah* represents a departure from the natural inclination towards goodness and virtue that is inherent in every human being. This corruption can manifest in various ways and is influenced by both internal and external factors. Without guidance, the *fitrah* may become corruptible but it cannot be destroyed. Shaykh Saalih bin Fawzaan bin Abdillaah al-Fawzaan (2013) suggested that "The soul, if it is left upon its *fitrah* (natural state) affirms Allāh's divinity and has love for Allāh, worships Him alone, and does not ascribe partners to Him. However, the *Shayaateen* [devil] from the *Jinn* and the *Ins* (mankind) corrupts and deviates it from that with what they reveal to one another by way of beautification in speech and deceptions. *Tawhîd* is centred in the *fitrah*. Shirk is foreign and inserted into it". This statement emphasises that when left in its natural state, the soul instinctively acknowledges and loves Allāh, worshiping Him alone without associating any partners with Him. Understanding and reflecting on this statement can deepen one's appreciation for the purity of the *fitrah* and the constant struggle against external influences that seek to corrupt it. It emphasises the importance of seeking knowledge, guidance, and protection from Allāh to safeguard the *fitrah* and maintain a steadfast commitment to *tawhîd* in the face of adversity. Table 5.3 outlines the internal and external factors contributing to the corruption of the fitrah.

Table 5.3 Internal and external factors contributing to the corruption of the *fitrah*

Internal factors	External factors
Desires and temptations Greed Lust Envy Arrogance	Societal influence Socialisation Societal norms promoting unethical behaviour Cultural practices encouraging moral deviation Peer pressure to conform to immoral standards Acculturation
Ignorance Lack of knowledge about moral principles Absence of understanding moral values	Environmental influences Upbringing and family dynamics shaping moral beliefs Exposure to violence or injustice affecting morality Traumatic experiences leading to compromised integrity
Spiritual neglect Neglecting spiritual well-being Failure to nurture connection with Divine	Misguidance Following misguided leaders or ideologies Being indoctrinated with false beliefs

At times, this innate spiritual disposition often becomes clouded due to the pervasive influence of corrupt societal and environmental factors. Individuals are bombarded with immoral messages and behaviours, leading to a desensitisation and acculturation to low ethical standards. As a result, moral compasses are suppressed, and many embrace immorality and deviant behaviours as societal norms. Ibn Taymīyyah (1991) writes, "The servants of God are inherently compelled by their *fitrah* to love God, though amongst them are those who corrupt this *fitrah*… and this love of God intensifies according to one's knowledge of Him and the soundness of one's *fitrah*. And it diminishes with diminished knowledge, and the pollution of one's *fitrah* with corruptive vain desires" (p. 67). What is Ibn Taymīyyah is suggesting highlights the inherent inclination of God's servants to love Him as a natural aspect of their *fitrah*. However, it acknowledges that some individuals corrupt this innate disposition. The intensity of this love for God correlates with one's knowledge of Him and the purity of their *fitrah*. As individuals deepen their understanding of God and maintain a sound *fitrah,* their love for Him strengthens. On the contrary, this love diminishes with decreased knowledge and the pollution of the *fitrah* by corruptive desires. This underlines the importance of seeking knowledge and purifying the soul to strengthen one's relationship with God.

The corruption of the *fitrah* is a multifaceted phenomenon influenced by both internal and external factors, each playing a role in distorting an individual's innate sense of morality and spiritual alignment. Internally, desires and temptations such as greed, lust, envy, and arrogance can exert a powerful sway over individuals, clouding their judgment and leading them astray from moral principles. These internal struggles often arise from innate human weaknesses and vulnerabilities, exacerbated by societal pressures and personal inclinations. For example, the desire for material wealth or physical pleasure can override considerations of ethical conduct, leading individuals to compromise their moral integrity. Furthermore, ignorance of moral principles due to a lack of guidance or education exacerbates the corruption of the *fitrah*. Without a solid foundation in ethical intelligence, individuals may struggle to discern right from wrong, making decisions that contradict their innate sense of morality. This ignorance can stem from various factors, including inadequate upbringing, limited access to education, or societal neglect of moral instruction. Spiritual neglect is another internal factor contributing to the corruption of the *fitrah*. When individuals become disconnected from their spiritual essence and fail to nurture a connection with the divine, they may prioritise worldly desires over moral principles. This disconnect often results from a preoccupation with material pursuits, a lack of spiritual fulfilment, or a failure to engage in practices that nourish the soul, such as prayer, reflection, and acts of worship.

Externally, societal norms, cultural practices, and peer pressure play a significant role in shaping individuals' moral behaviour. In societies where unethical conduct is normalised or even encouraged, individuals may become desensitised to moral wrongdoing, leading to a gradual erosion of their ethical standards. Cultural attitudes towards issues such as honesty, integrity, and compassion can influence individual behaviour, either reinforcing or undermining their innate sense of morality. Environmental factors, including upbringing, family dynamics, and exposure to trauma, also contribute to the corruption of the *fitrah*. Childhood experiences, familial influences, and traumatic events can profoundly impact an individual's moral development, shaping their attitudes, beliefs, and behaviours in significant ways. Adverse circumstances or dysfunctional family dynamics may lead individuals to adopt coping mechanisms that compromise their moral integrity, further distancing them from their innate sense of right and wrong. Furthermore, misguidance from leaders or ideologies promoting distorted morality can have a detrimental effect on individuals' spiritual well-being. When individuals are misled or indoctrinated with false beliefs, they may become disconnected from their innate sense of morality, blindly following ideologies that contradict their *fitrah*. This misguidance can lead to confusion, moral relativism, and a loss of spiritual direction, exacerbating the corruption of the *fitrah*.

5.8 Restoring and Realignment of the Fitrah

Seeking alignment with the *fitrah* is a profound journey of self-discovery and spiritual growth, requiring deliberate efforts to restore and realign oneself with the inherent disposition towards righteousness. Figure 5.1 shows the stages on restoration and realignment of the f*itrah*. Figure 4.1 shows the stages on restoration and realignment of the fitrah.

The journey which begins with a deep commitment with *niyyāh* (intention) is fundamental to all actions, influencing not only worship but all aspects of human activity. It is narrated on the authority of Umar bin al-Khattab (may Allāh be pleased

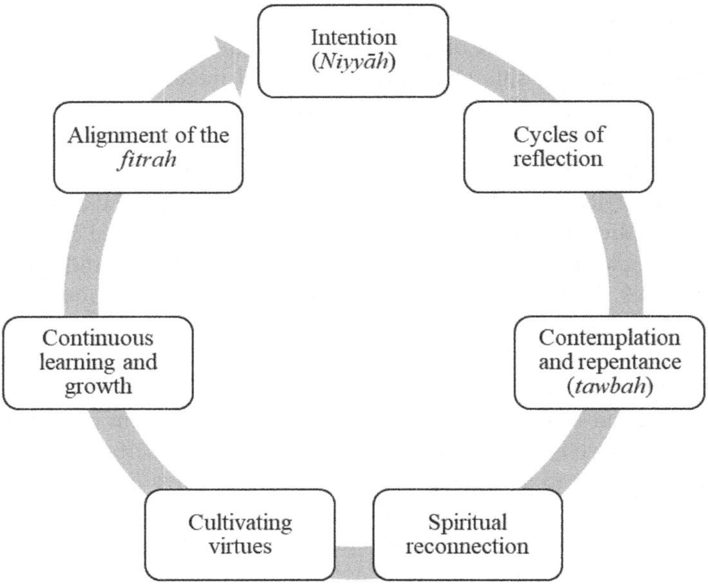

Fig. 5.1 Stages on restoration and realignment of the *fitrah*

with him) who said: I heard the Messenger of Allāh (ﷺ) say: "Actions are (judged) by motives (*niyyāh*), so each man will have what he intended" (Bukhârî & Muslim, n.d.). This *hadīth* emphasises the importance of sincere intention in all actions. Imam Al-Bukhârî and other scholars highlight its significance by starting their books or discussions with it, emphasising that seeking Allāh's pleasure should be the primary motive behind every action. Imam Ash-Shafi'i even went as far as to say that this *hadīth* encompasses a third of all knowledge, underlining its centrality to the principles of Islām and righteous deeds. Imam Ahmad said: "I like that for every action, from prayer, fasting or charity or any action of righteousness that there be an intention preceding the action. The Prophet said: 'actions are by intentions', and this is taken for every matter" (Cited in Islāmīcweb.net, 2018). Ibn Qayyim Al-Jawziyyah defined intention as the awareness and purpose behind an action, emphasising that a rational and willing person always understands and desires their actions. This internal conceptualisation and purpose form the essence of intention. Ibn Qayyim Al-Jawziyyah's definition of intention highlights the integral role of awareness and purpose in human actions. According to him, an intelligent and voluntary actor inherently understands and desires their actions, making intention an internal aspect of the individual's conceptualisation and purpose.

The second stage is that the cycles of reflection are integral to personal growth, self-awareness, and spiritual development. These cycles involve a systematic process of introspection, evaluation, and learning from past experiences. Reflection plays a crucial role in self-awareness by enabling individuals to gain insights into their thoughts, feelings, and behaviours, leading to a deeper understanding of themselves. Through this process, individuals can identify lessons learned from past experiences, recognise their strengths, and pinpoint areas for improvement, which facilitates both personal and professional growth. This reflective practice also enhances decision-making skills, as it allows individuals to consider past outcomes, leading to more informed and effective problem-solving. Cycles of reflection on the Qur'ânic commands and the *Sunnah* play a significant role in a believer's life, facilitating spiritual and moral development. By continuously revisiting and contemplating these foundational texts, individuals deepen their understanding of Islāmic teachings and principles, which guide their daily actions and decisions. This reflective practice helps integrate these teachings more profoundly into their lives, ensuring that their behaviour aligns with Islāmic values and practices. Furthermore, these cycles of reflection foster a stronger connection with one's faith and Allāh, the Almighty, enhancing spiritual growth. It is important for the individual to recognise the inherent goodness and spiritual potential in every person's *fitrah*. Understanding that deviations from *fitrah* are often a result of external influences and societal conditioning rather than inherent flaws. Through regular cycles of reflection, individuals can better navigate life's challenges and make choices that reflect their commitment to their faith, ultimately leading to a more fulfilling and spiritually enriched life.

Engaging in regular contemplation and self-reflection (*muraqabah*). Practicing contemplation and self-awareness to stay connected with one's inner self and moral values is a crucial aspect of spiritual growth, allowing individuals to identify areas where they may have deviated from their *fitrah* and strayed from righteous conduct. Through contemplation, individuals can introspectively examine their thoughts, actions, and intentions, assessing whether they align with Islāmic principles and values. This process of self-awareness enables individuals to recognise shortcomings and areas for improvement, fostering a deeper commitment to living in accordance with their innate moral compass. Practicing sincere repentance (*tawbah*) for past transgressions is essential in Islām, as it signifies remorse for wrongful actions and a genuine intention to rectify them. *Tawbah* involves acknowledging one's mistakes, seeking forgiveness from Allāh, and committing to abstain from repeating those actions in the future. Allāh says in the Qur'ân.

يَٰٓأَيُّهَا ٱلَّذِينَ ءَامَنُوا۟ تُوبُوٓا۟ إِلَى ٱللَّهِ تَوْبَةً نَّصُوحًا عَسَىٰ رَبُّكُمْ أَن يُكَفِّرَ عَنكُمْ سَيِّـَٔاتِكُمْ وَيُدْخِلَكُمْ جَنَّٰتٍ تَجْرِى مِن تَحْتِهَا
ٱلْأَنْهَٰرُ يَوْمَ لَا يُخْزِى ٱللَّهُ ٱلنَّبِىَّ وَٱلَّذِينَ ءَامَنُوا۟ مَعَهُۥ نُورُهُمْ يَسْعَىٰ بَيْنَ أَيْدِيهِمْ وَبِأَيْمَٰنِهِمْ يَقُولُونَ رَبَّنَآ أَتْمِمْ لَنَا نُورَنَا
وَٱغْفِرْ لَنَآ إِنَّكَ عَلَىٰ كُلِّ شَىْءٍ قَدِيرٌ

- *O you who have believed, repent to Allāh with sincere repentance. Perhaps your Lord will remove from you your misdeeds and admit you into gardens beneath which rivers flow [on] the Day when Allāh will not disgrace the Prophet and those who believed with him. Their light will proceed before them and on their right; they will say, 'Our Lord, perfect for us our light and forgive us. Indeed, You are over all things competent* (At-Tahrim 66:8, interpretation of the meaning).

The above verse begins with a direct address to the believers, emphasising that repentance is a fundamental aspect of their faith and relationship with Allāh. It highlights the importance of sincere repentance for believers, promising that genuine remorse and a commitment to abandon sinful behaviour can lead to the removal of misdeeds and the reward of paradise. The verse also includes a prayer for the perfection of this light and forgiveness, emphasising the believers' reliance on Allāh's omnipotence and mercy.

It was narrated from Abu Hurayrah (may Allāh be pleased with him) that the Prophet (ﷺ) said: "If you were to commit sin until your sins reach the heaven, then you were to repent, your repentance would be accepted" (Ibn Majah, n.d.). In another *hadīth*, Allāh's Messenger (ﷺ) said: "O people, repent to Allāh, for I verily repent to Him one hundred times a day" (Muslim, n.d.-c). Sincere repentance (*tawbah nasuhah*) highlights that repentance should be genuine and heartfelt. It involves a true feeling of remorse for past misdeeds, a firm resolution to abandon sinful behaviour, and a commitment to seek Allāh's forgiveness intensely. Sincere repentance in Islām strengthens the individual's relationship with Allāh, serving as a means of spiritual purification and renewal. It allows individuals to experience Allāh's mercy and forgiveness, restoring their spiritual well-being and facilitating personal growth and transformation.

To spiritually reconnect, individuals can deepen their relationship with the Divine through various practices such as prayer, reflection, and contemplation. Prayer serves as a direct means of communication with Allāh, providing solace, guidance, and a sense of closeness. Regularly engaging in *salah* (Islāmic prayer) allows individuals to centre themselves spiritually and seek Allāh's guidance in their lives. Reflecting on the beauty of creation and the signs of Allāh's presence in the world around them fosters a deeper appreciation for His blessings and strengthens the connection between the individual and their Creator. Furthermore, seeking guidance from the Qur'ân and the *Sunnah* is essential for realigning one's actions and beliefs with Islāmic principles. The Qur'ân serves as the ultimate source of guidance for Muslims, containing divine wisdom and teachings applicable to all aspects of life. Studying its verses and reflecting on their meanings helps individuals gain clarity and direction in their spiritual journey. Similarly, the *Sunnah* provides practical examples of how to live according to Islāmic principles. By following the guidance of the Qur'ân and *Sunnah*, individuals can strive to embody the values of compassion, justice, and righteousness in their daily lives. Relying on Allāh's guidance and assistance through sincere supplication (*dua'h*) and reliance (*tawakkul*) on His mercy and wisdom is a fundamental aspect of Islāmic faith and practice. Supplication is a means by which believers express their dependence on Allāh and seek His help, mercy, and guidance in all aspects of their lives. It is a manifestation of humility, trust, and devotion to the Creator. By turning to Allāh in prayer, individuals acknowledge their limitations and recognise Allāh as the ultimate source of guidance and support.

وَإِذَا سَأَلَكَ عِبَادِى عَنِّى فَإِنِّى قَرِيبٌ أُجِيبُ دَعْوَةَ ٱلدَّاعِ إِذَا دَعَانِ فَلْيَسْتَجِيبُوا۟ لِى وَلْيُؤْمِنُوا۟ بِى لَعَلَّهُمْ يَرْشُدُونَ

- *And when My servants ask you concerning Me, indeed I am near. I respond to the invocation of the supplicant when he calls upon Me. So let them respond to Me [by obedience] and believe in Me that they may be [rightly] guided* (Al-Baqarah 2:186, interpretation of the meaning).

In a *hadīth* Ibn 'Abbas (may Allāh be pleased with him) narrated, "When you ask (for anything), ask it from Allāh, and if you seek help, seek help from Allāh" (Tirmidhî, n.d.). The verse from Al-Baqarah (2:186) and the *hadīth* narrated by Ibn 'Abbas both emphasise Allāh's closeness to His servants and His responsiveness to their prayers, encouraging believers to seek help and make supplications directly to Him. They highlight the importance of sincere prayer, obedience, and faith, assuring believers that Allāh is always near, ready to assist and guide those who turn to Him with a genuine heart. *Tawakkul*, or reliance on Allāh, complements the act of supplication by entrusting one's affairs entirely to Allāh's wisdom and decree. It involves placing full trust in Allāh's plan and having faith that He will guide and support those who strive to restore their *fitrah*. *Tawakkul* does not imply passivity but rather an active reliance on Allāh while taking necessary actions. It strengthens one's connection with Allāh and provides a sense of peace and contentment, knowing that Allāh is in control of all outcomes. Allāh says in the Qur'ân:

وإِذَا سَأَلَكَ عِبَادِى عَنِّى فَإِنِّى قَرِيبٌ أُجِيبُ دَعْوَةَ ٱلدَّاعِ إِذَا دَعَانِ فَلْيَسْتَجِيبُواْ لِى وَلْيُؤْمِنُواْ بِى لَعَلَّهُمْ يَرْشُدُون

- *And will provide for him from where he does not expect. And whoever relies upon Allāh—then He is sufficient for him. Indeed, Allāh will accomplish His purpose. Allāh has already set for everything a [decreed] extent* (At-Talaq 65:3, interpretation of the meaning).

According to the exegesis of Ibn Kathir (2000) whoever has taqwa (God conscious] of Allāh in what He has commanded and avoids what He has forbidden, then Allāh will make a way out for him from every difficulty and will provide for him from resources he never anticipated or thought about.

However, to foster spiritual growth and maintain adherence to Islāmic values, individuals should surround themselves with positive influences and supportive communities. Being part of a nurturing environment where fellow believers encourage and uplift one another facilitates the cultivation of virtuous qualities and reinforces commitment to the path of righteousness. Positive influences from religious scholars, faith leaders, mentors, and like-minded individuals can provide guidance, support, and inspiration on the journey towards spiritual fulfilment. There are several *hadīths* that highlight the importance of having righteous friends. Here are a few notable ones: It is narrated by Abu Musa (may Allāh be pleased with him) Allāh's Messenger (ﷺ) said, "The example of a good companion (who sits with you) in comparison with a bad one, is like that of the musk seller and the blacksmith's bellows (or furnace); from the first you would either buy musk or enjoy its good smell while the bellows would either burn your clothes or your house, or you get a bad nasty smell thereof" (Bukhârî, n.d.-b). It is narrated by Abu Hurayrah (may Allāh be pleased with him) that the Prophet (ﷺ) said: "A man follows the religion of his friend; so, each one should consider whom he makes his friend" (Abū Dāwūd, n.d.). These *hadīths* emphasise the impact that friends can have on one's behaviour and faith, encouraging Muslims to choose friends who are righteous and who will positively influence their character and spirituality.

Cultivating virtues such as honesty, compassion, humility, and patience aligns individuals with their *fitrah*. Honesty is fundamental in maintaining trust and integrity in relationships and society at large. When individuals commit to honesty, they create an environment where others feel safe and respected. This quality is vital for the development of healthy, enduring relationships and fosters an atmosphere of mutual respect and understanding. Compassion involves empathy and concern for the suffering of others. By practicing compassion, individuals connect with others on a deeper level, fostering a sense of community and support. Humility is the recognition of one's limitations and the appreciation of others' strengths and contributions. This virtue allows for open-mindedness and the willingness to learn from others. It reduces conflicts and fosters cooperation and teamwork, as humble people are more likely to listen and value others' opinions and contributions. Developing patience (*sabr*) allows individuals to remain steadfast and persistent in the pursuit of their goals. In interpersonal relationships, patience helps in resolving conflicts amicably and reduces the likelihood of hasty and regrettable decisions. Virtuous qualities contribute significantly to growth and personal development. By consciously nurturing these virtues, individuals tap into their inherent moral compass and strive towards righteousness. The *fitrah* guides people towards natural goodness and moral behaviour. Cultivating these virtues aligns one's actions with this innate disposition, leading to a more fulfilling and righteous life Continuous learning and growth are fundamental aspects of deepening one's connection with Islām and strengthening the fitrah, the innate disposition towards goodness.

Islām places a high value on the pursuit of knowledge. The Qur'ân and *hadīths* emphasise the importance of seeking knowledge as a means to strengthen faith and understanding. The Qur'ân encourages the pursuit of knowledge, as seen in verses such as:

ٱقْرَأْ بِٱسْمِ رَبِّكَ ٱلَّذِى خَلَقَ

- *Read in the name of your Lord who created* (Al-'Alaq 96:1, interpretation of the meaning).

The verse "Read in the name of your Lord who created" serves as a profound reminder of the importance of knowledge in Islām. It marks the beginning of the Qur'ânic revelation, emphasising that the pursuit of learning is a divine directive. This foundational principle encourages Muslims to seek knowledge continuously, integrate it with their faith, and contribute to the betterment of themselves and society. Allāh says in another verse of the Qur'ân:

وَقُل رَّبِّ زِدْنِى عِلْمًا

- *And say, My Lord, increase me in knowledge* (Ta-Ha 20:114 interpretation of the meaning).

The above verse highlights a fundamental principle in Islām: the pursuit of knowledge. This directive emphasises the importance of continuously seeking knowledge, wisdom, and understanding. It stresses the spiritual, intellectual, and societal benefits of seeking knowledge and encourages believers to strive for intellectual humility and lifelong learning. This pursuit of knowledge is seen as a way to deepen one's faith, contribute positively to society, and lead a more fulfilling and meaningful life. The Prophet Muhammad (ﷺ) also stressed the importance of knowledge: Abu Hurayrah (may Allāh be pleased with him) reported: The Messenger of Allāh (ﷺ) said, "Allāh makes the way to *Jannah* [paradise] easy for him who treads the path in search of knowledge" (Muslim, n.d.-d). This *hadīth* indicates the spiritual rewards and ease in the afterlife for those who seek knowledge.

Recognising that restoring the *fitrah* is an ongoing process involves a commitment to lifelong spiritual growth and development. This concept is supported by Islāmic teachings that encourage continuous self-improvement and devotion. The Qur'ân highlights the importance of constant self-improvement and spiritual striving:

وَٱلَّذِينَ جَٰهَدُوا۟ فِينَا لَنَهْدِيَنَّهُمْ سُبُلَنَا ۚ وَإِنَّ ٱللَّهَ لَمَعَ ٱلْمُحْسِنِينَ

- *And those who strive for Us—We will surely guide them to Our ways. And indeed, Allāh is with the doers of good* (Al-Ankabūt 29:69, interpretation of the meaning).

The verse captures a core principle of Islāmic teaching: the importance of sincere effort in the pursuit of righteousness and the assurance of divine guidance and support for those who engage in seeking authentic knowledge and good deeds. Maududi, (n.d.) in his exegesis, explains that this verse highlights the importance of sincere effort and struggle (*jihad*) in the path of Allāh. The term "strive for Us" (*jahadu fina*) refers to those who exert their utmost efforts to seek the pleasure of Allāh through righteous deeds, worship, and self-purification. By emphasising the relationship between effort and divine assistance, Maududi's *tafsir* (exegesis) underlines the proactive role that believers must take in their spiritual journey and the assurance of Allāh's unwavering support for those who commit themselves to His path.

The Prophet Muhammad (ﷺ) emphasised the importance of consistent good deeds: It was narrated that 'Aishah (may Allāh be pleased with her) said: "The Messenger of Allāh (ﷺ) said: Do as much of good deeds as you can, for Allāh does not get tired (of giving reward) until you get tired. And the most beloved of deeds to Allāh are those that are continuous, even if they are few" (An-Nasai', n.d.). To cultivate continuous learning and spiritual growth, individuals can regularly study the Qur'ân and *hadīth* to gain deeper understanding of Islāmic teachings that resonate with the essence of *fitrah*. Attend Islāmic classes and lectures, and participate in community classes, online courses, and lectures to broaden knowledge of Islām. Regularly evaluate personal actions and intentions to ensure that they align with Islāmic principles and values. Engage in consistent worship and good deeds: maintain regular prayers, charity, and other acts of worship with sincerity and consistency.

5.9 Conclusions

The journey of realigning the *fitrah*, the innate disposition towards goodness and righteousness, involves several interconnected stages. It begins with the intention (*niyyah*) to seek spiritual growth and align oneself with the divine will. This intention sets the foundation for a series of reflective cycles where individuals engage in introspection, assessing their actions and intentions in light of Islāmic principles. Through contemplation and repentance (*tawbah*), individuals reflect on past mistakes, seek forgiveness from Allāh, and commit to avoiding sinful behaviour in the future. This process leads to a spiritual reconnection, strengthening the bond with Allāh through acts of worship, remembrance, and seeking closeness to Him. Simultaneously, individuals focus on cultivating virtues such as humility, compassion, patience, and gratitude, fostering these qualities through conscious effort and practice. Continuous learning and growth play a crucial role in this journey, as individuals actively pursue knowledge of Islām, engage in spiritual practices, and seek personal development to enhance their understanding and practice of faith. Together, these stages facilitate the purification of the soul (*tazkiyah*) and lead to the restoration of the *fitrah*, enabling individuals to realign themselves with their natural state of purity and deepen their spiritual connection with Allāh.

References

Abū Dāwūd. (n.d.). *Sunan Dāwūd. 4833*. In-book reference: Book 43, Hadith 61. English translation: Book 42, Hadith 4815. Hasan (Al-Albani). https://sunnah.com/abudawud:4833

Abū Dāwūd, & Tirmidhî. (n.d.). *Riyad as-Salihin 1388*. In-book reference: Book 12, Hadith 13. https://sunnah.com/riyadussalihin:1388

Al-Attas, S. M. N. (1985). *Islam, secularism and the philosophy of the future*. Mansell Publishing Limited.

Al-Faruqi, I. R. (1980). *Islam and culture*. Angkatan Bella Malaysia (ABIM).

Al-Qarni, A. i. A. A. (2003). *al-Fitrah: Haqiqatuha wa madhahib al-nas fiha*. Dar al-Muslimin li al Nashr wa al-Tawzi.

An-Nasa'i. (n.d.). *Sunan an-Nasa'i 762*. In-book reference: Book 9, Hadith 21.English translation: Vol. 1,. Book 9, Hadith 763. Sahih (Darussalam). https://sunnah.com/nasai:762.

An-Nawawi. (n.d.). *Forty Hadith of an-Nawawi*. Hadith 27, 40 Hadith an-Nawawi. Ahmed bin Hambal and Al- Darimi.

Azar, B. (2010). *A reason to believe*. American Psychological Association. http://www.apa.org/monitor/2010/12/believe.aspx. Accessed 29 May 2024.

Badawi, E. M., & Haleem, M. A. (2008). *Arabic–English dictionary of qur'anic usage* (Handbook of Oriental Studies/Handbuch der Orientalistik. Section One: The Near and Middle East). Brill.

Barrett, J. L. (2008). *BBC Radio 4's today*. http://www.telegraph.co.uk/news/religion/3512686/Children-are-born-believers-in- God-academic-claims.html. Accessed 29 May 2024.

Barrett, J. L. (2012). *Born believers: The science of children's religious belief*. Free Press.

Bering, J. (2011). *The belief instinct: The psychology of souls, destiny, and the meaning of life*. W. W. Norton & Company.

Bhat, M. A. (2016). Human psychology (*fitrah*) from Islāmic perspective. *International Journal of Nusantara Islam, 3*(4), 161–174.

Boyer, P. (2001). *Religion explained: The evolutionary origins of religious thought*. Basic Books.

Bukhârî. (n.d.-a). *Sahih al- Bukhârî 1385*. In-book reference: Book 23, Hadith 137. USC-MSA web (English) reference: Vol. 2, Book 23, Hadith 467. https://sunnah.com/bukhari:1385

Bukhârî. (n.d.-b). *Sahih al- Bukhârî* 2101. In-book reference: Book 34, Hadith 54.USC-MSA web (English) reference: Vol. 3, Book 34, Hadith 314. https://sunnah.com/bukhari:2101

Bukhârî, & Muslim. (n.d.). *Hadith 1, 40 Hadith an-Nawawi*. https://sunnah.com/nawawi40:1

Haque, A. (2018). Psychology from an Islāmic perspective. In S. Fernando & R. Moodley (Eds.), *Global psychologies* (pp. 137–150). Palgrave Macmillan.

Haque, A. (n.d.). *Psychology from Islāmic perspective*. https://www.academia.edu/13065499/Islāmic_Psychology. Accessed 28 May 2024.

Ibn Kathir. (2000). *Tafsir ibn Kathir* (J. Abualrub, N. Khitab, H. Khitab, A. Walker, M. Al-Jibali, & S. Ayoub, Trans.). Darussalam Publishers and Distributors.

Ibn Majah. (n.d.). *Sunan Ibn Majah 4248*. In-book reference: Book 37, Hadith 149. English translation: Vol. 5, Book 37, Hadith 4248. Hasan (Darussalam). https://sunnah.com/ibnmajah:4248

Ibn Manzûr. (1988). *Lisân al-'Arab, al-Muhît*. Vol. 4, ed. A. al-'Alayali. Dâru Lisân al-'Arab.

Ibn Qayyim Al-Jawziyyah. (n.d.). Saalih Al-Sadlaan, Al-Niyyāh vol. 1, pp. 98–99. Cited in Zarabozo J. M. (2008). *Commentary on the Forty Hadith of Al-Nawawi*. Vol 1. Al-Basheer Company for Publications and Translations.

Ibn Qutayba al-Daynuri. (1983). *Islah fi ghalat Abi Ubayd*. Dar al-Gharb al-Islami.

Ibn Taymīyyah, T. A. (1991). *Dar' ta'arud al-Aql wa'l-Naql* (Vol. 6, pp. 67–73). Sifatu Safwa Corporation.

Ibn Taymīyyah, T. A. (2000). *Expounds on Islam. Selected writings of Shaykh al-Islam Taqi ad-Din Ibn Taymīyyah on Islāmic faith, life, and society* (Compiled and translated by Muhammad 'Abdul-Haqq Ansari). The Institute of Islāmic and Arabic Sciences in America (IIASA).

Imam Al-Ghazālī. (1982). *Ihya Ulum Al Din*. Vol. 1 to 4. Al-Haj Maulana Fazul-Karim. Kitab Bhavan.

Islām Q&A. (2009). *What is the fault of children born in a kaafir environment*? https://islamqa.info/en/answers/11783/what-is-thefault-of-children-born-in-a-kaafir-environment. Accessed 29 May 2024.

Islām Q&A. (2017). *The covenant taken from the sons of Adam is the fitrah*. https://islamqa.info/en/answers/248517/the-covenanttaken-from-the-sons-of-adam-is-the-fitrah. Accessed 29 May 2024.

Islāmīcweb.net. (2018).*The intention is the foundation of every action*. https://islamweb.net/en/article/156996/the-intention-is-thefoundation-of-every-action. Accessed 30 May 2024.

Kelemen, D. (2004). Are children "intuitive theists"? Reasoning about purpose and design in nature. *Psychological Science, 15*(5), 295–301. https://doi.org/10.1111/j.0956-7976.2004.00672.x

Maududi – Sayyid Abul Ala Maududi. (n.d.). *Tafhim al-Qur'an*. http://www.englishtafsir.com/. Accessed 31 May 2024.

Mohamed, Y. (1996). *Fitrah: The Islāmic concept of human nature*. TA-HA Publishers Ltd.

Muslim. (n.d.-a). *Sahih Muslim 2710d*. The book pertaining to the remembrance of Allāh, supplication, repentance and seeking forgiveness. In-book reference: Book 48, Hadith 78. USC-MSA web (English) reference: Book 35, Hadith 6547. https://sunnah.com/muslim:2710d

Muslim. (n.d.-b). *Sahih Muslim 2999*. In-book reference: Book 55, Hadith 82. USC-MSA web (English) reference: Book 42, Hadith 7138. https://sunnah.com/muslim:2999

Muslim. (n.d.-c). *Muslim 4/2076*.Fortress of the Muslim (Hisn al-Muslim). https://sunnah.com/hisn:249

Muslim. (n.d.-d). *Riyad as-Salihin 1381*. In-book reference: Book 12, Hadith 6. https://sunnah.com/riyadussalihin:1381

Newberg, A., & D'Aquili, E. (2008). *Why god won't go away: Brain science and the biology of belief*. Random House Publishing Group.

Newberg, A., D'Aquili, E., & Rause, V. (2001). *Why god won't go away: Brain science and the biology of belief*. Ballantine Books.

Oziev, G. (2022). *The objectives of the lawgiver in legislation.* IKI Academy Course on Objectives of the Shar'iah, ITKI 6101. Topic 4 (Part 1). Accessed 30 May 2022.

Rassool, G. H. (2023). *Islāmic psychology: The basics.* Routledge.

Sherwood, H. (2018). *Religion: why faith is becoming more and more popular.* https://www.theguardian.com/news/2018/aug/27/religion-why-is-faith-growing-and-what-happens-next. Accessed 29 May 2024.

Tamir, C., Connaughton, A., & Salazar, A. M. (2020). *The global God divide people's thoughts on whether belief in God is necessary to be moral vary by economic development, education, and age.* Pew Research Center. https://www.pewresearch.org/global/wp content/uploads/sites/2/2020/07/PG_2020.07.20_Global-Religion_FINAL.pdf. Accessed 29 May 2024.

Tirmidhî. (n.d.). *Sunnah.com reference: Book 16, Hadith 36.*English translation: Book 16, Hadith 1515Arabic reference: Book 16, Hadith 1472. Hasan and Sahih. https://sunnah.com/bulugh/16/36

University of Oxford. (2011). Humans 'predisposed' to believe in gods and the afterlife. *ScienceDaily.* www.sciencedaily.com/releases/2011/07/110714103828.htm. Accessed 29 May 2024.

Chapter 6
The Psychology of the Self (Part 1): The *Nafs* and the *Rûh*

6.1 Introduction

The concept of the soul and its intricacies have long fascinated scholars, philosophers, and theologians across cultures and religions. In Islāmic psychology, the metaphysical elements and the inner psyche that influence human behaviours are the self (*nafs*), the soul (*rûh*), the heart (*qalb*), and the intellect (*aql*). These elements are in the inner world (*Alam-e-batin*) of humans from an Islāmīc perspective. These key metaphysical elements of the spiritual being are derived from Qur'ânic sources. Abu Hamid al-Ghazâlî viewed these four aspects as interconnected and interdependent, forming a holistic relationship that constitutes the human soul (Haque & Keshavarzi, 2014). To fully understand these elements, it is essential to distinguish their distinct purposes and characteristics as described in divine revelation. The theme "psychology of the self" is divided into two chapters: Chap. 6 Part 1 examines the concepts of *nafs* and *rûh*, while Chap. 7 Part 2 explores the *qalb* and *'aql*, analysing their intricate interrelationships.

6.2 *Nafs* (Self): Concept and Explanations

The study of the *nafs* is a central element of Islāmic psychology. Nafs (plural: anfus or nufus) is an Arabic term that lexically means self, soul, psyche, ego, life, person, heart, or mind (Al-'Akiti, 1997). In Islāmīc literature, *nafs* is synonymous with the concepts of self, psyche, or soul. The Qur'ān mentions the word *nafs* 295 times, using it in two primary ways: to indicate one's own self and to refer to elements of the self, such as desires, appetite, anger, passion, and lust (Ahmed, 2015). In Sufi literature, the concept of *nafs* is predominant and is often referred to as the lowest facet of an individual's inner animal and satanic psyche (Chittick, 1983, p. 12). The

G. H. Rassool, *Exploring the Intersection of Islāmic Spirituality and Psychotherapy*,
https://doi.org/10.1007/978-3-031-72724-5_6

Table 6.1 Summary of key points about the *nafs*

Aspect	Description	References
Spiritual soul	The *nafs* is referred to as the spiritual soul in Islamic tradition.	Al-Raghib; Ibn Sina; Ibn al-Arabi
Entire soul and self	The nafs encompasses the entire soul and self.	Ahmad (1992)
Lower self	Al-Ghazâlî describes the *nafs* as the "lower" part of the self/soul.	Al-Ghazâlî (2009)
Changing states	Ibn al-Qayyim explains that the nafs transitions between states: *Nafs al-Ammara*, *Nafs al-Lawwama*, and *Nafs al-Mutma'innah*, the latter being the aim of perfection.	Ibn al-Qayyim (n.d.-a, n.d.-b), p. 308
Human attributes	The *nafs* is an internal entity that combines various human attributes, directing behavior towards good or evil.	Karzoon (1997), p. 60
Behavioural influence	The *nafs* shapes human behavior in conjunction with personality, guiding actions towards good or evil.	Rassool (2021), p. 60
Totality of self	The *nafs* represents the totality of the human self and psyche.	General understanding in Islāmic tradition

nafs is recognised as the spiritual soul by scholars like Al-Raghib, Ibn Sina, and Ibn al-Arabi, and is considered the "lower" part of the self or soul by Al-Ghazâlî, indicating its association with base instincts and desires. The *nafs* is dynamic, capable of transitioning through different states from the commanding self (*Nafs al-Ammara*) to the tranquil self (*Nafs al-Mutma'innah*), reflecting its evolving nature. It combines various human attributes and influences behaviour towards good or evil, playing a crucial role in personal development and spiritual growth (Ahmad, 1992; Ibn al-Qayyim, n.d.-a; Karzoon, 1997; Rassool, 2021). Table 6.1 summarises the key points about the nafs. These perspectives highlight the multifaceted nature of the nafs and its profound impact on human behaviour and spiritual development.

In Islāmic psychology, the *nafs* is often viewed as a dynamic entity that evolves through various stages of refinement. The three levels, or states, of the *nafs* described in the Qur'ān: *Nafs al-Ammara Bissu'* (Yusuf 12: 53); *Nafs al-Lawwāmah* (Al-Qiyamah 75:2); *Nafs al-Muṭmaʾinnah.* (Fajr 89:27–28).

6.3 Al-Ghazālī's Concept of *Nafs*

Al-Ghazālī (1995) presents two distinct meanings for the *nafs* in his works. First, he defines the nafs as the principle that "unites the irascible and appetitive faculties, and constantly enjoins evil" (p. 233). Second, he refers to the *nafs* as the soul, representing a person's essence free of matter. Al-Ghazālī (2010) further expounds the *nafs* as the appetitive soul, which "united man's blameworthy qualities" (p. xvi), contrasting it with the rational soul. Additionally, he describes the *nafs* as the vehicle (*markab*) of the heart and states that Sufis refer to the *nafs* as the animal spirit (*al-riih al-hayawdni an nafs*). Al-Ghazālī offers an alternative understanding of the *nafs*, viewing it as both a subtle spiritual substance, which is the essence of man, and as a principle that encompasses the faculties of anger and appetence, representing the blameworthy qualities within individuals. He expresses the complexity of the *nafs* by stating, "Never have I dealt with anything more difficult than my own soul, which sometimes helps me and sometimes opposes me" (Cited in Abu Zainab, 2015).

6.4 Levels of *Nafs*

Allāh says in the Qur'ān

وَيَسْأَلُونَكَ عَنِ الرُّوحِ ۖ قُلِ الرُّوحُ مِنْ أَمْرِ رَبِّي وَمَا أُوتِيتُم مِّنَ الْعِلْمِ إِلَّا قَلِيلًا

- *And they ask you, [O Muhammad], about the soul. Say, "The soul is of the affair of my Lord. And mankind has not been given of knowledge except a little*" (Al-Isrā 17:85, interpretation of the meaning).

This verse emphasises the profound mystery of the soul. It underlines that the nature and essence of the soul are beyond human comprehension and are known only to Allāh. The soul's intricacies and its true nature remain a divine secret, reflecting the limitations of human knowledge. It teaches believers to recognise the limits of human knowledge and to trust in Allah's wisdom, focusing instead on living a life that aligns with divine guidance and spiritual growth. The knowledge of the *nafs* is based on the Qur'ān, traditional knowledge, and scholarly interpretation of the Qur'ān. There is a general consensus that among the scholars that Allāh has described, at least 3 levels of the *nafs* as presented in Fig. 6.1

- *Nafs al-Ammara Bissu'* (The Commanding Self) is the base level of the *nafs*, characterised by its propensity to incite evil and succumb to carnal desires. It represents the unrefined, egoistic aspect of the self that is dominated by worldly attachments and impulses.
- *Nafs al-Lawwāmah* (The Reproachful Self): At this stage, the self becomes self-aware and begins to recognise its own faults and wrongdoings. This state is marked by inner conflict and self-reproach as the individual strives to overcome base desires and align with higher moral and spiritual values.
- *Nafs al-Mutma'innah* (The Tranquil Self): The highest state of the nafs is one of peace and contentment, where the self has achieved harmony with divine will and is free from the turmoil of lower desires. It represents a state of spiritual tranquillity and closeness to God.

These three levels represent a progression in the spiritual development of individuals, reflecting their evolving relationship with their inner selves and their Creator as outlined in Islāmic tradition and expounded upon by the Qur'ân. Starting from the commanding self (*Nafs al-Ammara*), characterised by indulgence in

Fig. 6.1 The three levels of the *nafs*

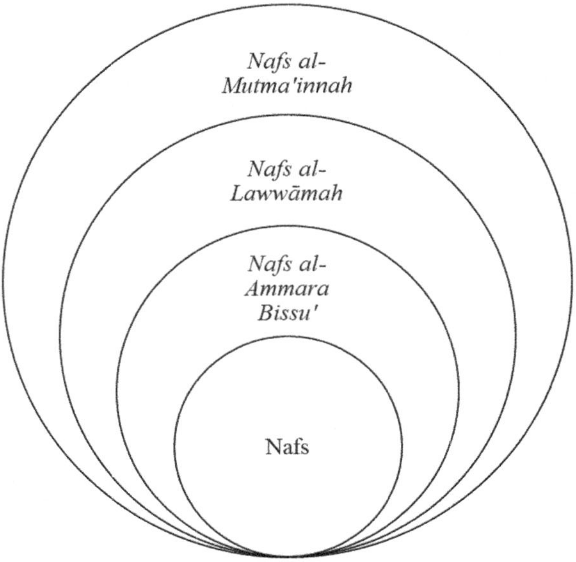

worldly desires and disobedience, individuals progress towards the reproaching self (*Nafs al-Lawwāmah*), where they become aware of their moral shortcomings and seek repentance. Ultimately, they strive to attain the tranquil self (*Nafs al-Mutma'innah*), marked by inner peace, contentment, and submission to the will of Allāh. This progression signifies an evolving relationship with one's inner self and with the Creator, as individuals move closer to spiritual enlightenment and a deeper understanding of their purpose in accordance with the teachings of the Qur'ân.

6.5 *Nafs al-Ammara Bissu'* (the Commanding Self)

The *Nafs al-Ammara Bissu'* is found Surah Yusuf 12 verse 53. Allāh says in the Qur'ān:

إِنَّ ٱلنَّفْسَ لَأَمَّارَةٌۢ بِٱلسُّوٓءِ

- *Indeed, the soul is a persistent enjoiner of evil* (Yusuf 12:53, interpretation of the meaning).

This verse highlights the inherent tendency of the *nafs* to urge individuals towards wrongdoing. It underlines the natural inclinations and base desires within the human psyche that drive towards sinful actions. It highlights human imperfection and the need for divine assistance in the spiritual journey towards righteousness. This concept is illustrated in the story of Zuleika and Prophet Yusuf in the Qur'ân (Chap. 12). This narrative highlights the struggle between base desires and moral integrity, serving as a profound lesson on the nature of the *nafs* and the importance of divine guidance and self-control. Zuleika, the wife of al-Aziz (meaning "The Mighty" or The

Powerful) becomes infatuated with Yusuf, who is a young, handsome servant in her household. Overcome by her desires, she attempts to seduce him. Despite her persistent advances, Yusuf resists, demonstrating his strong faith and commitment to moral integrity. Yusuf's resistance to Zuleika's temptation is a testament to his righteous character. He seeks refuge in Allāh, acknowledging the inherent weakness of the *nafs* and the need for divine assistance to remain steadfast. His plea to Allāh highlights his awareness of the soul's propensity to enjoin evil and his reliance on divine protection.

The nafs' behavioural intention is impulsively inclined towards wants and desires, leading to evil actions. According to Al-Ghazālī, this evil is rooted in the human aspects as a social animal, driven by survival/aggressive instincts (*quwwat ghaḍabiyyah*) and appetitive/carnal drives (*quwwat shahawiyyah*) (Keshavarzi & Ali, 2021). Al-Tabari in his exegesis of the above verse [Yusuf 12:53] commented that it is this *nafs* that brings punishment itself. He further commented that Allāh also says:

يَـٰٓأَيُّهَا ٱلَّذِينَ ءَامَنُوا۟ لَا تَتَّبِعُوا۟ خُطُوَٰتِ ٱلشَّيْطَـٰنِ ۚ وَمَن يَتَّبِعْ خُطُوَٰتِ ٱلشَّيْطَـٰنِ فَإِنَّهُۥ يَأْمُرُ بِٱلْفَحْشَآءِ وَٱلْمُنكَرِ ۚ وَلَوْلَا فَضْلُ ٱللَّهِ
عَلَيْكُمْ وَرَحْمَتُهُۥ مَا زَكَىٰ مِنكُم مِّنْ أَحَدٍ أَبَدًا وَلَـٰكِنَّ ٱللَّهَ يُزَكِّى مَن يَشَآءُ ۗ وَٱللَّهُ سَمِيعٌ عَلِيمٌ

- *O you who have believed, do not follow the footsteps of Satan. And whoever follows the footsteps of Satan—indeed, he enjoins immorality and wrongdoing. And if not for the favour of Allāh upon you and His mercy, not one of you would have been pure, ever, but Allāh purifies whom He wills, and Allāh is Hearing and Knowing* (An-Nur 24:21, Interpretation of the meaning).

Al-Tabari explains that the *nafs* exists in the realm of the senses and is driven by earthly desires and passions. This *nafs* contains hidden evil, which leads it to commit wrongdoings. Without Allāh's guidance, a person would be overwhelmed by this evil. At its lowest level, the *nafs* is inclined towards disobedience and sin due to its attraction to evil, failing to submit to Allāh. Zarabozo (2002) notes that the soul's predisposition to evil makes it susceptible to Satan's whispers, leading to sinful actions. When individuals let the soul dominate, they gradually lose feelings of remorse or guilt for their sins. From a psychological perspective, when individuals let their base desires (*Nafs al-Ammara Bissu'*) take control, they may experience a decreased capacity for guilt or remorse and a decline in moral reasoning. This can be explained by cognitive dissonance theory, where continuous engagement in harmful behaviours without consequences or self-reflection causes a shift in one's moral compass, diminishing feelings of guilt or responsibility for those actions. This state has been described as having their hearts blocked from believing in the truth. Allāh also says:

كَلَّآ إِنَّهُمْ عَن رَّبِّهِمْ يَوْمَئِذٍ لَّمَحْجُوبُونَ

- *No! Rather, the stain has covered their hearts of that which they were earning* (Al-Mutaffifin 83:14-interpretation of the meaning).

According to exegesis of Ibn Kathir (2000), "It is the dark covering that cast over it from the many sins and wrong they committed that has covered up their hearts." This verse also suggests that persistent engagement in sinful or immoral actions leaves a metaphorical stain on the heart. This stain represents the accumulation of the negative consequences of one's deeds, leading to a hardened heart or a desensitised conscience. Over time, these actions corrupt the individual's moral compass, making it difficult for them to feel remorse or recognise the wrongness of their behaviours. This concept aligns with the psychological idea that repeated harmful actions without self-reflection or consequences can lead to a diminished sense of guilt and responsibility.

6.6 *Nafs al-Lawwāmah* (the Reproachful Self)

Allāh mentions in the Qur'ān:

وَلَآ أُقْسِمُ بِٱلنَّفْسِ ٱللَّوَّامَةِ

- *And I swear by the reproaching soul* (Al-Qiyamah75:2, interpretation of the meaning).

The self-reproaching soul, also known as the self-critical or self-accusing soul, is a stage of self-awareness where an individual becomes conscious of their moral shortcomings and wrongdoings. This type of self is characterised by an acute awareness of its evil deeds and a tendency to critically evaluate its actions. The individual in this state frequently reflects on their behaviour, feeling a strong sense of guilt or remorse for their past sins and moral failings. This self-reproaching self does not just regret harmful actions; it also feels a profound sense of responsibility for not engaging in more positive or virtuous behaviours. The internal dialogue often involves questioning why better choices were not made and lamenting missed opportunities to do good. Hasan al-Basri said, "You always see the believer blaming himself and saying things like 'Did I want this? Why did I do that? Was this better than that?'" (Cited in Al-'Akiti, 1997). This may be regarded as the policing of "ethical intelligence" of the self (Rassool, 2023).

In this stage, the *nafs*, being conscious of its own imperfections, individuals have a sense of guilt would seek repentance from Allāh and attempt to address their transgressions [*Fahishah* (immoral sin)].

وَالَّذِينَ إِذَا فَعَلُوا فَاحِشَةً أَوْ ظَلَمُوا أَنْفُسَهُمْ ذَكَرُوا اللَّهَ فَاسْتَغْفَرُوا لِذُنُوبِهِمْ وَمَنْ يَغْفِرُ الذُّنُوبَ إِلَّا اللَّهُ وَلَمْ يُصِرُّوا عَلَىٰ مَا فَعَلُوا وَهُمْ يَعْلَمُونَ

- *And those who, when they commit an immorality or wrong themselves [by transgression], remember Allāh and seek forgiveness for their sins—and who can forgive sins except Allāh?- and [who] do not persist in what they have done while they know* (Ali 'Imran 3: 135, interpretation of the meaning).

This is the stage of contemplation and spiritual awakening in repentance and seeking forgiveness. From a psychological perspective, the verse describes a process of moral and cognitive restoration following immoral actions or transgressions. When individuals commit wrongful acts, they experience cognitive dissonance, a psychological anxiety arising from the conflict between their actions and their moral standards. Remembering Allāh and seeking forgiveness can be seen as coping mechanisms to resolve this dissonance. Anas (may Allāh be pleased with him) reported that the Messenger of Allāh.

(ﷺ) said, "Allāh, the Exalted, has said: 'O son of Adam, I forgive you as long as you pray to Me and hope for My forgiveness, whatever sins you have committed. O son of 'Adam, I do not care if your sins reach the height of the heaven, then you asks for my forgiveness, I will forgive you. O son of 'Adam, if you come to Me with an earth load of sins, and meet Me associating nothing to Me, I would match it with an earth load of forgiveness" (Tirmidhî, Tirmidhî, n.d.-a, n.d.-b).

6.7 *Nafs al-Mutma'innah* (the Tranquil Self)

Allāh mentions in the Qur'ān about this stage of the *Nafs*.

يَا أَيَّتُهَا النَّفْسُ الْمُطْمَئِنَّةُ
ارْجِعِي إِلَىٰ رَبِّكِ رَاضِيَةً مَرْضِيَّةً
فَادْخُلِي فِي عِبَادِي
وَادْخُلِي جَنَّتِي

- *[To the righteous it will be said]: O reassured soul, return to your Lord, well pleased and pleasing [to Him]. And enter among My [righteous] servants. And enter My paradise* (Al-Fajr 89: 27–30, interpretation of the meaning):

The state known as the *Nafs al-Mutma'innah*, or the soul at peace, represents a level of spiritual tranquillity and inner peace achieved through a strong connection with and submission to Allāh. This stage is marked by a profound sense of serenity and contentment that comes from spiritual health and alignment with divine will. According to Imam Al-Tabari, Ibn Abbas described the tranquil soul as a believing soul. Al-Qatadah elaborated that it is the soul of a believer who is calm due to Allāh's promises. Such a soul is at peace and content with knowledge of Allāh's names, attributes, and His messages about the afterlife, including the *Barzakh* [referring to the barrier or intermediate state between the physical world and the afterlife, where souls reside after death until the Day of Judgement]. This believer has such strong faith that he almost perceives these events as real. He fully submits to Allāh's will, remains content, does not waver in faith, and understands that all gains and afflictions were preordained by Allah even before his creation (cited in Al-'Akiti, 1997). Ibn Qayyim Al-Jawziyyah described the *Nafs al-Lawwāmah* as a restless and fluctuating soul, constantly changing states, remembering and forgetting, loving and hating, rejoicing and becoming sad, accepting and rejecting, and obeying and rebelling. This soul is also associated with believers. On the Day of Judgement, the *Nafs al-Lawwāmah* will blame itself, whether for its many wrong actions or for its shortcomings in good deeds. This self-reproach is considered accurate for everyone. Imam al-Ghazālī (2010) suggests that "When it is at rest under

His command, and agitation has left it on account of its opposition to the fleshly appetites, it is called 'the soul at rest'" (*al-nafi mutma'innah* (p. 10).

Striving for a strong connection with the Creator is similar to achieving self-actualisation, but it is attained through the purification of the soul (*Tazkiyah an-nafs*). The *Nafs al-Mutma'innah* represents the fulfilment of one's spiritual potential and the attainment of a harmonious state where one's actions are in perfect alignment with their spiritual beliefs and values. The serenity (*sakinah*) experienced at this stage can be seen as the result of resolving internal conflicts and achieving a harmonious state of the psyche. This state allows individuals to experience a stable and enduring sense of peace and contentment. Having a high moral compass consistently displays virtues such as goodness, piety, and righteousness and is indicative of a well-integrated moral and ethical framework. This integration helps in reducing cognitive dissonance, leading to a stable sense of self and moral integrity. Individuals in this state are better equipped to handle life's challenges and adversities because their strong spiritual foundation provides them with resilience and a sense of purpose. This resilience is not just emotional but also spiritual, as their faith provides them with a source of strength and guidance. This process allows us to fulfil our true purpose: the worship and obedience of Allāh.

إِلَّا مَنْ أَتَى ٱللَّهَ بِقَلْبٍ سَلِيمٍ

- *The Day when neither wealth nor sons will benefit, except he who comes to Allah with a sound heart* (Ash Shu'ara 26:89, interpretation of the meaning).

Qalbīn Salīm (The *sound heart*) refers to a heart that is pure and free from spiritual diseases such as envy, pride, and malice. It embodies a sincere devotion to Allāh and a moral integrity that influences both thoughts and actions. The concepts of *Nafs al-Mutma'innah* and *Qalbīn Salīm* are deeply related. Thus, achieving a tranquil soul (*Nafs al-Mutma'innah*) often involves cultivating a pure or sound heart (*Qalbīn Salīm*). The tranquillity of the self is supported by the purity and sincerity of the heart. Both states represent high levels of spiritual development, where an individual's internal state (heart) and external actions (self) are aligned with Islāmic teachings. A tranquil soul is a result of a sound heart, where moral integrity and inner peace go hand in hand. To achieve *Nafs al-Mutma'innah* and *Qalbīn Salīm*, one must engage in continuous spiritual practices, such as *Tazkiyah an-nafs* (Purification of the soul).

6.8 Freudian's Psychosexual Development and the Nafs

Freud's constructs of Id, Ego, and Superego (Freud, 1923) provide a foundational framework for comprehending the complexities of human behaviour and psychological development. The Id, often described as the reservoir of instinctual energy, represents the raw and primal impulses within individuals. It operates on the pleasure principle, seeking immediate gratification of desires without regard for consequences or societal norms. Essentially, the Id embodies the inherent drives for survival, reproduction, and pleasure-seeking that are fundamental to human existence. In contrast, the Ego serves as the executive part of the psyche, navigating the demands of both the Id and the external world. It operates on the reality principle, seeking to satisfy the needs and desires of the Id in a manner that is socially acceptable and aligned with the constraints of reality. The Ego acts as a rational mediator, balancing the instinctual impulses of the Id with the moral standards and societal expectations imposed by the Superego. This role requires constant negotiation and adaptation, as the Ego strives to maintain equilibrium amidst competing internal and external forces. Thus, the Ego plays a crucial role in mediating conflicts between primal urges and moral considerations, facilitating adaptive and socially appropriate behaviour.

In the literature on Islāmic psychology, there exists a common misconception that equates the Islāmic concept of the *nafs* with Freudian psychosexual development, particularly the constructs of the id, ego, and superego. For instance, Keshavarzi and Ali (2021) proposed that "It is possible to liken the *nafs* in this sense to Freud's conceptualisation of the id." (p. 28). This notion has been rejected by contemporary scholars and thinkers of Islāmic psychology of its Orientalist approach including the doyen of Islāmic psychology, Malik Badri. Badri (2021) stated that "A good and widely held example at the time was their proposition that the Freudian seminal theory of the three structures of personality-namely the id, ego, and superego-are the same as the three spiritual ego states of the soul that are mentioned in the Qur'ān. They claimed that the commanding soul *Nafs Ammāra* stands for the id, the soul *nafs* is exemplified by the ego, and the tranquil soul *Nafs Mutma'innah* stands for the superego. This undermined the richer and metaphysical nature of these Qur'ānic concepts. In the late 1950s I personally witnessed many Muslim psychologists strongly defend this false belief as if Freud were a spiritually motivated scholar" (p. xxi).

However, this oversimplification overlooks significant differences in the underlying frameworks and perspectives of these concepts. While both the *nafs* and Freudian constructs explore aspects of human psychology and behaviour, they originate from distinct philosophical and cultural contexts. The *nafs*, rooted in Islāmic spirituality, encompasses a broader understanding of the human soul and its development, including moral, spiritual, and ethical dimensions. In contrast, Freudian psychoanalytic theory focuses primarily on individual psychology, emphasising the role of unconscious drives and early childhood experiences in shaping personality and behaviour. Students of Islāmic psychology should familiarise themselves with authentic literature that addresses the nafs from an Islāmic perspective. There is existing literature, available in both print and web-based formats, that highlights the misconceptions and challenges inherent in equating these two frameworks (Rassool, 2021, 2023).

6.9 Disciplining the *Nafs*

Disciplining the *nafs*, or self-discipline, is a central concept in Islāmic spirituality aimed at achieving moral and spiritual growth. It involves exerting control over one's desires, impulses, and inclinations in alignment with Islāmic teachings and values. Despite the evil nature of the nafs, according to Al-Ghazālī, the *nafs* is the essence by which man can get to know God. Khan (2020) suggested that "Contrary to the popular usage of the term among Muslims, the *nafs*, by its very nature, is not intrinsically evil. It can be trained and disciplined, leading to its ultimate state: *Mutma'innah*"(p. 119). The Qur'ān emphasises purifying the soul repeatedly. This is reflected in the following verse:

قَدۡ أَفۡلَحَ مَن تَزَكَّىٰ

- *He has certainly succeeded who purifies himself* (Al A'la 87: 14, interpretation of the meaning).

This verse highlights the profound importance of spiritual and psychological purification in Islām. Spiritually, the purification of the self involves cleansing the heart from impurities such as arrogance, envy, and greed, while cultivating virtues like humility, compassion, and sincerity. It entails striving for a deeper connection with the Divine through acts of worship, remembrance of Allāh, and adherence to moral principles. By purifying the heart and aligning one's intentions with the pleasure of Allāh, individuals can attain spiritual clarity, inner peace, and closeness to the Divine. Psychologically, the process of purification involves introspection, self-awareness, and the cultivation of healthy thought patterns and behaviours. It entails confronting and overcoming negative emotions, such as anger, anxiety, and despair, through techniques like cognitive reframing, Islāmic contemplation, and self-discipline. By purifying the mind from toxic influences and harmful thought patterns, individuals can achieve emotional balance, psychological well-being, and resilience in the face of life's challenges.

Jihad al-nafs, or the struggle against the self, is a significant aspect of spiritual striving in Islām, often considered to be a greater struggle than physical combat (*al-jihad al-akbar*). It involves combating evil ideas, desires, and behaviours such as lust, anger, and deviance. According to Ibn al-Qayyim Al-Jawziyyah (b), this struggle entails purging oneself of animalistic and satanic influences, striving to learn true guidance, following it, and inviting others to it with patience. *Jihad al-Shaytan*, on the other hand, involves resisting Satan's temptations, doubts, and corrupt desires, striving to maintain faith and righteousness despite his influences. In essence, both forms of *jihad* require steadfastness, self-discipline, and a commitment to upholding moral principles in the face of internal and external challenges. Skinner (2019) draws upon Al-Ghazâlî's analogy of the rider on a horse to illustrate the process of disciplining the nafs, or self. In this analogy, the horse represents the *hawā*, or animal self, which operates in its natural state, guided by the reins (*'aql*) and controlled by the rider centred in the *qalb* (heart) under divine guidance. Various manifestations of psychopathology can be observed within this framework: the horse may be out of control, directed by the reins in an irrational manner, or firmly controlled but contrary to its natural disposition, resulting in destructive behaviour. Thus, disciplining the *nafs* involves restraining and guiding the hawā, aligning it with divine guidance and the innate *fiṭrah* (natural disposition) of the individual. In some way, it is the *hawā* of the *nafs* (self) that need to be restrained or disciplined.

Al-Ghazālī illustrates the believer's struggle against internal enemies, likening the body to a city and the intellect to its ruling king. The senses and faculties serve as soldiers and aides, while the *Nafs al-Ammāra*—representing base desires like lust and anger—poses as a challenging enemy within. The believer must defend against these internal adversaries, striving to control them and align their actions with divine guidance. By resisting these urges and striving in the way of God [*An-Nisa'*4:95], the believer earns commendation and promises of reward. Al-Ghazālī's analogy highlights the importance of self-discipline and moral striving in the journey towards spiritual fulfilment (Sunnah Online.Com). The purification of the soul in Islām involves cleansing the heart of vices and immoral traits by minimising the influence of *hawā* (base desires) and disciplining the nafs (self). Key approaches include seeking authentic religious knowledge, making sincere intentions, reading and reflecting on the Qur'ân, nourishing the soul with the remembrance of Allāh (*zikr*), enjoining good and forbidding wrong, performing obligatory prayers, increasing small acts of kindness, avoiding sins and evil deeds, resisting the nafs' demands by meeting only basic needs, making supplications (the weapon of the believer), and being charitable. These practices collectively aim to strengthen moral character and foster spiritual growth. Table 6.2 provides a summary of the approaches to purifying the soul

Allāh says in the Qurʾān.

قَدْ أَفْلَحَ مَن تَزَكَّىٰ
وَذَكَرَ ٱسْمَ رَبِّهِۦ فَصَلَّىٰ

- *He has certainly succeeded who purifies himself.*
- *And mentions the name of his Lord and prays* (Al A'la 87: 14–15, interpretation of the meaning).

The verses emphasise the significance of both spiritual and psychological well-being. Spiritually, these verses highlight the importance of self-purification and remembrance of Allāh as key components of faith and success. Purifying oneself from vices and immoral traits aligns the soul with divine guidance, fostering a deeper connection with Allāh. Psychologically, this purification process promotes inner peace and mental clarity. Regular remembrance and prayer can reduce stress, enhance emotional stability, and provide a sense of purpose and fulfilment. Together, these practices contribute to a holistic approach to well-being, integrating spiritual growth with psychological resilience.

On the authority of Abu Abbas Abdullah bin Abbas (may Allāh be pleased with him) who said: One day I was behind the Prophet (ﷺ) [riding on the same mount] and he said, "O young man, I shall teach you some words [of advice]: Be mindful of Allāh and Allāh will protect you. Be mindful of Allāh and you will find Him in

Table 6.2 A summary of the approaches to purifying the soul

Approach	Description
Seeking authentic religious knowledge	Gaining true understanding of Islāmic teachings.
Making sincere intentions	Ensuring all actions are done with genuine and pure motives.
Reading and reflecting on the Qur'ân	Engaging with the holy text to internalise its teachings.
Making sincere intentions	Ensuring all actions are done with genuine and pure motives.
Reading and reflecting on the Qur'ân	Engaging with the holy text to internalise its teachings.
Remembrance of Allāh (*zikr*)	Regularly remembering and glorifying Allāh to nourish the soul.
Enjoining good and forbidding wrong	Promoting virtuous behaviour and discouraging immoral actions.
Performing obligatory prayers	Maintaining regular prayers to stay spiritually disciplined.
Increasing small acts of kindness	Performing minor good deeds to cultivate a generous and kind spirit.
Avoiding sins and evil deeds	Abstaining from actions that corrupt the soul and lead to moral decay.
Resisting the nafs' demands	Controlling desires and fulfilling only basic needs, avoiding indulgence in fantasies.
Making supplications	Praying to Allāh for guidance and strength (considered the weapon of the believer).
Being charitable	Giving to others to purify wealth and promote empathy and compassion.

front of you. If you ask, then ask Allāh [alone]; and if you seek help, then seek help from Allāh [alone]. And know that if the nation were to gather together to benefit you with anything, they would not benefit you except with what Allāh had already prescribed for you. And if they were to gather together to harm you with anything, they would not harm you except with what Allāh had already prescribed against you. The pens have been lifted and the pages have dried." (Tirmidhî n.d.-a). The Messenger of Allāh (ﷺ) commanded us to say:

> اللَّهُمَّ إِنِّي أَعُوذُ بِكَ مِنَ الْعَجْزِ وَالْكَسَلِ وَالْبُخْلِ وَالْجُبْنِ وَالْهَرَمِ وَعَذَابِ الْقَبْرِ اللَّهُمَّ آتِ نَفْسِي تَقْوَاهَا وَزَكِّهَا أَنْتَ خَيْرُ مَنْ زَكَّاهَا أَنْتَ وَلِيُّهَا وَمَوْلَاهَا اللَّهُمَّ إِنِّي أَعُوذُ بِكَ مِنْ نَفْسٍ لَا تَشْبَعُ وَمِنْ قَلْبٍ لَا يَخْشَعُ وَمِنْ عِلْمٍ لَا يَنْفَعُ وَدَعْوَةٍ لَا تُسْتَجَابُ
>
> O Allāh, I seek refuge in You from incapacity, laziness, miserliness, cowardice, old age, the torment of the grave. O Allāh, make my soul obedient and purify it, for You are the best One to purify it, You are its Guardian and Lord. O Allāh, I seek refuge in You from a soul that is not satisfied, a heart that is not humble, knowledge that is of no benefit and a supplication that is not answered. (An-Nasa'i, n.d.)

Thus, it is through the process of the purification of the soul (*Tazkiyah-an-nafs*) that the behavioural inclinations of *nafs* can be controlled and disciplined.

6.9.1 The Rûh (Spirit): An Introduction

In the Qur'ân, the term rûh (spirit, soul, or breath of life) is mentioned 21 times in 20 verses and is used to refer to various metaphysical entities such as angels, revelation, or divine inspiration. It also signifies the inner human nature or soul, which animates the mind and body, influencing feelings, thoughts, behaviours, and volition. The concepts of *nafs* and rûh are often regarded as synonymous and interchangeable by most Islāmic scholars, depending on the context. Both terms highlight the notion of the soul as a vital component of human existence, essential for life and spiritual connection.

Allāh says in the Qur'ān:

ۗوَلَوْ تَرَىٰ إِذِ الظَّالِمُونَ فِي غَمَرَاتِ الْمَوْتِ وَالْمَلَائِكَةُ بَاسِطُو أَيْدِيهِمْ أَخْرِجُوا أَنْفُسَكُمُ

- *And if you could but see when the wrongdoers are in the overwhelming pangs of death while the angels extend their hands, [saying], "Discharge your souls*! (Al An'ām 6:93, interpretation of the meaning).

ۚللَّهُ يَتَوَفَّى الْأَنْفُسَ حِينَ مَوْتِهَا وَالَّتِي لَمْ تَمُتْ فِي مَنَامِهَاۖ فَيُمْسِكُ الَّتِي قَضَىٰ عَلَيْهَا الْمَوْتَ وَيُرْسِلُ الْأُخْرَىٰ إِلَىٰ أَجَلٍ مُسَمًّى

- *Allāh takes the souls at the time of their death, and those that do not die [He takes] during their sleep. Then He keeps those for which He has decreed death and releases the others for a specified term* (Az-Zumar 39:42, interpretation of the meaning).

These verses from the Qur'ân provide profound insights into the concepts of death and the soul's journey. In Al-An'ām 6:93 (interpretation of the meaning), the imagery of wrongdoers experiencing the overwhelming pangs of death and the angels demanding the discharge of their souls highlights the inevitability and severity of death for those who have transgressed. It illustrates the moment of death as a significant and intense transition, highlighting the spiritual consequences of a life led in wrongdoing. Az-Zumar 39:42 (interpretation of the meaning), offers a broader understanding of Allāh's control over life and death. It explains that Allāh takes souls both at death and during sleep, emphasising His ultimate authority over human existence. The verse highlights that sleep is a temporary state similar to death, from which souls are either returned to life or held back if their decreed time has come. This conveys the transient nature of life and the continuous presence of divine will in the processes of life and death. Both verses serve as a reminder of the spiritual realities governing human existence and the importance of living a righteous life in preparation for the hereafter. The essence of the *rûh's* true essence is known only to Allāh. This is illustrated in a *hadīth* narrated by Ibn 'Abbas. The Quraysh asked the Jews for a question to challenge Prophet Muhammad, (ﷺ). They suggested asking about the rûh. When the Quraysh did so, Allāh revealed: "They ask you concerning the rûh. Say: The rûh is one of the things, the knowledge of which is only with my Lord. And of knowledge, you have been given only a little" (Al-Isrā 17:85, interpretation of the meaning (Tirmidhî, n.d.-b).

6.10 Relationship of *Nafs* and *Rûh*

Scholars of *Ahlus-Sunnah wal Jam'aah*, including Ibn Taymiyyah and Ibn Qayyim al-Jawziyyah, argue that the terms "*nafs*" and "rûh" are interchangeable. They base this on the Qur'ânic descriptions of the three states of *Nafs Ammara, Nafs Lawwāmah, and Nafs Mutma'innah*-suggesting these states can also describe *rûh*. Other scholars distinguish between the two, positing that life exists in humans when the *rûh* enters the heart *(qalb)*. According to this view, the soul is referred to as *nafs* when it is within the body and as *rûh* when it is separated from the body. Sharfuddin (2021) posits that "*nafs*" refers to the state of a person when the "*rûh*" is within the body, equating nafs with the heart (*qalb*) and describing it as the ego or the arrogant "I" within every individual, which can be destructive if excessive. Table 6.3 summarises the different meanings and contexts for the soul (nafs/rûh) in the Qur'ân.

Al-Tuwaijri (2016) contends that the essence of the "*rûh*" is distinct from that of the physical body, asserting that the body ceases to function once the soul is removed. However, there are several *hadīths* that indicate that the *nafs* and the *rûh* is the same thing. Umm Salamah reported that the Messenger of Allāh (ﷺ) said: "When the rûh is taken out, the eyesight follows it" (Muslim, n.d.-a). In another *hadīth*, Abu Hurayrah (may Allāh be pleased with him) reported that the Messenger of Allāh (ﷺ) said, "Do you not see that when a person dies his gaze is fixed intently? That occurs when his eyesight follows his *nafs* [as it comes out]." (Muslim, n.d.-b). However, as "these terms may be used interchangeably in relation to their essence, the difference between them is merely a difference in attributes and usage (Al-Kanadi, 1996). In the context of Islāmic psychology, the *nafs* is considered as the self and the *rûh* as the soul. However, depending on the context of use, the two terms are considered interchangeable by the majority of scholars.

Table 6.3 Summarising the different meanings and contexts for the soul (nafs/rûh) in the Qur'ân

Category	Description	Qur'anic evidence
Creation and origin	The soul as the source of human creation	An-Nisā 4:1, Az-Zumar 39:6, Al-A'raf 7:189, Al-An'ām 6:98
Life and death	The inevitability of death for every soul	Al-'Ankabūt 29:57, Al-Anbiya 21:35, Ali 'Imran 3:185
	Allāh taking the souls at the time of death and during sleep	Az-Zumar 39:42
Spiritual and moral dimensions	The soul's accountability and the consequences of wrongdoing	Al-An'ām 6:93
	Self-discipline and purification of the soul	Al-A'la 87:14–15
Divine inspiration and revelation	The Spirit (rûh) as divine inspiration and the bringer of revelation	An-Nahl 16:2, An-Nahl 16:102

References

Abu Zainab. (2015). *30 Quotes of Imam Al-Ghazālī.* https://topIslāmic.com/30-quotes-imam-ghazali/. Accessed 7 June 2024.

Ahmad, A. (1992). Qur'anic concepts of human psyche. In Z. A. Ansari (Ed.), *Quranic concepts of human psyche*. International Institute of Islāmic Thought and Islāmic Research Institute Press.

Ahmed, S. K. (2015). *An introduction to the three types of Nafs.* https://www.ilmgate.org/an-introduction-to-the-three-types-of-Nafs/. Accessed 7 June 2024.

Al-Akiti, M. A. (1997). *The meaning of Nafs.* https://www.livingislam.org/nafs.html. Accessed 7 June 2024.

Al-Ghazālī, A. H. (1995). *Disciplining the soul, refining the character, and curing the sicknesses of the heart.* Islāmic Texts Society.

Al-Ghazālī, A. H. (2009). *The book of knowledge* (The Revival of the Religious Sciences #1). Adam Publishers.

Al-Ghazālī, A. H. (2010). The marvels of the heart: Science of the spirit. Book 21, in *Iḥyā' 'ulūm al-dīn (The Revival of the Religious Sciences*). Walter James Skellie (Translation). Fons Vitae.

Al-Kanadi, Abu Bilal Mustafa. (1996). *Mysteries of the soul expounded.* Abul- Qasim Publishing House.

Al-Tabari, Abu Ja'afar Muhammad ibn Jarir. (n.d.). *Tafsir of al-Tabari: Jami' al-Bayan fi Tafsir al-Qur'an*, 30 vols., Chapter 12, V. 53. Bulaq1323.

Al-Tuwaijri, Muhammad Ibn 'Abdul Mohsin. (2016). *Psychology from an Islāmic perspective.* https://societysstranger.wordpress.com/category/Islāmic-psychology/. Accessed 16 June 2024.

An-Nasa'i. (n.d.). *Sunan an-Nasa'i 5538.* Book 50, Hadith 111. English translation: Vol. 6, Book 50, Hadith 5540. Sahih (Darussalam). https://sunnah.com/nasai:5538

Chittick, W. (1983). *The Sufi path of love. The spiritual teachings of Rumi.* State University of New York Press.

Freud, S. (1923). *The ego and the id.* Hogarth Press and the Institute of Psycho-Analysis.

Haque, A., & Keshavarzi, H. (2014). Integrating indigenous healing methods in therapy: Muslim beliefs and practices. *International Journal of Culture and Mental Health, 7*(3), 297–314.

Ibn al-Qayyim Al-Jawziyyah. (n.d.-a). *Madarij as-Salikin* fi Manazili Iyyaka Na'budu wa Iyyaka Nasta'in, vol. 1. Cited in Al-Akiti, M.A. (1997). *The Meaning of Nafs..* https://www.livingislam.org/nafs.html. Accessed 7 June 2024.

Ibn al-Qayyim Al-Jawziyyah. (n.d.-b). *Zaad al-Ma'aad* (3/9–12). Cited in Islam Q&A. (2001). *Greater and lesser jihaad.* https://islamqa.info/en/answers/10455/greater-and-lesser-jihaad. Accessed 8 June 2024.

Ibn Kathir. (2000). *Tafsir ibn Kathir* (J. Abualrub, N. Khitab, H. Khitab, A. Walker, M. Al-Jibali, & S. Ayoub, Trans.). Darussalam Publishers and Distributors.

Karzoon, A. (1997). *Manhaj al-Islaam fi Tazkiyah al-Nafs* (p. 1). Daar Noor al-Maktabaat, Vol.

Keshavarzi, H., & Ali, B. (2021). Foundations of traditionally Islāmically integrated psychotherapy (TIIP). In H. Keshavarzi et al. (Eds.), *Applying Islāmic principles to clinical mental health care: Traditional Islāmically integrated psychotherapy.* Routledge.

Khan, F. (2020). Quantitative and qualitative assessment of the ontological domains of the psyche of TIIP. In H. Keshavarzi, F. Khan, B. Ali, & R. Awaad (Eds.), *Applying Islāmic principles to clinical mental health care: Traditional Islāmically integrated psychotherapy.* Routledge.

Muslim. (n.d.-a). And Qurtubi's at-Tadhkirah. Cited from Abu Bilal Mustafa al-Kanadi (1996). *Mysteries of the Soul Expounded.* Abul-Qasim Publishing House.

Muslim. (n.d.-b). *Sahih Muslim 144 a. The Book of Faith.* In-book reference: Book 1, Hadith 276USC-MSA web (English) reference: Book 1, Hadith 267. https://sunnah.com/muslim:144a

Rassool, G. H. (2021). *Islāmic psychology: Human behaviour and experience from an Islāmic perspective.* Routledge.

Rassool, G. H. (2023). *Islāmic psychology: The basics.* Routledge.

Sharfuddin, S. (2021). *The concept of Rûh in Islam.* http://rahbar.co.uk/the-concept-of-rûh-in-islam/. Accessed 16 June 2024.

Skinner, R. (2019). A beginner's guide to the concept of Islāmic psychology. *Journal of the British Islāmic Medical Association, 3*(1), 22–26.
Sunnah Online.Com. (n.d.). *Jihad an-Nafs* (Striving against the Soul). Al-Ghazālī's *The Soldiers of the Heart. rom Ihya 'Ulum ad-Din* (The Revival of the Religious Sciences). Cited in https://sunnahonline.com/library/purification-of-the-soul/224-jihad-an-nafsstriving-against-the-soul. Accessed 8 June 2024.
Tirmidhî. (n.d.-a). An-Nawawi. *Forty Hadith of an-Nawawi.* Hadith 19, 40 Hadith an-Nawawi. https://sunnah.com/riyadussalihin/introduction/40
Tirmidhî. (n.d.-b). *Riyad as-Salihin. The Book of Miscellany.* Arabic/English book reference: Book 1, Hadith 442. Tirmidhî, who classified it as Hadith Hasan. https://sunnah.com/riyadussalihin/introduction/442
Zarabozo, J. (2002). *Purification of the soul: Process, concept, and means.* Al-Basheer Company for Publications and Translations.

Chapter 7
The Psychology of the Soul (Part II): The *Qalb* and the *'Aql*

7.1 Introduction

The first part of this chapter focuses on the *qalb* and the second part on the *aql'* (intellect). The chapter will also examine the complex relationship between the self (*nafs*), the soul (*rûh*), the heart (*qalb*), and the intellect (*'aql*).

In Islāmic tradition, the heart (قلب) (*qalb*)—or spiritual heart—is considered the seat of emotions, intuition, and spiritual insight. Al-Ghazālī (1995) suggested that the heart has a dual nature. The first one is "the physical heart which contains a cavity filled with blood and is the locus of the Spirit" the (*rûh*)," and the second meaning is spiritual, which is of a "spiritual, divine subtlety connected to the physical heart, which is the reality or real essence of man, which perceived, knows and intuits" (p. 234). He went on to maintain that the spiritual heart is "the essence of a man. In man, it is what perceives, knows, is aware, is spoken to, punishes, blames and is responsible. It has connection with the corporeal heart, and the minds of most men have been baffled in trying to grasp the mode of the connection... It [the heart] is like king and the soldiers are like servants and helpers." (Al-Ghazālī, 1980 p. 3). Unlike the physical heart, the *qalb* is a metaphysical entity that reflects the true essence of a person, serving as the core of their spiritual and moral being. It is through the *qalb* that individuals experience profound spiritual states, gaining insights and intuitions that transcend ordinary perception. This spiritual heart is not merely a seat of emotions but a dynamic centre of consciousness and divine connection, enabling individuals to perceive, know, and engage with higher realities. The *qalb* facilitates a deep, personal relationship with the divine, guiding one's inner journey towards self-awareness and spiritual fulfilment. Through the *qalb*, the human soul interacts with and responds to divine influences, shaping the individual's ethical and spiritual character.

G. H. Rassool, *Exploring the Intersection of Islāmic Spirituality and Psychotherapy*,
https://doi.org/10.1007/978-3-031-72724-5_7

7.2 Ibn Al-Qayyim's Types of Hearts

It is narrated by An-Nu'man bin Bashir that I heard Allāh's Messenger (ﷺ) saying, "Beware! There is a piece of flesh in the body if it becomes good (reformed) the whole body becomes good but if it gets spoilt the whole body gets spoilt and that is the heart." (Bukhari (a)). This *hadīth* highlights the profound significance of the heart, both physically and spiritually, in shaping an individual's overall well-being. In Islāmic thought, the heart (*qalb*) is not just a physical organ but a central spiritual entity that governs one's moral and ethical state. When the heart is pure and reformed, it positively influences the entire person's character and actions, leading to a virtuous life. Conversely, if the heart becomes corrupted, it negatively impacts the person's entire being, resulting in moral and ethical decay. This concept highlights the importance of nurturing and purifying the heart to achieve overall goodness and integrity in life.

Ibn al-Qayyim classified the *qalb* into three types due to its functional aspect of life and death. Ibn al-Qayyim describes "the first type of heart is the living, humble, soft, attentive and heedful heart. The second type is the brittle, dry and dead heart. The third type is the diseased heart, either it is closer to securing itself or it is closer to its devastation." (p. 141). The sound or healthy heart, as described by Ibn al-Qayyim, is one that is psychologically robust and free from doubts about Allāh and His Messenger. This "truthful and sound (*salīm*) heart" is characterised by its constant truthfulness and security. A *salīm* heart is protected from committing *shirk* (idolatry or polytheism) and is free from carnal desires, adhering strictly to Allāh's commands and prohibitions. It becomes sound through love for Allāh, seeking His rulings, and showing fear, hope, trust, reliance, penitence, and humility. Such a heart prioritises what pleases Allāh and distances itself from what displeases Him, embodying true servitude (*ʿubūdiyyah*) to Allāh alone. Its actions, desires, love, trust, reliance, repentance, humility, and reverential hope are solely for Allāh's sake. A summary of the key components of a sound heart is presented in Table 7.1.

Table 7.1 Key components of the *salīm* heart

Component	Description
Psychological robustness	Free from doubts and hindrances about Allāh and His Messenger
Truthfulness and security	Characterised by unwavering truthfulness and established security
Freedom from *shirk*	Secure from committing idolatry or polytheism
Adherence to Divine commands	Free from carnal desires and obedient to Allāh's orders and prohibitions
Love and devotion to Allāh	Gains soundness through loving Allāh, seeking His rulings, and preferring His pleasure
Servitude to Allāh (ʿUbūdiyyah)	Exhibits fear, hope, trust, reliance, penitence, humility, and seeks Allāh's pleasure in all circumstances.
Pure intentions	Acts solely for Allāh's sake, directing all love, trust, and reliance towards Him.

The spiritually dead heart, in contrast to the sound heart, is devoid of life and knowledge of its Lord and His commands, being immersed in worldly temptations, fantasies, desires, and pleasures. Ibn al-Qayyim describes this heart as one that "worships other than Allāh," directing its love, dread, hope, pleasure, displeasure, glorification, and submission to things other than Allāh. He explains that this heart acts solely based on its base desires: "if it loves, it loves for the sake of its base desires; if it hates, it hates for the sake of its base desires; if it gives, it gives for the sake of its base desires; if it withholds, it withholds for the sake of its base desires" (p. 140). This heart prioritises its desires over the Pleasure of its Master, illustrating its profound spiritual decay and misalignment. The diseased heart is the type of heart that is alive but flawed, balancing between two dimensions. On one side, it possesses sincerity, reliance, faith, and love for Allāh, which sustain its life. On the other, it craves worldly lust and pleasure, striving to fulfil these desires. This heart responds to whichever influence, spiritual, or worldly dominates at a given moment. Shafi (2011) explains, "It is constantly being tried by two callers, one calling it to Allāh—His Messenger—and the abode of the Hereafter and the other calling it to temporal, worldly matters. It responds to the one that is closest and most predominant at that time." Thus, this heart oscillates between moral goodness and deviant behaviours.

7.3 Qur'ānic, Hadīth and Scholars' View of the Types of Heart

Allāh has mentioned these types of the hearts in His saying in the Qur'ān:

وَمَا أَرْسَلْنَا مِنْ قَبْلِكَ مِنْ رَسُولٍ وَلَا نَبِيٍّ إِلَّا إِذَا تَمَنَّىٰ أَلْقَى الشَّيْطَانُ فِي أُمْنِيَّتِهِ فَيَنْسَخُ اللَّهُ مَا يُلْقِي الشَّيْطَانُ
ثُمَّ يُحْكِمُ اللَّهُ آيَاتِهِ ۗ وَاللَّهُ عَلِيمٌ حَكِيمٌ

لِيَجْعَلَ مَا يُلْقِي الشَّيْطَانُ فِتْنَةً لِلَّذِينَ فِي قُلُوبِهِمْ مَرَضٌ وَالْقَاسِيَةِ قُلُوبُهُمْ ۗ وَإِنَّ الظَّالِمِينَ لَفِي شِقَاقٍ بَعِيدٍ
وَلِيَعْلَمَ الَّذِينَ أُوتُوا الْعِلْمَ أَنَّهُ الْحَقُّ مِنْ رَبِّكَ فَيُؤْمِنُوا بِهِ فَتُخْبِتَ لَهُ قُلُوبُهُمْ ۗ وَإِنَّ
اللَّهَ لَهَادِ الَّذِينَ آمَنُوا إِلَىٰ صِرَاطٍ مُسْتَقِيمٍ

- *And We did not send before you any messenger or prophet except that when he spoke [or recited], Satan threw into it [some misunderstanding]. But Allāh abolishes that which Satan throws in; then Allāh makes precise His verses. And Allāh is Knowing and Wise. [That is] so He may make what Satan throws in a trial for those within whose hearts is disease and those hard of heart. And indeed, the wrongdoers are in extreme dissension. And so those who were given knowledge may know that it is the truth from your Lord and [therefore] believe in it, and their hearts humbly submit to it. And indeed, is Allāh the Guide of those who have believed to a straight path.* (Al-Haj 22: 52–54, interpretation of the meaning)

Ibn al-Qayyim comments on the verses by identifying "two types of hearts put to trial and one type that is victorious." The hearts put to trial are "the diseased and the harsh and dry." In contrast, the victorious heart is "the heart of the believer that is humble before its Lord, it is at rest and satisfaction with Him, submissive and obedient to Him" (pp. 142–143). This victorious heart possesses a soundness that aligns with the natural inclination (*fitrah*) in the worship of God.

Ibn al-Qayyim mentions that the Companions of the Messenger of Allāh (ﷺ) (may Allāh be pleased with them) divided the hearts into four categories based on their spiritual conditions and inclinations. The believer's heart is solely devoted to Allāh and His Messenger (ﷺ), secure from doubts and carnal desires, illuminated by the light of knowledge and faith, and detached from all but the truth. The disbeliever's heart is encased, veiled, and covered, preventing the light of knowledge and faith from penetrating it. The hypocrite's heart is inverted, knowing the truth only to reject it, seeing the light only to become blind, and filled with the worst evils, causing it to relapse into falsehood and display enmity towards the truth while allying with falsehood. The heart caught between faith and hypocrisy has two conflicting desires and inclinations, not firmly established in faith, and fluctuates between belief and disbelief based on the prevailing influence within it, sometimes leaning closer to faith and at other times to disbelief.

In clarifying the four categories of the heart, Shafi (2011) cites Ibn Abî Shaybah's commentary, which provides insight into the heart that has dual urges: one towards faith and the other towards hypocrisy. This type of heart is characterised by its fluctuating state, responding to whichever urge predominates at a given time. It is not firmly established in either faith or hypocrisy, leading to an unstable spiritual condition. This heart's dual nature reflects the ongoing internal struggle, highlighting the battle between good and evil inclinations within a person. In relation to the "encased heart" immersed by a veil and covering the light of knowledge and faith, Allāh said in the Qur'ān:

وَقَالُوا قُلُوبُنَا غُلْفٌ ۚ

- *And they said, "Our hearts are wrapped."* (Al-Baqarah 2: 88, interpretation of the meaning).

Ibn Kathir (2000) and Ibn al-Qayyim explain that the verse "Allāh has set a seal upon their hearts because of their disbelief, so they believe not but a little" signifies a punishment from Allāh upon those who rejected the truth. Ibn al-Qayyim elaborates that this punishment manifests as a covering or veil over their hearts, sealing their capacity to fully accept faith. He describes it as "a covering upon the hearts, a seal for the ears and blindness for the eyes. This is the obscuring screen upon the eyes" (p. 146). This sealing and veiling by Allāh represent a spiritual consequence for their persistent disbelief and rejection of divine guidance, restricting their ability to see and understand the truth. This is reflected in the following verse of the Qur'ān.

وَإِذَا قَرَأْتَ الْقُرْآنَ جَعَلْنَا بَيْنَكَ وَبَيْنَ الَّذِينَ لَا يُؤْمِنُونَ بِالْآخِرَةِ حِجَابًا مَّسْتُورًا
وَجَعَلْنَا عَلَىٰ قُلُوبِهِمْ أَكِنَّةً أَن يَفْقَهُوهُ وَفِي آذَانِهِمْ وَقْرًا ۚ وَإِذَا ذَكَرْتَ رَبَّكَ فِي الْقُرْآنِ وَحْدَهُ وَلَّوْا عَلَىٰ أَدْبَارِهِمْ
نُفُورًا

- *And when you recite the* Qur'ān, *We put between you and those who do not believe in the Hereafter a concealed partition. And We have placed over their hearts coverings, lest they understand it, and in their ears deafness.* (Al-Isra' 17:45–46, interpretation of the meaning).

Ibn al-Qayyim comments that people with these types of hearts are rebuked "to purify their *Tawhīd* and following innovation or imitation (*ittibāʿ*) they turn on their heels and run! The 'inverted heart' refers to the heart of the hypocrite." The individual with the characteristics of a dead heart is exemplified in the following verse. Allāh said in the Qur'ān:

صُمٌّ بُكْمٌ عُمْيٌ فَهُمْ لَا يَرْجِعُونَ

- *Deaf, dumb, and blind-so they will not return [to the right path].* (Al-Baqarah 2: 18, interpretation of the meaning).

According to the exegesis of Ibn Kathir (2000), deaf means that they cannot hear the guidance, dumb means they cannot utter the words that might benefit them, and blind means they are in total darkness and deviation. This is one with the dead heart. It was narrated that 'Abdullah bin 'Amr said: "It was said to the Messenger of Allāh (ﷺ) 'Which of the people is best?' He said: 'Everyone who is pure of heart and sincere in speech.' They said: 'Sincere in speech, we know what this is, but what is pure of heart?' He said: 'It is (the heart) that is pious and pure, with no sin, injustice, rancour, or envy in it.'" (Ibn Majah).

There is a *hadīth* relating to the four kinds of hearts based in faith, unbelief, and hypocrisy as is authentically reported from Hudhayfah b. al-Yamān. Abu Sa'id reported: The Messenger of Allāh (ﷺ) said, "There are four kinds of hearts: a polished heart as shiny as a radiant lamp, a sealed heart with a knot tied around it, a heart that is turned upside down, and a heart that is wrapped. As for the polished heart, it is the heart of the believer and its lamp is the light of faith. The sealed heart is the heart of the unbeliever. The heart that is turned upside down is the heart of a pure hypocrite, for he had knowledge, but he denied it. As for the heart that is wrapped, it is the heart that contains both faith and hypocrisy. The parable of faith in this heart is the parable of the herb that is sustained by pure water, and the parable of the hypocrisy in it is the parable of an ulcer that thrives upon puss and blood; whichever of the two is greater will dominate." (Ahmad).

This narration divides hearts into four categories, each symbolising distinct spiritual conditions. The "polished heart" represents the believer, whose heart shines brightly with the light of faith, similar to a radiant lamp. It signifies purity, clarity, and illumination brought about by sincere devotion to Allāh. In contrast, the "sealed heart" belongs to the disbeliever, tightly closed off from faith and divine guidance, symbolised by a knot preventing the entry of spiritual light. The "upside down heart" characterises the pure hypocrite, who outwardly displays adherence to faith while inwardly concealing disbelief or insincerity, symbolising a state of inversion despite possessing knowledge of the truth. Finally, the "wrapped heart" encapsulates both faith and hypocrisy within, depicting an internal struggle where either belief or hypocrisy can dominate. It compares faith to a herb nourished by pure water and hypocrisy to an ulcer thriving on impurities, with the stronger prevailing influence dictating the heart's spiritual state. This categorisation serves as a profound reflection on the diversity of spiritual conditions and emphasises the importance of sincerity, steadfastness in faith, and the constant battle between belief and hypocrisy within the hearts of individuals.

7.4 Trials and Tribulations of the Heart

Trials and tribulations of the heart refer to the spiritual challenges and tests that individuals face in maintaining their faith, sincerity, and connection with Allāh. These trials can manifest in various forms, testing the purity and strength of one's heart. Common trials include doubts, temptations, hardships, and worldly distractions that can sway a person's faith or lead them astray from the path of righteousness. In Islāmic teachings, trials are seen as opportunities for spiritual growth and purification. They serve to strengthen a believer's resolve, deepen their trust in Allāh, and refine their character. Enduring trials with patience and steadfastness is highly valued, as it demonstrates faith and submission to Allāh's will. Furthermore, trials of the heart also include internal struggles against base desires, arrogance, jealousy, and other negative traits that can cloud one's spiritual clarity. Overcoming these internal battles requires self-discipline, self-awareness, and continuous effort to align one's actions with Islāmic teachings and values. In essence, trials and tribulations of the heart are integral to the spiritual journey of a believer, serving as tests that shape their character, deepen their faith, and ultimately lead them closer to Allāh.

The heart (*qalb*) in Islāmic spirituality faces both trials and responsibilities. It can be corrupted through deviation, leading to suffering and punishment. On the contrary, when guided by true divine teachings, the heart receives rewards and ascends spiritually, similar to a "polished mirror" reflecting Divine knowledge. A diseased or dead heart, on the other hand, becomes hardened, sick, blind, sealed, and lacks spiritual inclinations. Therefore, individuals are urged to consistently examine their hearts to identify problems, purify their souls urgently, and align themselves with Allāh's guidance for spiritual elevation and fulfilment. This process of self-reflection and purification is crucial in maintaining a healthy spiritual state and achieving closeness to Allāh. Hudhyafah b. al-Yamān said: I heard the Messenger of Allāh (ﷺ) observing: Temptations will be presented to men's hearts as reed mat is woven stick by stick and any heart which is impregnated by them will have a black mark put into it, but any heart which rejects them will have a white mark put in it. The result is that there will be two types of hearts: one white like a white stone which will not be harmed by any turmoil or temptation, so long as the heavens and the earth endure; and the other black and dust-coloured like a vessel which is upset, not recognising what is good or rejecting what is abominable but being impregnated with passion (Muslim). According to Ibn al-Qayyim "The trials that are presented to the hearts are the causes of its disease. They are the trials of carnal desires and doubts, the trials of aimless wandering and misguidance, the trials of sins and innovations and the trials of oppression and ignorance. The first type [i.e., carnal desires] leads to the corruption of desire and intent and the second type [i.e., doubts] leads to the corruption of knowledge and belief" (p. 145). Despite its negative elements of satanic and carnal temptations, it also has another function in bringing the connection of divine guidance to reach the individual through the *fitrah*. This is the polished mirror.

7.5 ‘Aql (Intellect): An Introduction

The term "‘*aql*" originates from the Arabic root "*aqala*," meaning "to restrain" or "to tie." reflecting its original connotation of intellect and comprehension. Over time, it evolved to signify reason or intellect in Islāmic psychology. In Islāmic thought, the concept of "‘*aql*" is approached from various perspectives by different scholars. Imam Ahmad and al-Muhasibi viewed *‘aql* as an inherent attribute of humanity, similar to an inborn light facilitating perception and understanding. This perspective emphasises *‘aql's* innate nature as a divine gift, essential for moral discernment and spiritual growth.

Ibn Taymiyyah (1988), contrasting this view, emphasised that true intelligence (*al-aqil*) entails acting consistently with one's knowledge. Those who act contrary to their understanding are not considered truly wise in Islāmic terms, highlighting the ethical dimension of *‘aql*. Al-Jawzi (2004) narrowed down *‘aql* to four principal meanings:

- As a sensory-cognitive process for acquiring knowledge.
- A tool for recognising self-evident truths.
- Knowledge gained through personal experience.
- Faculty that restrains one's desires, promoting ethical intelligence.

Dalhat (2015) further elaborates that *‘aql* involves the intellectual capacity to comprehend factual evidence presented in information or messages, underscoring its role in discerning truth and making informed decisions. According to Esposito (2004), *‘aql* can be understood as "dialectical reasoning," emphasising its role in logical thought processes (p. 22). Skinner (2019) elaborates that the root meaning of ‘*aql* as "shackle" highlights its function as the faculty that reins in the animalistic impulses of the *hawā* (the lower self) (p. 23). Together, these perspectives portray *‘aql* not only as a cognitive faculty but also as a moral compass guiding human behaviour towards righteousness. It integrates reason with ethical considerations, emphasising its pivotal role in fostering personal integrity, understanding divine guidance, and navigating life's complexities with wisdom and clarity.

In Islāmic theology, *‘aql* is viewed as a divine gift from Allāh, bestowed upon humanity to uphold moral goodness and develop ethical intelligence. *‘Aql* in Islāmic thought involves balancing the emotional and instinctual aspects of the *nafs* (self). It serves as a rational faculty that guides individuals to align their actions with higher spiritual and ethical principles. This rational faculty enables individuals to discern right from wrong, make sound judgements, and understand ethical principles. It serves as a guiding light that helps believers navigate life's challenges, adhere to Islāmic teachings, and fulfil their moral responsibilities. *'Aql* plays an important role in integrating reason with spirituality, promoting virtuous conduct, and fostering a deeper connection with Allāh's guidance and divine wisdom. Its significance lies in its ability to facilitate ethical decision-making and uphold moral integrity, reflecting the balance between intellect and faith in Islamic teachings.

7.6 Anatomical Seat of *'Aql*

In Islāmic thought, the concept of *'aql* (intellect or cognition) and its anatomical seat have been debated among scholars throughout history. Muslim physicians and jurists, such as Al-Bayjūrī, often aligned with the view that *'aql* is associated with the physical brain. They saw cognitive functions as rooted in neurological processes, linking the capacity for rational thought and understanding to the brain's anatomical structure. This perspective reflects an understanding influenced by medical knowledge of the time and rational discourse within Islāmic scholarship. Imam Ahmad and Imam Abu Hanifa, two influential figures in Islāmic jurisprudence and theology, generally held the view that *'aql* (intellect or cognition) is associated with the physical brain. Their perspectives were grounded in the rational and logical faculties attributed to the brain as the organ responsible for cognitive functions.

In contrast, other prominent figures like Imam al-Shafi'i, Ibn al-Jawzi, Al-Ghazālī, and some Hanbali scholars argue for *'aql* being located in the heart (*qalb*). They draw upon Qur'ânic verses and spiritual teachings that attribute intellectual and moral reasoning to the heart's metaphysical significance. Al-Ghazālī (2010) stated that "'Intellect' may be used with the force of knowledge (*'ilm*) of the real nature of things and is thus an expression for the quality of knowledge whose seat is the heart" (p. 9). Ibn Taymiyyah (1988) observed that "Where does intellect, reason (*'aql*) reside within it (the body)?" Then, reason is established with the soul that displays reason (grasps, understands). And as for the body, then it is connected to his heart, just as Allāh, the Most High said, "Do they not traverse through the Earth wherewith they have hearts with which they understand" (Al-Haj 22:46, interpretation of the meaning). And it was said to Ibn Abbas, "How did you acquire knowledge?" He said, "With an inquisitive tongue and an understanding heart." (pp. 53–55). This interpretation emphasises the heart as not merely a physical organ but also a centre of spiritual consciousness and moral discernment. According to this view, the heart is seen as the seat of *'aql* because it symbolises deeper emotional and cognitive faculties, guiding individuals in ethical decision-making and spiritual growth.

It is significant to clarify the position of Ibn Taymiyyah (1988) on the relationship between the heart and the brain. He stated that "However, that which is correct (in the matter) is that the spirit, which is the soul, it has a connection to this (the heart) and to that (the brain), and that which it is described of intellect is connected to both this and that."(pp. 53–55). What Ibn Taymiyyah attempts to do was to synthesise the two opposite views by explaining that "cognition is related to both heart and brain. He said the foundation of the will and decision making is in the heart, and the foundation of thought is the brain" (Dalhat, 2015, p. 81). According to Abu Iyaad (2013), the concept of *'aql* is not confined to any single organ but rather involves a complex interaction between the soul, heart, and brain. These components collectively contribute to the development and expression of intellect within an individual. The heart is emphasised as the central seat of *'aql*, playing a pivotal role in moral and spiritual discernment. It guides and directs cognitive processes, influencing ethical decisions and actions. In contrast, the brain is viewed as a supportive element, assisting in the rational and logical aspects of intellectual functions. However, the essence of *'aql* is ultimately rooted in the presence of the soul, which imbues life and vitality, essential for the functioning of intellect. This perspective integrates spiritual, metaphysical, physiological, and philosophical dimensions, highlighting the interconnectedness of body, mind, and soul in the manifestation of human intellect and reasoning.

Dalhat (2015) argues—based on a review of evidence from the Qur'ân, *Sunnah*, Arabic language, and related sources—that the heart is centrally the seat of intelligence rather than the brain. This perspective emphasises the heart's role in cognitive functions, moral discernment, and spiritual awareness as depicted in Islamic teachings. Additionally, recent findings in neuro-cardiology support this view, revealing the presence of about 40,000 sensory neurites in the heart that communicate with the brain (Armour, 2007). The intricate nervous network within the heart, as studied by Kukanova and Mravec (2006)—along with the existence of the intracardiac nervous system (Durães Campos et al., 2018)—further highlight the physiological complexity of the heart's role beyond mere circulation. These discoveries contribute to understanding the heart not only as a physical organ but also as a significant centre influencing emotional, cognitive, and physiological processes, thereby enriching the discourse on the seat of intelligence in human beings. Al-Ghazālī (2010) describes *'aql* as having five functions. Four of these functions are essentially describing the cognitive operations, such as logical reasoning. The fifth function articulates the knowledge of the heart (*qalb*).

7.7 Qur'ânic Verse: Absence of 'Aql

There are a number of verses in the Qur'ān that focus on those with an absence of intellect or power of reasoning, or the failure to use the intellect for guidance. Those who have deficit in intellect or absence of intellect or reason would be absolved from accountability, responsibility, and liability under Islāmic *Shar'iah* [jurisprudence]. However, Allāh rebukes those who fail to use this ability (Al-Anfal 8:22, interpretation of the meaning). Allāh also mentions the individuals who failed to use their intellect to understand and be guided (Al-Mulk 67:10, interpretation of the meaning). There is also metaphorical blindness that refers to spiritual and moral understanding being obscured or neglected despite possessing the ability to reason and perceive through hearing and sight (Al-Haj 22:46, interpretation of the meaning). The verse invites reflection on the state of one's heart, urging individuals to use their intellect and sensory faculties to comprehend deeper truths and divine guidance, thereby emphasizing the internal clarity needed to perceive the world with wisdom and insight. The Qur'ān sums up the failure of these people to use their faculties of the heart, vision, and hearing as a means of gaining guidance or denying the truth (Al-A'raf 7:179, interpretation of the meaning).

7.8 Interrelationship Between the *Qalb*, *'Aql,* and *Nafs*

The interrelationship between the *qalb* (heart), *'aql* (intellect), and *nafs* (self) forms a foundational aspect of Islāmic psychology and spirituality, intertwining their roles in human consciousness and behaviour.

The *qalb*, often depicted metaphorically as the seat of spiritual understanding and moral consciousness in Islāmic tradition, plays a central role in guiding human actions and intentions. It is considered the locus of faith and sincerity, where spiritual insights and divine inspirations are received and processed. The purity or corruption of the *qalb* directly influences one's ethical choices and spiritual growth, as it is through the *qalb* that individuals experience and nurture their relationship with Allāh. *'Aql*, on the other hand, represents the rational faculty that enables critical thinking, reasoning, and decision-making. It complements the *qalb* by providing the intellect necessary to discern *halāl* and *harām*, right from wrong, understand religious teachings, and apply moral principles in daily life. While *'aql* operates through cognitive processes associated with the brain, its alignment with the *qalb* ensures that intellectual pursuits are guided by ethical considerations and spiritual values. The *nafs* encompasses the broader concept of the self, encompassing desires, inclinations, and ego. It interacts with both the *qalb* and *'aql*, often wavering between spiritual aspirations and worldly temptations. Depending on its state, whether it is *Nafs Ammara* (the commanding self), *Nafs Lawwāmah* (the reproaching self), or *Nafs Mutma'innah* (the tranquil self, the *nafs* influence how the *qalb* and *'aql* collaborate or conflict in shaping moral behaviour and spiritual development.

It is through the purification of the self (*nafs*) that there is sense of equilibrium and synthesis between these three elements, giving rise towards the *fitrah.* Allāh mentions in the Qur'ān:

وَنَفْسٍ وَمَا سَوَّىٰهَا
فَأَلْهَمَهَا فُجُورَهَا وَتَقْوَىٰهَا
قَدْ أَفْلَحَ مَن زَكَّىٰهَا
وَقَدْ خَابَ مَن دَسَّىٰهَا

- *And [by] the soul and He who proportioned it*
- *And inspired it [with discernment of] its wickedness and its righteousness,*
- *He has succeeded who purifies it,*

- *And he has failed who instils it [with corruption]* (Ash-Shams 91:7–10, interpretation of the meaning)

The commentaries from the above verses from Saheeh International suggest that

> That God after giving the human self-powers of the body, sense and mind has not left it uninformed in the world but has instilled into his unconscious by means of a natural inspiration the distinction between good and evil, right and wrong, and the sense of the good to be good and of the evil to be evil. That the future of man depends on how by using the powers of discrimination, will and judgment that God has endowed him with, he develops the good and suppresses the evil tendencies of the self. If he develops the good inclination and frees his self of the evil inclinations, he will attain to eternal success, and if, on the contrary, he suppresses the good and promotes the evil, he will meet with disappointment and failure. (Al-Mehri, 2010, p. 617).

This passage highlights God's provision to humanity with powers of the body, senses, and mind, complemented by an innate moral compass. It highlights that humans are inherently endowed with a natural inspiration that distinguishes between good and evil, guiding them towards what is right and virtuous. The future of individuals hinges on their conscious use of God-given faculties such as discrimination, willpower, and judgement. By nurturing and cultivating their inherent inclination towards goodness while restraining and overcoming tendencies towards evil, humans can achieve eternal success. Equally, neglecting the good and fostering evil inclinations leads to disappointment and failure. This perspective emphasises personal responsibility in moral development and spiritual growth, aligning with the belief in divine guidance and human agency in shaping one's destiny.

In his exegesis, Ibn Kathir (2000) explained that verses 7–10 indicate that Allāh created it sound and well-proportioned upon the correct nature (*Al-fitrah*). Allāh He explained the good and the evil to it (the *nafs*). He showed him to his transgression and his *taqwa* [God consciousness]. This means that "He clarified that for it and He guided it to what has been ordained for him." Al-Ghazālī (1993) provides an analogy to explain the relationship between these three elements. Al-Ghazālī suggests that the

> Soul is a king over body as a king over an empire. In the empire of soul, hands, feet and other organs are like different businessmen and industrialists in town. Greed is a collector of revenue in that town, anger is its police, intellect is it minister and soul is its king. The collector greed is like one who collects food and anger is like a police who keeps guard over it. The collector greed is a downright liar and a deceiver. It ostensibly wishes good but there is destructive poison in it. The reign of soul over the region of body is similar. It goes on well if all organs and attributes are under the rule of soul. When soul takes the help of its minister intellect, it rules over greed keeping anger in control (pp. 5–6).

This metaphorical description illustrates the internal governance of the human being, likening the soul to a king who rules over the body as an empire. In this analogy, each part of the body and its faculties, such as hands, feet, intellect, greed, and anger, are portrayed as distinct entities fulfilling specific roles within the empire of the soul. Greed is depicted as a collector of revenue, symbolising the desires and cravings that seek to accumulate worldly goods and pleasures. Anger serves as the police force, maintaining order but also capable of causing harm if unchecked. The intellect acts as the minister, advising the soul on how to govern wisely and make decisions that benefit the whole. The analogy emphasises the delicate balance required for the soul to maintain control over its domain. When the soul, guided by intellect, effectively manages greed and keeps anger restrained, harmony prevails within the body. However, if greed dominates unchecked, it can deceive and lead to destructive outcomes, similar to poison undermining the well-being of the soul's empire. Thus, a mature intellect (*'aql*) enables the heart (*qalb*) to connect with God, fostering a virtuous and spiritually aligned life. On the contrary, an intellect with limited knowledge struggles to control the impulsiveness and desires of the *nafs* (self), causing the *qalb* to become tarnished and not shinning like a mirror which reflect evils rather than virtues. This results in the heart reflecting evils rather than virtues, highlighting the importance of a well-developed *'aql* in maintaining spiritual and moral purity.

Gulam (2018) explores the relationship between the *qalb*, *nafs*, and *'aql* in shaping human nature and personality. He emphasises that the self must be polished like a mirror, asserting that the *qalb* can be refined through efforts such as resisting desires, cultivating good characteristics, seeking seclusion and solitude, and constantly remembering (zikr) Allāh (Cited in Solihin, 2012). This approach underlines the importance of spiritual and moral development in achieving a pure and virtuous heart. This means that after the purification of the *nafs*, the *qalb* also need to be purified to be shinned as a polished mirror with the right virtues and absence of evils. Al-Ghazālī cites a famous saying from the Prophet (ﷺ), An-Nu'man b. Bashir, reported God's Messenger as saying, "In the body there is a piece of flesh, and the whole body is sound if it is sound, but the whole body is corrupt if it is corrupt. It is the heart." (Bukhāri & Muslim). This means that the sound *qalb* acts as a shield from the both the *'aql* and the *nafs* from evil temptations. It has been suggested that "a strong *qalb* can protect the *aql* from deviation and wrongful thought and raise the *nafs* in status to *al-Muṭmaʾinnah.*" (Gulam, 2018, p. 207). It is through the process of purification of the *nafs* and the *qalb* that can bind the *'aql*, *nafs*, and *qalb*, despite their inequalities and function, in an integrated whole.

In summary, the *qalb*, *'aql*, and *nafs* form a dynamic interplay within human psychology, wherein the heart provides spiritual insight, the intellect offers rational guidance, and the self-navigates between spiritual elevation and worldly distractions. Understanding their interrelationship is essential for cultivating a balanced and righteous life according to Islāmic teachings.

References

Abu Iyaad. (2013). *Where does the intellect ('Aql) reside, in the heart or the brain?* http://www.ibntaymiyyah.com/articles/jxazygi-where-does-the-intellect-aql-reside-the-heart-or-the-brain.cfm. Accessed 16 June 2024.

Ahmad. *Hiss al-Muslim* 120. 1/391. Al-Albani graded it authentic in al-Silsilah al-Saheehah, 199.

Al-Ghazālī, A. H. (1980). Ihya' 'Ulum al-Din. Vol. 3. Beirut, 1982, p 3; ibid. Vol. 1, p. 5; cf. R. J. McCarthy, *Freedom and fulfilment; an annotated translation of al-Ghazali's al-Munqidh min al-Dalal and other relevant works of al-Ghazali*, Boston. Appendix V, p. 365.

Al-Ghazālī, A. H. (1993). The book of destructive evils. In A. H. Al-Ghazālī (Ed.), *Revival of religious learnings (Ihya Ulum-Id-Din)* (Al-Haj Maulana Fazlul-Ul Karim, Trans.) (Vol. 3). Darul-Ishaa.

Al-Ghazālī, A. H. (1995). *Disciplining the soul, refining the character, and curing the sicknesses of the heart*. Islāmic Texts Society.

Al-Ghazālī, A. H. (2010). The marvels of the heart: Science of the spirit. Book 21. In *Iḥyāʾ ʿulūm al-dīn (The Revival of the Religious Sciences)* (W. J. Skellie, Trans.). Fons Vitae.

Al-Jawzi, A. A. (2004). *Akhbar al-Azkiya'*. Dar Ibn Hazm.

Al-Mehri, A. B. (2010). *The Qur'an*. With Surah Introductions and Appendices. Saheeh International Translation. Maktabah Booksellers and Publishers.

Armour, J. A. (*2007*). The little brain on the heart. *Cleveland Clinic Journal of Medicine, 74*(Suppl 1), S48–S51. https://doi.org/10.3949/ccjm.74.suppl1.s48

Bukhāri. *Sahih al-Bukhari* 52. In-book reference: Book 2, Hadith 45. USC-MSA web (English) reference: Vol. 1, Book 2, Hadith 50. https://sunnah.com/bukhari/2/45

Bukhāri, & Muslim. *Mishkat al-Masabih 2762*. In-book reference: Book 11, Hadith 4. https://sunnah.com/mishkat:2762

Dalhat, Y. (2015). Concept of *al-Aql* (Reason) in Islam. *International Journal of Humanities and Social Science, 5*(9), 77–83.

Durães Campos, I., Pinto, V., Sousa, N., & Pereira, V. H. (2018). A brain within the heart: A review on the intracardiac nervous system. *Journal of Molecular and Cellular Cardiology, 119*, 1–9. https://doi.org/10.1016/j.yjmcc.2018.04.005

Esposito, J. (2004). *The Oxford Dictionary of Islam* (Oxford paperback reference). Oxford University Press.

Gulam, H. (2018). The intertwined relationship between the Nafs (Carnal Soul), Aql (Reasoning) Qalb (Heart). *Jurnal Ilmiah Islam Futura, 17*(2), 200–213.

Ibn al-Qayyim Al-Jawziyyah (a). Ighathatu'l-Lahfan fi Masayid al-Shaytan, vol. 1, 11 / 11–191. Cited in Ibn al-Qayyim. *Diseases of the hearts & their cures*. Translated From The Original Arabic By All, (pp. 33–42). Rumaysah. Daar Us-Sunnah Publishers.

Ibn Kathir. (2000). *Tafsir ibn Kathir* (J. Abualrub, N. Khitab, H. Khitab, A. Walker, M. Al-Jibali, & S. Ayoub, Trans.). Darussalam Publishers and Distributors.

Ibn Majah. *Sunan Ibn Majah. Zuhd*. English reference: Vol. 5. Book 37, Hadith 4216. Arabic reference: Book 37, Hadith 4356. Sahih (Darussalam). https://sunnah.com/ibnmajah/5/37

Ibn Taymīyyah, T. A. (1988). *Risalah fi al-Aql wa al-Rûh*. Darr al-Hijrah.

Kukanova, B., & Mravec, B. (2006). Complex intracardiac nervous system. *Bratislavske lekarskelisty, 107*(3), 45–51.

Muslim. *Sahih Muslim 144 a. he Book of Faith*. In-book reference: Book 1, Hadith 276USC-MSA web (English) reference: Book 1, Hadith 267. https://sunnah.com/muslim:144a

Shafi, S. A. R. R. (2011). *The types of hearts*. https://www.islam21c.com/spirituality/3333-three-types-of-hearts/. Accessed 16 Jue 2024.

Skinner, R. (2019). A beginner's guide to the concept of Islāmic psychology. *Journal of the British Islāmic Medical Association, 3*(1), 22–26.

Solihin, M. (2012). Ghazali's Tazkiyat Al-Nafs & its relation with individual's development & mental health. In *Psychology and Islam*. http://spychology-ofislam.blogspot.sg/2012/03/ghazali-tazkiyat-al-nafs-its-relation.html. Accessed 16 June 2024

Chapter 8
Psychoanalytic, Client-Centred, and Cognitive-Behaviour Therapy: Congruence or Dissonance with Islāmic Spirituality

8.1 Introduction

In contemporary psychological practice, the integration of spiritual dimensions into therapeutic approaches has gained significant traction, reflecting a growing recognition of the role faith plays in many individuals' lives. For clinicians working with Muslim clients, understanding the interplay between modern psychological methods and Islāmic spirituality is particularly important. The congruence of various psychosocial interventions with Islāmic beliefs and practices is important for Muslim clients seeking therapy, as it ensures that therapeutic practices respect and align with their religious beliefs and values. However, some therapeutic approaches may be incongruent with Islāmic teachings due to differing foundational principles, philosophical underpinnings, and cultural contexts from which these therapies originate. Many Western-developed therapies, such as humanistic therapy and certain aspects of existential therapy, emphasise individual autonomy, self-actualisation, and subjective experiences, which can sometimes clash with the communal and theocentric focus of Islāmic teachings.

Moreover, therapies that prioritise secular worldviews or materialistic interpretations of human experience may overlook the spiritual dimensions of well-being that are central to Islām. For instance, the emphasis on self-reliance in these therapies might conflict with the Islāmic principle of reliance on Allāh (*tawakkul*). Furthermore, therapies that do not account for the importance of religious practices, community support, and spiritual growth might not fully resonate with Muslim clients who view these aspects as integral to their mental health and overall well-being. Therefore, it is essential for therapists to adapt these approaches to include and respect the spiritual and religious values of Muslim clients, ensuring a holistic and culturally sensitive therapeutic experience. Muslim clients often express reservations about psychotherapy, preferring spiritual healing, familial support, or medical advice over conventional psychotherapeutic practices, citing perceived conflicts

G. H. Rassool, *Exploring the Intersection of Islāmic Spirituality and Psychotherapy*,
https://doi.org/10.1007/978-3-031-72724-5_8

with Islāmic beliefs and ineffectiveness (Smith, 2011). This chapter provides an overview of the congruence and incongruence of various psychotherapeutic and counselling approaches when working with Muslim clients. It highlights how certain therapies can be aligned with Islāmic teachings to ensure they respect and support the client's religious beliefs and values. The therapies explored include the psychoanalytic therapy, client-centred therapy (CCT), and cognitive behavioural therapy (CBT).

8.2 Psychoanalytic Therapy: An Overview

Psychoanalytic theory, developed by Sigmund Freud, posits that human behaviour is largely influenced by unconscious drives and experiences from early childhood. It emphasises the role of unconscious processes, including repressed memories, desires, and conflicts, which shape an individual's thoughts, feelings, and behaviours. The theory introduces key concepts such as the id, ego, and superego, which represent different aspects of the personality and their interactions. Techniques like free association, dream analysis, and the interpretation of transference and defence mechanisms are used to uncover and understand these unconscious influences. The ultimate aim is to bring these hidden elements to consciousness, allowing individuals to gain insight and achieve psychological healing. Psychoanalytic therapy is often a long-term process, requiring a strong therapeutic alliance between the therapist and the patient. Despite facing criticism and evolving over time, psychoanalytic theory remains a foundational framework in psychology for understanding the depth and complexity of human behaviour.

8.2.1 Dissonance with Islāmic Beliefs

The Freudian tradition's general disregard for religion makes it incompatible with Islāmic culture, highlighting the complexities of integrating psychological approaches with religious and cultural beliefs (Badri, 1979; Amer & Jalal, 2012). Freudian psychoanalysis—similar to behaviourist and humanistic psychology—is grounded in a secular view of human nature, and neglects the moral and spiritual dimensions of human existence, focusing instead on rationalist, mind-body dualist theories rooted in Judaeo-Christian teachings (Webster, 2005).

Freud's psychosexual development theory posits that early childhood experiences significantly shape adult behaviour and personality through fixation or regression. Islāmic teachings present an alternative perspective where human nature is viewed as inherently good, and any deviation is attributed to external influences rather than deterministic internal drives. According to Islāmic teachings, a newborn starts life in a state of *fitrah*, whereas Freud sees a newborn as driven entirely by the id until the development of the ego and superego. Freudian psychoanalysis presents a deterministic view of human behaviour, attributing it to unconscious drives and early life experiences, which overshadow conscious intentions. Similarly, the deterministic aspects of psychoanalysis can clash with the Islāmic belief in personal responsibility and the potential for repentance (*tawbah*) and transformation.

This deterministic perspective clashes with Islāmic beliefs that emphasise free will, personal responsibility, and moral accountability. In Islām, humans are created with *fitrah,* an inherent predisposition to recognise and follow the truth of Allāh's existence. While individuals have the capacity to make moral choices, their actions are ultimately guided by Allāh's divine will, highlighting the understanding of free will within the framework of divine decree. This contrasts sharply with Freud's theory, which discounts the role of moral agency and the spiritual dimensions that Islām holds central to human behaviour and personality development.

Even Freudian's dream analysis, a cornerstone of psychoanalytic therapy, is not congruent with Islāmic beliefs and practices. Freudian theory suggests that dreams are manifestations of unconscious desires and conflicts, often involving sexual and aggressive themes. This approach contrasts sharply with Islāmic teachings on dreams, which hold that dreams can be meaningful and may convey messages or guidance from Allāh. In Islam, dreams are considered a spiritual experience, sometimes offering insights into future events or serving as a means of communication with the divine. The emphasis on unconscious drives and psychological conflicts in Freudian dream analysis does not align with the spiritual and interpretative framework through which dreams are understood in the Prophetic dream tradition. The Islāmic methodology of dream interpretation is characterised by a multifaceted approach that draws upon various sources within the Islāmic tradition. Imām al-Baghawi emphasised the diversity of sources utilised in Islāmic dream interpretation, which encompass not only religious texts but also indigenous proverbs, linguistic analysis, and the consideration of opposites. This comprehensive approach highlights the richness and flexibility inherent in Islāmic dream interpretation, showcasing a holistic perspective that integrates spiritual, cultural, and linguistic dimensions to unravel the profound messages conveyed in dreams.

Psychoanalysis—credited with developing talking therapy—has introduced valuable techniques to psychotherapy despite its fundamental misalignment with Islāmic principles. The focus on individual unconscious motivations in psychoanalytic approaches contrasts sharply with the holistic nature of Islāmic ideas and practices, which emphasise spiritual dimensions alongside individual psychology. Islām provides a holistic view of human existence, encompassing their origins, purpose in life, and ultimate return after completing their earthly journey (Abdul Razak & Hisham, 2012). In Islāmic communities, psychoanalytic approaches are not widely accepted as a form of therapy and counselling due to a significant degree of incongruence with Islāmic values and practices (Al-Abdul-Jabbar & Al-Issa, 2000; Azhar & Varma, 2000; Rassool, 2016, 2025; Sabry & Vohra, 2013). The potential for adaptation and finding points of congruence between psychoanalytic approaches and Islāmic values highlights the need for careful evaluation. However, there is a general consensus that the psychoanalytical and psychodynamic approaches to therapy and counselling, as espoused by Muslims Freud, are not congruent with Islāmic principles (Rassool, 2025). It is questionable whether it is possible to present Islām in a positive light when operating from a psychoanalytic perspective with its own frameworks and conceptions that are not in accordance with theological and spiritual aspects of Islām.

8.3 Client-Centred Therapy: An Overview

Client-centred therapy (CCT), developed by Carl Rogers in the 1940s and 1950s, is based on the belief that individuals possess the capacity for personal growth and change. In this approach, the therapist is authentic and transparent, fostering trust and openness in the therapeutic relationship. The therapist also shows complete support and acceptance of the client without judgment, creating a safe and valued environment, and deeply understands the client's feelings and experiences from their perspective, helping the client feel heard and validated. The goals of CCT include helping clients achieve self-actualisation by realising their potential and becoming more authentic, fostering self-understanding by encouraging exploration and awareness of their thoughts, feelings, and behaviours, and empowering clients to take control of their lives and make decisions that reflect their true selves.

8.3.1 CCT: Congruence with Islāmic Beliefs

Client-centred therapy aligns with Islāmic teachings by emphasising the inherent goodness and potential for growth within individuals, mirroring Islāmic beliefs in the innate capacity of humans for spiritual and personal development. Islāmic traditions advocate for self-purification of the soul (*Tazkiyah an-nafs*) as a pathway to higher spirituality, paralleling CCT's focus on self-actualisation. Furthermore, CCT's emphasis on individual autonomy and the freedom to make life choices resonates with Islāmic principles that prioritise personal responsibility and the exercise of free will. In Islām, individuals are encouraged to make moral decisions based on ethical intelligence and a deep understanding of Islāmic values, underlining a shared emphasis on autonomy and personal accountability. CCT and Islāmic teachings converge on the importance of qualities like empathy, rapport, active listening, and compassion within therapeutic relationships and daily interactions. Both emphasise the significance of empathy and compassion as foundational virtues for human relationships. In Islāmic tradition, the Prophet Muhammad (ﷺ) serves as a model of empathy and compassion, demonstrating genuine concern and sympathy for all individuals regardless of background or beliefs. CCT similarly values these qualities, viewing them as essential for fostering genuine connections and personal growth. Additionally, both perspectives underline the importance of moral and ethical values in guiding behaviour, with Islāmic teachings providing a well-defined ethical framework emphasising personal responsibility, accountability, and the pursuit of righteousness.

CCT and Islāmic teachings converge on valuing inner peace, happiness, and leading a virtuous life. Both emphasise the pursuit of fulfilment and well-being through a balanced and meaningful existence aligned with personal growth and ethical principles. However, while both perspectives endorse holistic approaches to well-being, client-centred therapy, rooted in humanistic principles, often focuses on personal growth and self-actualisation without explicitly integrating the spiritual dimension central to Islāmic teachings in the pursuit of happiness and wellness. Al-Thani (2012) highlights the significant positive similarities between the CCT and the Islāmic perspective, particularly regarding the nature of human beings, spirituality, self-responsibility, and the goal of becoming fully functioning individuals. Both frameworks value human beings and emphasise individual responsibility for personal actions and inner change. They encourage clients to develop a positive attitude towards themselves and others, taking responsibility for their choices and behaviours. Both perspectives stress the importance of self-awareness for facilitating individual change and prioritize the therapeutic relationship, encouraging clients to be active and accountable in their personal growth. The client-centred approach is notably aligned with Islāmic psychotherapy and counselling in these aspects.

8.3.2 CCT: Dissonance with Islāmic Beliefs

The applicability of CCT to non-Western clients, particularly in the Islāmic context, has been debated, with studies highlighting its incongruence with Islāmic principles due to the lack of formal recognition of spirituality in person-centred theory (AbdAllāh, 2011; Al-Thani, 2012; Badri, 2014; Mohamad et al., 2011, Rassool, 2016, 2025). While Islāmic psychotherapy integrates spirituality and religiosity as essential elements, CCT does not explicitly address these aspects. Nonetheless, Carl Rogers acknowledged the spiritual dimension in his work, describing moments of deep connection and healing as transcending the individual and becoming part of a larger, spiritual experience (Rogers, 1980). The statement reflects Rogers' deep and transformative experience of connecting with the unknown aspects within oneself, where actions become healing and intuitively right despite seeming unconventional. It emphasises a profound interpersonal connection where one's inner spirit touches another's, indicating a spiritual and holistic perspective on human connection and personal growth. This spiritual essence is echoed by Al-Thani (2012), who notes that both Islāmic society and the person-centred approach (PCA) value the application of spirituality in helping and supporting clients psychologically, aiming to create a safe environment where individuals feel accepted and loved.

One primary area of potential conflict is the emphasis on individual autonomy and self-determination in CCT. In Islām, personal autonomy is balanced with a strong emphasis on submission to the will of Allāh and adherence to the guidance provided in the Qur'ân and *hadīth*. This religious framework emphasises that ultimate knowledge and authority rest with Allāh, and that personal decisions should align with Islāmic principles and communal well-being. Therefore, the CCT approach of encouraging clients to rely primarily on their inner experiences and personal judgments might be seen as conflicting with the Islāmic emphasis on seeking divine guidance and adhering to prescribed religious duties. Islāmic cultures often value tradition and authority, limiting open expression of emotion and favouring collective over individualistic approaches (AbdAllāh, 2011; Nassar-McMillan & Hakim-Larson, 2003).

From an Islāmic perspective, CCT's non-directive and egalitarian therapist-client relationship is seen as problematic due to its perceived lack of structure and guidance. Islāmic cultural norms often expect therapists to be authoritative figures who provide clear direction and support in addressing client issues. The non-directive nature of CCT, focusing on the client's self-discovery and growth facilitated by the therapist's personal qualities, may initially confuse Muslim clients who expect more active and structured guidance (Mohamad et al., 2011; Dwairy, 2006). Research suggests that a more structured and directive therapeutic approach is generally preferred and considered more effective within Islāmic cultural contexts (Basit & Hamid, 2010). Moreover, the principle of unconditional positive regard in CCT, which involves accepting clients without judgment, can be at odds with the Islāmic emphasis on moral and ethical behaviour. Islāmic teachings explicitly outline behaviours and actions that are considered sinful or inappropriate, and followers are encouraged to correct and avoid such behaviours. This moral framework suggests a need for addressing certain actions rather than accepting them unconditionally, which can create a tension with the CCT approach.

Critics of client-centred therapy argue that maintaining congruence and genuine, non-judgmental relationships with clients is unrealistic due to inherent social judgments (Badri, 2014). The principle of congruence, which calls for the therapist's authenticity and transparency, needs careful consideration in the context of Islāmic cultural and religious norms. Many Islāmic cultures place a high value on modesty, discretion, and respectful behaviour. This cultural norm can influence how both therapists and clients perceive appropriate levels of self-disclosure and openness. Concerns also arise that striving for non-judgmental support may compromise therapists' congruence and authenticity in their responses (Yusoff, 2011).

In multicultural counselling, the concept of unconditional positive regard faces challenges, particularly in societies like Islāmic communities where moral and religious teachings strongly influence social norms (MacDougall, 2002). Critics highlight the cultural incongruence of unconditional positive regard within Islāmic faith, noting that certain behaviours deemed unacceptable in Islām may challenge therapists' ability to maintain unconditional acceptance (Badri, 2014). Client-centred therapy promotes self-actualisation as integral to personal growth, emphasising the development of aspects such as self-esteem and self-concept (Ozsoy, 2010). This concept aligns with Islāmic beliefs that stress self-transformation and human potential (Amer & Jalal, 2012). In Islām, self-actualisation involves fulfilling one's role as vicegerent on earth, guided by divine principles and the teachings of the Prophet Muhammad (ﷺ) across physical, social, psychological, and spiritual dimensions (Al-Baqarah 2:30). However, criticism within Islāmic societies suggests that self-actualization may conflict with collective values and community harmony, potentially leading to social rejection (Al-Bahadel, 2004; Al-Thani, 2012; Rassool, 2025). Dwairy (2009) warns that emphasising individual self-actualisation in collectivistic cultures could provoke familial and societal confrontations, contrasting with alternative views that integrate spiritual practices like fasting and prayer into the path of personal and social reform (Choudhury, 2010).

8.4 Cognitive-Behaviour Therapy: An Overview

Cognitive Behavioural Therapy (CBT) is a structured and evidence-based therapeutic approach that addresses the interplay between thoughts, emotions, and behaviouurs. Central to CBT is the principle of cognitive restructuring, which involves identifying and challenging negative thought patterns that contribute to emotional distress or maladaptive behaviours. By replacing these thoughts with more balanced and realistic alternatives, CBT aims to modify emotional responses and improve overall well-being. This process empowers individuals to gain insight into their thinking patterns and equips them with tools to manage their mental health more effectively in daily life. Another key component of CBT is behavioural activation, which focuses on increasing engagement in positive and adaptive behaviours. CBT emphasises problem-solving skills to cope with life stressors and challenges. Therapists and clients collaborate closely to set specific therapeutic goals, working together through structured sessions and assignments aimed at achieving these objectives.

8.4.1 CBT: Congruence with Islāmic Beliefs

While CBT is generally secular and rooted in Western psychological traditions, there can be some congruence between its principles and Islāmic beliefs. CBT emphasises identifying and challenging negative thoughts to promote more positive thinking patterns, which aligns closely with Islāmic principles of positive thinking (*Husn al-dhan*) and gratitude (*shukr*). Allāh states in the Qur'ân that "Indeed, Allah will not change the condition of a people until they change what is in themselves." (Ar-Ra'd 13:11, interpretation of the meaning). This verse aligns closely with the principles of CBT, which emphasises personal responsibility and the power of individuals to change their own thoughts and behaviours to improve their mental health.

In CBT, cultivating gratitude can help shift focus from negative to positive thoughts, thereby reducing psychospiritual symptoms. Regularly practicing gratitude can rewire the brain to recognise and appreciate positive experiences more readily. Allāh encourages believers to be grateful: "If you are grateful, I will surely increase you [in favour]" (Ibraheem 14:7, interpretation of the meaning). This spiritual practice helps Muslims maintain a positive outlook and trust in Allāh's plan, promoting psychological resilience and a sense of spiritual fulfilment.

Islāmic teachings encourage believers to maintain a positive outlook and trust in Allāh's plan (*tawakkul*), even during trials and tribulations. This is reflected in the practice of expressing gratitude for all blessings—big and small—which fosters a mindset of appreciation and optimism. By encouraging a focus on positive cognitive patterns and gratitude, both CBT and Islāmic teachings promote mental well-being and resilience, helping individuals to reframe negative thoughts and focus on the positive aspects of their lives, thereby improving overall psychological and spiritual health. CBT encourages individuals to engage in activities that bring pleasure and a sense of achievement to combat depression and anxiety, a concept known as behavioural activation. This principle aligns well with Islāmic teachings, which emphasise engaging in good deeds (*amal salih*) and productive activities as essential aspects of a faithful life. Acts of worship—such as prayer (*salat*) and fasting (*siyam*)—along with charitable activities (*sadaqah*) and community involvement, are seen as beneficial both spiritually and psychologically in Islām. For instance, Allāh states in the Qur'ân: "And whoever volunteers good – then indeed, Allāh is appreciative and knowing (AL-Baqarah 2:158, interpretation of the meaning). In the exegesis of Ibn Kathir (2000), it was stated that one of the meanings of this verse from Al-Hasan Al-Basri "is volunteering to do good works in general; and that Allāh's reward is immense for the little deed, and He knows about the sufficiency of the reward. Hence, He will not award insufficient rewards to anyone." In effect, this verse highlights the spiritual reward and psychological benefits of good deeds. Engaging in such activities provides a sense of purpose, community, and fulfilment, which can heal psychospiritual problems, thus supporting the effectiveness of behavioural activation in CBT through the framework of Islāmic values.

Both CBT and Islāmic beliefs teach effective coping strategies: CBT through practical techniques to manage stress and anxiety, and Islām through patience (*sabr*), prayer (*salah*), and reliance on Allāh (*tawakkul*). Additionally, both value self-reflection and contemplation, with CBT encouraging self-awareness to modify thought patterns, and Islām promoting *muhasabah* (self-reflection) and *dhikr* (remembrance of Allāh). Finally, both recognise the importance of social support in mental health, with CBT highlighting the value of social networks, and Islām emphasising community (*Ummah*), brotherhood, and mutual aid.

8.4.2 CBT: Dissonance with Islāmic Beliefs

The examination of CBT's philosophical foundations by Dozois et al. (2019) and Besai et al. (2012a) reveals potential dissonance with Islāmic traditions. Conflicts arise in areas such as the nature of reality (empiricism vs spiritual beliefs), views on individual misfortune, methods of behavioural and emotional change, concepts of self-control, and the balance between individual rights and reliance on God's guidance. These differences in philosophical perspectives and beliefs about predestination and control, moral conduct, and autonomy necessitate careful exploration to reconcile CBT principles with Islāmic teachings effectively.

Islāmic principles and CBT may encounter conflicts due to differing epistemological foundations, with Islām aligning more closely with rationalism and CBT often incorporating constructivist elements. CBT emphasises evidence-based psychological techniques supported by scientific research to address mental health challenges. In contrast, Islāmic perspectives place significant emphasis on seeking healing and guidance through religious texts such as the Qur'ân, prayer (*salah*), and adherence to the *Sunnah* (the teachings and practices of Prophet Muhammad (ﷺ)). While CBT emphasises empirical methods and behavioural change, Islām incorporates spiritual practices that provide comfort, strength, and direction aligned with divine guidance, offering a holistic approach to healing that integrates psychological and spiritual dimensions. Islāmic tradition emphasises the existence of an absolute, objective reality accessible through the senses and reason (*'aql*), encouraging believers to study, reflect, and use their intellect to comprehend God's signs in nature. Classical Islāmic scholars like Ibn Al-Haytham, Ibn Ḥayyān, Ibn Sînâ, Al-Bīrūnī, and Ibn Khaldūn laid the groundwork for empirical, experimental, and quantitative scientific inquiry (Rassool, 2023). In their quest for knowledge, these scholars employed various methodologies suited to the nature of their investigations. Importantly, in Islāmic thought, rationalism, reason, and revelation are viewed as complementary rather than antagonistic, allowing for a harmonious integration of empirical inquiry and spiritual understanding (Rassool, 2023).

Islāmic beliefs incorporate the concept of "*qadr*" or divine decree, which asserts that both positive and negative events are ultimately determined by Allah's will. This theological principle, integral to the faith as the sixth pillar of *imān* (faith), encompasses the belief in predestination (*qadar*). This is clearly reflected in the Qur'ân. Allāh says: "Indeed, all things We created with predestination" (Al-Qamar 54:49 interpretation of the meaning). This is further reinforced in many other verses in the Qur'ân, including: "Say, 'Never will we be struck except by what Allāh has decreed for us; He is our protector.' And upon Allāh let the believers rely." (At-Tawbah 9:51, interpretation of the meaning). So good, evil, and whatever happens in this world happens by Allah's will. Allāh says in the Qur'ân: "But if good comes to them, they say, 'This is from Allāh;' and if evil befalls them, they say, 'This is from you.' Say, 'All [things] are from Allāh.' So, what is [the matter] with those people that they can hardly understand any statement?" (An-Nisā' 4:78 interpretation of the meaning). Muslims recognise that Allāh is the ultimate architect of all aspects of life, including moments of ease and hardship. Consequently, Muslim clients may not perceive themselves as solely responsible for their challenges, attributing life circumstances to Allāh's divine plan and acknowledging His sovereignty over all events. In contrast, CBT focuses on personal responsibility and the idea that individuals have the power to change their thoughts and behaviours.

In CBT, therapists aim to help clients modify behaviours and thoughts that contribute to their distress, promoting mental health. However, in the context of Muslim clients, certain behaviours targeted by CBT may clash with Islāmic ethical norms and principles. For example, exposure therapies that involve scenarios or activities considered morally unacceptable in Islām could cause significant discomfort or internal conflict for Muslim clients. This clash highlights the importance of therapists approaching treatment with cultural competence and sensitivity to religious beliefs. Understanding how specific therapeutic techniques align with Islāmic ethical frameworks is essential.

In CBT, the conceptualisation of the self tends to focus on individualistic principles such as self-awareness, autonomy, and the protection of individual rights. However, Islāmic principles present an alternative perspective where the self is viewed as inseparable from the collective community (*ummah*), prioritising communal rights and interests (*Fard kifayah*) over individual ones. This collectivistic approach emphasises unity, cooperation, and working towards the common good as essential components of Islāmic ethics. While Islām acknowledges individual free will and accountability, it underlines the importance of considering community well-being and fostering harmony within society. This difference in perspective can pose challenges in therapy for Muslim clients, highlighting the need for therapists to understand and respect Islāmic values that prioritise communal welfare alongside individual growth and development. Therapeutic approaches should aim to integrate these cultural and religious values sensitively to support clients in navigating their mental health challenges while staying true to their faith.

From an Islāmic perspective, psychological disorders are often perceived as part of Allāh's divine plan, either as tests of faith, opportunities for spiritual growth, or as purification from sins. Muslim clients may view these challenges through a lens of patience, resilience, and acceptance of Allāh's will, finding solace in the belief that enduring difficulties can lead to spiritual blessings. This theological viewpoint shapes how individuals from various Islāmic cultures perceive and cope with mental health issues, with some seeing afflictions as a chance for self-reflection, repentance, and seeking forgiveness from Allāh. Ultimately, these interpretations highlight the importance of adhering to Allāh's natural and moral laws, demonstrating faith through perseverance and spiritual development amidst adversity (Abu-Ras et al., 2008; Haque, 2004b; Padela et al., 2012; Rassool, 2000). In contrast, mental health issues are generally seen as resulting from dysfunctional thought patterns and behaviours, which can be modified through therapy.

8.4.3 *Islāmic Cognitive Behavioural Therapy Approach*

The integration of cognitive-behavioural principles with Islāmic teachings has deep historical roots, dating back to early Islāmic scholars who demonstrated a sophisticated understanding of psychology.

One significant figure is Abū Zayd Ahmad ibn Sahl al-Balkhī (850–934)—Persian polymath and scholar—made significant contributions to various fields, including medicine, psychology, geography, and philosophy. He is renowned for his pioneering work in mental health, particularly his treatise "*Masabih al-Abdan wa al-Anfus*" ("Sustenance for Bodies and Souls") (Badri, 2013), where he introduced reciprocal inhibition and "rational cognitive therapy", emphasising the treatment of emotional disorders through cognitive restructuring and rational thinking. Al-Balkhi's methods also included a psycho-spiritual religious cognitive approach, recognising the interplay between spiritual beliefs and mental health. He is the father of cognitive behavioural therapy. Cognitive restructuring—a technique widely used in modern cognitive-behavioural therapy—finds resonance in the thinking style advocated by early Muslim scholars like Ibn al-Qayyim (Yusaf, 2019). This method involves identifying and challenging irrational or maladaptive thoughts to promote healthier cognitive patterns and emotional well-being. The alignment of cognitive restructuring with Islāmic thinking is evident in the works of these scholars, who emphasised the role of rational thinking in influencing emotions and behaviours. Their contributions reflect a profound psychological insight that predates contemporary cognitive therapies, illustrating the enduring relevance of their ideas in modern psychological practices (Badri, 1976, 2013; Haque, 2004a; Yusaf, 2019).

Opposite therapy, as proposed by Al-Ghazālī, is a therapeutic strategy designed to help individuals overcome spiritual deficiencies by cultivating opposing positive attributes to counteract their negative tendencies (Rosila & Yaacob, 2013). This imaginative technique involves clients acting as if the opposite quality is already present. For example, if a person struggles with ignorance, Al-Ghazālī suggests that they should imagine actively seeking knowledge and engage with knowledgeable individuals. Similarly, if someone experiences feelings of hatred, the therapy encourages them to redirect their attention towards cultivating love, imagining, and practicing this positive trait to replace the negative feeling. This approach emphasises the intentional selection and practice of virtuous characteristics to foster personal and spiritual growth. By consciously developing positive traits that oppose and replace negative aspects, individuals can overcome spiritual obstacles and deficiencies. The method underlines the belief that through deliberate practice and imagination, one can cultivate qualities such as knowledge and love, thereby promoting overall well-being and spiritual development (Al-Ghazālī, 1998; Badri, 2000; Rizvi, 1989; Rosila & Yaacob, 2013). This therapeutic concept highlights the transformative power of positive thinking and action in achieving personal and spiritual excellence.

Islāmically adjusted Cognitive-Behavioural Therapy (I-CBT) incorporates unique facets and techniques derived from Islāmic teachings, tailored to address the specific needs of Muslim clients. These interventions leverage significant cognitions from the Islāmic faith, such as the understanding of the world's temporality (Al-Qasas 28:60; 29:64), the focus on the Hereafter (Ali 'Imran 3:15), and the purpose and effects of distress and afflictions (Al Baqarah 2:155–6). This approach also emphasises trusting and relying on Allāh (*tawakkul*) (Ali 'Imran 3:159), recognising that ease follows hardship (Inshirah 94:5–6), focusing on Allah's blessings, remembering Allāh, reading the Qur'an (Ar-Ra'd 13:28), and making supplications (*dua'hs*) (Al Baqarah 2:186). When these spiritual elements are integrated into CBT, they can lead to several positive outcomes for spiritually motivated Muslims, including quicker recovery, improved treatment adherence, lower recurrence rates, and reduced treatment inequities (Husain & Hodge, 2016). Examples of spiritually modified cognitive interventions include emphasising self-control, self-worth in Allāh, high frustration tolerance, acceptance of others, the pursuit of achievement, the need for approval and love, accepting responsibility, self-direction, and self-acceptance (Hodge & Nadir, 2008). By aligning therapeutic techniques with Islāmic values, therapists can create a culturally sensitive framework that resonates deeply with Muslim clients, enhancing the effectiveness of therapy and ensuring that it respects and integrates their religious beliefs.

In the cognitive restructuring model suggested by Hamdan (2008), clients are guided to identify and evaluate automatic thoughts and dysfunctional core beliefs that lead to problem behaviours. This process involves discussing their most distressing issues, modifying automatic thoughts, and then addressing core beliefs by examining evidence and considering alternative explanations. For Muslim clients, these alternative explanations can be derived from Islāmic teachings, tailored to align with their faith and specific needs. However, it is crucial to recognise that cognitive restructuring may not be suitable for addressing fundamental Islāmic principles such as *tawhîd* (the belief in the Oneness of God), Islāmic religious practices and obligations, or obedience to parental wishes. Challenging these core beliefs could be inappropriate and counterproductive. Instead, CBT therapists should focus on fostering healthy communication skills, creating boundaries, and integrating Islāmic principles with individual autonomy and personal growth. For example, while it is not acceptable to dispute the concept of *tawhîd* or modify fundamental religious practices, therapists can work with clients to improve their communication within the framework of their faith, help them set healthy boundaries, and support personal development in ways that respect and uphold Islāmic values (Walpole et al., 2013). This culturally sensitive approach ensures that therapy is both respectful of and harmonious with the client's religious beliefs, promoting mental health and spiritual well-being simultaneously.

In I-CBT, contemplation—or deep thought—is a technique highly emphasised in the Qur'ân and *Sunnah.* This practice involves meditating on Allāh's creation and bounties, which is believed to strengthen faith and lead to better deeds and behaviour. Contemplation is seen as the beginning and key to all good and is considered the best function of the heart. Verses such as Al-Imran 3:190–1, Al-Mulk 67:3–4, and Al-Mu'minun 23:62 highlight the importance of contemplation, including its relevance to life hereafter, the ultimate goal for individuals (Badri, 2000; Ibn al-Qayyim al-Jawziyyah, n.d.; Rosila & Yaacob, 2013). Additionally, other techniques compatible with CBT within an Islāmic context include supplications, prayers, the power of suggestion, and remembered wellness. These practices align well with CBT's more directive approach, its focus on current and future functioning, and its emphasis on practical assignments or homework. This approach is particularly effective with Muslim clients, as it resonates with Islāmic values and traditions (Abudabbeh & Hays, 2006; Benson, 1996; Carter & Rashidi, 2004; Hamdan, 2008; Husain & Hodge, 2016; Rosila & Yaacob, 2013). The incorporation of practical, outside-of-session assignment, a hallmark of CBT, mirrors Islāmic traditions and may be especially appealing to Muslim clients. By blending these cognitive-behavioural techniques with Islāmic practices, therapists can offer culturally sensitive and effective therapy that respects and integrates the client's religious beliefs. This integrated approach not only enhances therapeutic outcomes but also supports the spiritual growth and well-being of Muslim clients.

In (I-CBT), the therapeutic approach integrates Islāmic teachings and practices to address psychological challenges effectively while honouring the client's religious beliefs. Central to this approach is guiding Muslim clients to reflect on relevant Qur'ânic verses that address their specific issues, such as patience, gratitude, or seeking forgiveness. This involves reading and discussing these verses in the context of the client's circumstances, providing a spiritual framework for coping and growth. Additionally, personalised positive affirmations based on Islāmic teachings are encouraged to combat negative self-talk and reinforce constructive thinking on a daily basis. Self-reflection and *tawbah* (repentance) play crucial roles in Islāmic modified CBT, fostering personal development and resilience. Clients engage in honest introspection, acknowledging mistakes without self-judgment, and taking responsibility for their actions in alignment with Islāmic principles of seeking forgiveness and embracing divine kindness for personal growth. Gratitude journaling—which involves documenting blessings and experiences as per the Islāmic concept of *shukr* (gratitude)—further strengthens the connection to Allāh's blessings and enhances overall well-being and contentment (Rassool, 2025). These techniques are designed to respect and integrate Islāmic beliefs, values, and practices into the therapeutic process, promoting psychological healing within a spiritually meaningful framework (Rassool, 2021). It is important to note that the application of these techniques varies based on individual client needs and the therapist's expertise in Islāmic modified CBT.

Research studies have demonstrated the effectiveness of culturally adapted therapeutic approaches for Muslim clients across different contexts. Mir et al., (2019) explored the use of culturally adapted behavioural activation for depression among Muslim clients, highlighting its efficacy, particularly when individuals utilised positive religious coping strategies as a health resource. This approach stresses the importance of integrating religious beliefs and practices into therapeutic interventions to enhance outcomes. Similarly, Perry et al., (2019) applied acceptance and commitment therapy (ACT) with a Turkish population in London, reporting significant reductions in depression, anxiety, and emotional distress. This study illustrates the adaptability of evidence-based therapies like ACT across cultural contexts while addressing the specific needs and values of Muslim clients. Furthermore, a case report by Alatiq and Alrshoud (2018) on family-based cognitive-behavioural therapy for obsessive-compulsive disorder in Saudi Arabia showcased the potential applicability of CBT in the region when tailored thoughtfully to cultural norms and sensitivities. These studies collectively emphasise the importance of culturally sensitive adaptations in psychotherapy to effectively address mental health issues within diverse Muslim populations. Bhatti-Ali (2024) has proposed a psychotherapeutic interventions integrating Islāmic psychotherapy with Acceptance Commitment Therapy (ACT) in the management of pain with Muslim clients. These findings highlight the potential benefits of integrating cultural and religious considerations into therapeutic practices, enhancing engagement, effectiveness, and relevance for Muslim clients seeking mental health support (Mir et al., 2019; Perry et al., 2019; Alatiq & Alrshoud, 2018).

Religion-adapted cognitive-behavioural therapy (R-CBT) has demonstrated effectiveness—as evidenced by systematic reviews. This approach involves integrating religious content into various therapeutic techniques such as cognitive restructuring, psychoeducation, and motivation. Adaptations also include incorporating religious activities like behavioural activation, meditation, or prayer to support cognitive restructuring, while emphasising religious values and coping strategies relevant to the client's faith. The systematic review highlights the efficacy of culturally adapted cognitive-behavioural therapy, particularly in addressing the needs of Muslim clients (de Abreu Costa & Moreira-Almeida, 2022). This adaptation recognises the significance of religion in clients' lives and tailors therapeutic interventions to align with their religious beliefs and practices. By integrating religious components into CBT, therapists can enhance treatment engagement and effectiveness, addressing psychological issues within a framework that respects and integrates cultural and religious identities.

The effectiveness of CBT within Muslim populations has raised concerns primarily because much of the existing research on CBT efficacy has been conducted with individuals from Western, Judeo-Christian backgrounds (Besai et al., 2012b; Hodge, 2004). While there is growing evidence suggesting the efficacy of cognitive interventions adapted to incorporate Islāmic principles, several methodological issues and gaps in research quality remain as significant concerns. Studies exploring CBT adapted for Islāmic spiritual interventions often face challenges such as small sample sizes, lack of diverse cultural representation, and variations in how Islāmic principles are integrated into therapy. These methodological limitations hinder the ability to draw definitive conclusions about the empirical soundness and universal applicability of modified CBT within Muslim communities. To address these concerns, there is a pressing need for more robust research methodologies, including larger and more diverse participant samples, rigorous study designs, and standardised outcome measures. Further research and clinical application are essential to continue refining and validating these approaches in diverse Muslim communities and geographic settings.

References

AbdAllāh, S. S. (2011). *Islāmic theological and spiritual foundations of resilience: Implications for counseling and psychotherapy with Muslims*. Paper presented at the international conference on the psychology of resilience.

Abdul Razak, M. A., & Hisham, N. A. (2012). Islāmic psychology and the call for Islāmization of modern psychology. *Journal of Islām in Asia, 9*(1), 156–183.

Abudabbeh, N., & Hays, P. A. (2006). Cognitive-behavioral therapy with people of Arab heritage. In P. A. Hays & G. Y. Iwamasa (Eds.), *Culturally responsive cognitive-behavioral therapy: Assessment, practice, and supervision* (pp. 141–159). American Psychological Association.

Abu-Ras, W., Gheith, A., & Cournos, F. (2008). The Imam's role in mental health promotion: A study at 22 mosques in New York City's Muslim Community. *Journal of Muslim Mental Health, 3*(2), 155–176. https://doi.org/10.1080/15564900802487576

Al-Abdul-Jabbar, J., & Al-Issa, I. (2000). Psychotherapy in Islāmic society. In I. Al-Issa (Ed.), *Al-Junn: Mental illness in the Islāmic World* (pp. 277–293). International Universities Press.

Alatiq, Y., & Alrshoud, H. (2018). Family-based cognitive behavioural therapy for obsessive-compulsive disorder with family accommodation: Case report from Saudi Arabia. *The Cognitive Behaviour Therapist, 11*. https://doi.org/10.1017/S1754470X1800017X

Al-Bahadel, D. (2004). *The feasibility of introducing counseling for woman and family therapy into society within Saudi Arabia*. Unpublished PhD thesis, University of East Anglia.

Al-Ghazālī, A. H. (1998). *Iḥyā' 'ulūm al-Dīn* [The Revival of the Religious Sciences] (Vol. 2). Dar al-Kutub al-Ilmiah.

Al-Thani, A. S. (2012). *An Islāmic Modification of the Person-Centred Counselling Approach*. QScience.com. Online at www.qscience.com/page/books/impcca. Accessed 19 June 2024.

Amer, M. A., & Jalal, B. (2012). Individual psychotherapy/counselling. In S. Ahmed & M. M. Amer (Eds.), *Counseling Muslims: Handbook of mental health issues and interventions*. Routledge.

Azhar, M. Z., & Varma, S. L. (2000). Mental illness and its treatment in Malaysia. In I. al-Issa (Ed.), *Al-Junūn: Mental illness in the Islāmic World* (pp. 163–185). International Universities Press.

Badri, M. (1976). *Islām and Alcoholism*. American Trust Publications.

Badri, M. (1979). *The Dilemma of Muslim psychologists*. MWH London Publishers.

Badri, M. (2000). *Contemplation: An Islāmic Psychospiritual Study*. International Institute of Islāmic Thought.

Badri, M. (2013). *Abu Zayd al-Balkhi's sustenance of the soul: The cognitive behavior therapy of a ninth century physician*. International Institute of Islāmic Thought (IIIT).

Badri, M. B. (2014). *Can the psychotherapy of Muslim patients be of real help to them without being Islāmised?*. Islāmic-World.net. http://Islāmic187.rssing.com/browser.php?indx=7717208&item=27. Accessed 19 June 2024.

Basit, A., & Hamid, M. (2010). Mental health issues of Muslim Americans. *Journal of the Islāmic Medical Association of North America, 42*(3), 106–110. https://doi.org/10.5915/42-3-5507

Benson, H. (1996). *Timeless healing: The power and biology of belief*. Simon & Schuster.

Besai, S., Clark, C. M., & Dobson, K. S. (2012a). Conceptual and pragmatic considerations in the use of cognitive-behavioral therapy with Muslim clients. *Cognitive Therapy and Research, 37*(1), 197–206. https://doi.org/10.1007/s10608-012-9450-y

Besai, S., Dobson, K. S., & Adel, A. (2012b). Cognition and dysphoria in Egypt and Canada: An examination of the cognitive triad. *Canadian Journal of Behavioural Science, 44*(1), 29–39.

Bhatti-Ali,, R. (2024). *Integrating Acceptance and Commitment Therapy with Islāmic Psychotherapy for Managing Chronic Pain*. 1st Edition. Focus Series on Islāmic Psychology & Psychotherapy. Oxford: Routledge.

Carter, D. J., & Rashidi, A. (2004). East meets West: Integrating psychotherapy approaches for Muslim women. *Holistic Nursing Practice, 18*(3), 152–159.

Choudhury, M. A. (2010). Self-actualization: Experience of Ramadan. Horizon, 197, 4. www.squ.edu.om/Portals/33/almasar/Horizon%20197%20.pdf. Accessed 14 Oct 2024.

de Abreu Costa, M., & Moreira-Almeida, A. (2022). Religion-adapted cognitive behavioral therapy: A review and description of techniques. *Journal of Religion and Health, 61*(1), 443–466. https://doi.org/10.1007/s10943-021-01345-z

Dozois, D. J. A., Dobson, K. S., & Rnic, K. (2019). Historical and philosophical bases of the cognitive-behavioral therapies. In K. S. Dobson & D. J. A. Dozois (Eds.), *Handbook of cognitive-behavioral therapies* (pp. 3–31). The Guilford Press.

Dwairy, M. (2006). *Counseling and psychotherapy with Arabs and Muslims: A culturally sensitive approach.* Columbia University Teachers' College.

Dwairy, M. (2009). Culture analysis and metaphor psychotherapy with Arab-Muslim clients. *Journal of Clinical Psychology: In Session, 65*(2), 199–209. https://doi.org/10.1002/jclp.20568

Hamdan, A. (2008). Cognitive restructuring: An Islāmic Perspective. *Journal of Muslim Mental Health, 3*(1), 99–116.

Haque, A. (2004a). Psychology from Islāmic perspective: Contributions of Early Muslim Scholars and challenges to contemporary Muslim psychologists. *Journal of Religion and Health, 43*(4), 357–377. https://doi.org/10.1007/s10943-004-4302-z

Haque, A. (2004b). Religion and mental health: The case of American Muslims. *Journal of Religion and Health, 43*(1), 45–58.

Hodge, D. R. (2004). Working with Hindu clients in a spiritually sensitive manner. *Social Work, 49*(1), 27–38.

Hodge, D. R., & Nadir, A. (2008). Moving toward culturally competent practice with Muslims: Modifying cognitive therapy with Islāmic tenets. *Social Work, 53*(1), 31–41.

Husain, A., & Hodge, D. R. (2016). Islāmically modified cognitive behavioral therapy: Enhancing outcomes by increasing the cultural congruence of cognitive behavioral therapy self-statements. *International Social Work, 59*(3), 393–405.

Ibn al-Qayyim al-Jawziyyah. (n.d.). *The Key to the House of Bliss (Miftah Dar al-Sa'adah).* Ri'asat al-Ifta.

Ibn Kathir. (2000). *Tafsir ibn Kathir* (J. Abualrub, N. Khitab, H. Khitab, A. Walker, M. Al-Jibali, & S. Ayoub, Trans.). Darussalam Publishers and Distributors.

Imām al-Baghawi. Sharh al-Sunnah [(Explanation of the Sunnah] 12/220. Cited in Cited in Islām Q&A. (1999). 6537 *Dreams and Dream Interpretation.* https://Islāmqa.info/en/answers/6537/dreams-and-dream-interpretation. Accessed 17 June 2024.

MacDougall, C. (2002). Rogers's person-centered approach: Consideration for use in multicultural counseling. *Journal of Humanistic Psychology, 42*(2), 48–55. https://doi.org/10.1177/0022167802422005

Mir, G., Ghani, R., Meer, S., & Hussain, G. (2019). Delivering a culturally adapted therapy for Muslim clients with depression. *The Cognitive Behaviour Therapist, 12*(1–14), E26. https://doi.org/10.1017/S1754470X19000059

Mohamad, M., Mokhtar, H. H., & Abu Sama, A. (2011). Person-centered counseling with Malay clients: Spirituality as an indicator of personal growth. *Procedia – Social and Behavioral Sciences, 30*, 2117–2123. https://doi.org/10.1016/j.sbspro.2011.10.411

Nassar-McMillan, S. C., & Hakim-Larson, J. (2003). Counseling considerations among Arab Americans. *Journal of Counseling and Development, 81*(2), 150–159.

Ozsoy, Z. (2010). A true understanding of self for self-actualization. *The Fountain Magazine.* www.fountainmagazine.com/Issue/detail/A-True-Understanding-of-Self-for-Self-Actualization. Accessed 19 June 2024.

Padela, A. I., Killawi, A., Forman, J., DeMonner, S., & Heisler, M. (2012). American Muslim perceptions of healing key agents in healing, and their roles. *Qualitative Health Research, 22*(6), 846–858.

Perry, A., Gardener, C., Oliver, J. E., Taş, Ç., & Özenç, C. (2019). Exploring the cultural flexibility of the ACT model as an effective therapeutic group intervention for Turkish speaking communities in East London. *The Cognitive Behaviour Therapist, 12.* https://doi.org/10.1017/S1754470X18000041

Rassool, G. H. (2000). The crescent and Islām: Healing, nursing, and the spiritual dimension: Some considerations towards an understanding of the Islāmic perspectives on caring. *Journal of Advanced Nursing, 32*(6), 1476–1484.
Rassool, G. H. (2021). *Islamic psychology: Human behaviour and experience from an Islamic perspective*. Routledge.
Rassool, G. H. (2016). *Islāmic counselling: An introduction to theory and practice*. Routledge.
Rassool, G. H. (2023). *Integrated research methodologies in Islāmic psychology. Focus series on Islāmic psychology and psychotherapy*. Routledge.
Rassool, G. H. (2025). *Islāmic Counselling & Psychotherapy: An introduction to theory and practice* (2nd ed.). Routledge.
Rizvi, S. A. A. (1989). *Muslim tradition in psychotherapy and modern trends*. Seraj Munir.
Rogers, C. (1980). *A way of being*. Houghton Mifflin Company.
Rosila, N., & Yaacob, N. (2013). Cognitive therapy approach from Islāmic psycho-spiritual conception. *Procedia -Social and Behavioral Sciences, 97*(6), 182–187.
Smith, J. (2011). *Removing barriers to therapy with Muslim-Arab-American clients*, Psy. D. thesis, Antioch. University New England. http://rave.ohiolink.edu/etdc/view?acc_num=antioch1319727578. Accessed 14 Oct 2024.
Sabry, W. M., & Vohra, A. (2013). Role of Islām in the management of psychiatric disorders. *Indian Journal of Psychiatry, 13*(55(Suppl. 2)), S205–S214. https://doi.org/10.4103/0019-5545.105534
Walpole, S. C., McMillan, D., House, A., Cottrell, D., & Mir, G. (2013). Interventions for treating depression in Muslim patients: A systematic review. *Journal of Affective Disorders, 145*(1), 11–20.
Webster, R. (2005). *Why Freud was wrong: Sin, science and psychoanalysis*. Orwell Press.
Yusoff, Y. B. M. (2011). *Counselling and religious and spiritual values: A Malaysian study*. PhD thesis, The University of Waikato. Online at http://researchcommons.waikato.ac.nz/bitstream/handle/10289/5834/thesis.pdf?sequence=5. Accessed14 Oct 2024.
Yusaf, S. (2019). *Spirituality in clinical practice: An Islāmic perspective* (PowerPoint). https://www.slideserve.com/callieflores/spirituality-in-clinical-practice-an-Islāmic-perspective-powerpoint-ppt-presentation. Accessed 20 June 2024.

Chapter 9
Post-modern Therapies: Congruence or Dissonance with Islāmic Spirituality

9.1 An Introduction to Post-modern Therapies

Post-modern therapy approaches—including solution-focused brief therapy (SFBT), narrative therapy, and hope therapy—represent a shift from traditional, modernist paradigms of psychotherapy towards more flexible, collaborative, and client-centred models. These therapies emerged in response to the limitations of conventional methods that often emphasised pathology, diagnosis, and the therapist's role as an expert. Post-modern approaches—on the contrary—focus on clients' strengths, stories, and the context of their experiences, aligning with contemporary understandings of the multifaceted nature of human identity and experience. Solution-focused brief therapy (SFBT) is a goal-directed, collaborative approach that emphasises solutions rather than problems. This approach aligns with post-modernism by prioritising the client's perspective and rejecting the idea of universal truths. It emphasises the collaborative construction of reality between the therapist and client. Narrative therapy posits that individuals construct their identities and realities through the stories they tell about their lives. Narrative therapy's post-modern roots lie in its emphasis on the multiplicity of truths and the deconstruction of dominant discourses that shape individuals' experiences. Hope therapy is centred on fostering a positive outlook and enhancing clients' sense of hope. Hope therapy aligns with post-modernism by prioritising the subjective experience of hope and recognising the diverse ways individuals find and maintain hope in their lives. It challenges the notion of a one-size-fits-all approach to therapy, instead advocating for a personalised and client-driven process. These post-modern therapy approaches share common principles: they emphasise collaboration, respect clients' perspectives, and focus on strengths and resources rather than deficits. By moving away from traditional pathologising frameworks, these therapies offer flexible, empowering strategies that respect the complexity and uniqueness of each client's

G. H. Rassool, *Exploring the Intersection of Islāmic Spirituality and Psychotherapy*,
https://doi.org/10.1007/978-3-031-72724-5_9

experience. In the chapters that follow, we will examine these post-modern therapies and their congruence and dissonance with Islāmic spirituality.

9.2 Solution-Focused Brief Therapy (SFBT): An Overview

Solution-Focused Brief Therapy (SFBT) is grounded in constructivist theory (Cepeda & Davenport, 2006), which posits that reality is subjectively constructed by individuals based on their experiences and perceptions. SFBT operates on the principle that changing one's perspective can lead to new solutions and possibilities, rather than focusing on the pathology or root causes of problems (de Shazer, 1985; de Shazer et al., 1986). It is a goal-oriented, short-term therapeutic approach developed by Steve de Shazer and Insoo Kim Berg. It emphasises building solutions rather than focusing on problems. SFBT operates on the premise that clients possess the resources and strengths to resolve their issues.

Key techniques include the miracle question, which helps clients envision their desired future, and scaling questions to assess progress and set achievable goals. By focusing on exception—times when the problem did not occur—therapists help clients identify effective strategies and reinforce their strengths through compliments and affirmations. This therapy is applicable to a variety of issues such as mental health disorders, relationship problems, and behavioural issues. Research supports the efficacy of Solution-Focused Brief Therapy (SFBT) in addressing a variety of issues. Studies indicate its success in reducing depression, anxiety, and mood-related disorders in adults (Maljanen et al., 2012), treating addiction and decreasing severity and trauma symptoms (Kim et al., 2018), and managing child behavioural problems (Bond et al., 2013). Additionally, SFBT has been found effective in addressing emotional, behavioural, and interpersonal issues (Kim et al., 2018). Its client-centred approach, which emphasises rapid progress and building on existing resources, makes it suitable for settings like mental health clinics, schools, and workplaces. Overall, SFBT's structured yet flexible methodology provides a practical and positive framework for facilitating meaningful change.

9.2.1 SFBT: Congruence with Islāmic Beliefs

The SFBT model generally aligns with Islāmic beliefs and Rassool (2016, 2025) highlighted SFBT aspects resonating with Islāmic principles, such as minimal self-disclosure, empowerment, positive orientation, pre-session change, goal setting, and competence seeking. SFBT supports the Islāmic concept of individual responsibility and accountability. Valiante (2003) noted Qur'ânic concepts that align with SFBT, emphasising action, free will, personal responsibility, kinship, and the capacity for change (*jihad* and nafs). The Qur'ân guides holistic solutions for body, mind, and soul, with Islām seen as a practical guide for daily actions. Similar to the tenets of SFBT, Islāmic principles emphasise individual behaviour and strengths, focusing more on action than retrospective insight. Success in this life and the Hereafter is measured by personal growth in relation to others and to God (Valiante, 2003). The Qur'ân highlights this, stating "Indeed, Allah will not change the condition of a people until they change what is in themselves" (Ar-Ra'd 13:11, interpretation of the meaning), emphasising the importance of initiating meaningful self-change. This aligns with the concept of incremental progress, where even minor positive actions can lead to significant improvements. Bidwell (1999) suggests that change offers a chance to enhance life and that problems are temporary, existing only because of the power attributed to them, thus encouraging the understanding that small, meaningful changes can bring about positive transformations.

The congruence between SFBT and Islāmic principles is evident in several key aspects. Both emphasise individuality, free will, and accountability, regardless of gender, as stated in the Qur'ân (An-Naĥl 16:97, interpretation of the meaning). The emphasis on goal setting in SFBT mirrors the Qur'ânic worldview that integrates thought and action (Valiante, 2003), reflecting the verse that "there is no man except that [good] for which he strives" (An-Najm 53:39, interpretation of the meaning). Moreover, SFBT's focus on individual behaviour for initiating change aligns with the Qur'ânic concept of "vicegerency," where humans are entrusted with responsibility on earth (Al-Baqarah 2:30, interpretation of the meaning). This parallel highlights how both SFBT and Islāmic principles emphasise personal agency and responsibility in achieving positive outcomes. Rassool (2025) highlights that the concepts of hope and possibilities, central to the theory of SFBT, resonate with Islāmic beliefs. In Islām, believers face trials with hope and patience, trusting in Allāh and finding solace in religious practices. The emphasis on patience in adversity promises rewards in both this life and the Hereafter, paralleling the focus on hope and resilience in SFBT. This underlines the compatibility between SFBT principles and Islāmic teachings, emphasising positivity and perseverance in overcoming challenges.

Both SFBT and Islāmic beliefs emphasise the inherent capacity of individuals to overcome challenges and achieve positive transformations in their lives. SFBT focuses on leveraging existing strengths and resources while promoting optimism and envisioning a better future, steering clear of negativity. Similarly, Islāmic teachings encourage hope, optimism, and trust in God's mercy, advocating for patience, perseverance, and positive actions in the face of difficulties. Both SFBT and Islāmic beliefs stress maintaining a positive outlook and embracing the potential for positive change, aligning closely in their emphasis on hope and optimism. This parallels with Qur'ânic verses such as "For indeed, with hardship [will be] ease" (Inshirah 94:5–6, interpretation of the meaning) and "So do not weaken or grieve, and you will be superior if you are [true] believers" (Ali-'Imran 3:139, interpretation of the meaning), which underline the importance of resilience and faith in overcoming adversity.

In a *hadīth*, it was narrated from Anas that the Prophet (ﷺ) entered upon a young man who was dying and said: "How do you feel?" He said: "I have hope in

Allāh, O Messenger of Allāh, but I fear my sins." The Messenger of Allāh (ﷺ) said: "These two things (hope and fear) do not coexist in the heart of a person in a situation like this, but Allah will give him that which he hopes for and keep him safe from that which he fears." (Ibn Majah). The *hadīth* underlines the Islāmic perspective on hope and fear, emphasising that in challenging situations, Allāh grants what one hopes for and protects from feared consequences. Rassool and Khan (2023) highlight the contemporary relevance of maintaining hope rooted in faith and trust in Allāh's mercy amidst despair. Lala (2023) explores how the Qur'ânic influences emotions of hope and fear, guiding believers towards positive actions and nurturing a lasting positive outlook. Both SFBT and Islāmic principles emphasise individual empowerment, accountability, and ethical decision-making. SFBT empowers clients to identify and implement solutions, while Islāmic values encourage self-improvement and ethical conduct. This alignment centres on agency and active participation in shaping one's life.

SFBT's emphasis on collaboration between therapist and client parallels the Islāmic principle of *shura*, which advocates for consultation and group decision-making. This principle is reflected in Qur'ânic verses urging consultation in matters (Ali-'Imran 3:159, Ash-Shura 42:38), emphasising the importance of seeking guidance and making decisions collectively. Consultation—known as *mashwara* in Islāmic teachings—was practiced and advocated by the Prophet Muhammad (ﷺ), emphasising its importance in decision-making and daily life. Al-Hasan noted that seeking advice leads people to the best possible outcomes, as mentioned in the *hadīth*, "and manage their affairs by mutual consultation" (Al-Adab Al-Mufrad). Both SFBT and Islāmic values emphasise collaboration, whether in therapeutic settings or decision-making processes, recognising the benefits of combining perspectives for positive results. However, it is important to acknowledge that while there are parallels, SFBT is a psychological approach that may not perfectly align with all aspects of Islāmic principles and practices.

9.2.2 SFBT: Dissonance with Islāmic Beliefs

SFBT operates within a secular framework, focusing on practical and solution-oriented approaches without explicit religious or spiritual themes. This secular nature of SFBT may create a disconnect for individuals with a monotheistic worldview. In contrast, the Islāmic perspective, centred on the belief in the oneness of Allāh, profoundly shapes Muslim views and behaviours. Islāmic principles, derived from the Qur'ân and teachings of Prophet Muhammad (ﷺ), offer comprehensive guidance on morality and personal conduct across various life aspects. SFBT and Islāmic principles differ notably in their approach to problem orientation. SFBT is future-oriented, emphasising the identification and pursuit of desired outcomes and solutions, whereas Islāmic principles focus on addressing and resolving current difficulties within the framework of religious teachings and moral norms, promoting progress. In family conflicts, SFBT envisions a better future through strengthened family relations and solution-focused strategies. On the contrary, an Islāmic approach addresses current disputes by emphasising concepts such as repentance (*tawbah*), seeking forgiveness (*istighfar*), patience (*sabr*), and communication (*muwajaha*) are fundamental to resolving conflicts and improving relationships which are grounded in Islāmic values.

The fundamental difference between Islāmic beliefs and SFBT lies in the concept of divine intervention. Islāmic teachings emphasise *tawakkul,* which involves surrendering to God's will and trusting in divine guidance, whereas SFBT focuses on the client's potential for change through practical means without explicitly addressing divine direction. For Muslim clients, incorporating prayer and trust in divine intervention is significant, particularly during challenging life circumstances. While SFBT empowers clients to achieve tangible changes, it may not explicitly acknowledge the spiritual dimension or divine guidance sought by Muslim clients.

The use of techniques like the miracle question in SFBT reveals a dissonance with Islāmic principles, particularly concerning concepts of sin, evil, and social hierarchy within Islāmic society. While the miracle question is effective for Muslim clients seeking quick resolutions to their issues, it may not fully align with Islāmic beliefs. SFBT employs this technique to help clients envision a future free from their problems and establish clear therapeutic goals. Valiante (2003) suggests that the miracle question holds both clinical significance (setting specific goals) and religious connotations (belief in divine intervention), paralleling the Islāmic principle of *tawhīd* (the unicity of God). This approach acknowledges human actions in initiating change while recognising God's role as the ultimate controller in alleviating life's challenges through miracles. Chaudhry and Li (2011) assert that the miracle question can be beneficial for Muslim clients seeking swift problem resolution. Muhammad (2012) supports this view, stating that the miracle question links actions to change and reinforces the Islāmic perspective on God's intervention in easing life's trials. Muslim clients may not resonate with the concept or language of a "miracle" as used in SFBT. Rassool (2016, 2025) argues that for Muslims, miracles are attributed solely to Allāh, who is seen as the Creator and ultimate authority capable of changing human conditions. Instead of the traditional "miracle question" in SFBT, Rassool (2016, 2025) suggests alternative approaches that respect cultural and religious beliefs. For instance, therapists can frame outcome questions in a way that reflects Islāmic perspectives, such as asking, "If God accepts your prayer, how would you be different from what you are now?" This alternative maintains a future-oriented focus while aligning more closely with the spiritual and cultural values of Muslim clients. This approach allows therapists to achieve therapeutic goals effectively while respecting and incorporating the religious beliefs and practices of their Muslim clients.

Islāmic teachings also emphasise that Allāh answers the prayers of those who call upon Him, urging believers not to despair of His mercy and emphasising His forgiveness of all sins (Az-Zumar 39:53, interpretation of the meaning). The statements from Islāmic teachings affirm that every supplication made by a Muslim receives a response from Allāh, though the nature of the response may vary.

According to Al-Haafiz Ibn Hajar (cited in Islām Q&A, 2012), supplicants may receive exactly what they asked for—or they may receive compensation in some form. Additionally, the Messenger of Allāh (ﷺ), as reported by Ahmad mentioned that when a Muslim makes supplication, even if there are sins or issues in their life, Allāh responds in one of three ways: granting the supplication swiftly, storing up reward for the Hereafter, or diverting an equivalent harm from them cited in Islām Q&A (2012). These teachings underline the belief in Allāh's mercy and responsiveness to the prayers of believers, demonstrating the understanding of supplication and divine intervention in Islāmic faith.

SFBT has a theoretical flaw in its assumption that human intentions are always good, failing to acknowledge the existence of sin and evil in individuals and social systems. This perspective contrasts with Islāmic beliefs, which emphasise the concept of *fitrah*, indicating a neutral state inclined towards good, and stress human free will and personal responsibility for choices between good and evil (Bidwell, 1999; Rassool, 2016, 2025). Bidwell (1999) questions whether the preferred "solutions" in SFBT might conflict with Islāmic principles or replace one undesirable behaviour with another, which Muslim clients might reject. Additionally, self-disclosure in therapy can be challenging for Muslim clients due to cultural and religious norms, leading to reluctance in sharing personal or family information outside the family context. Chaudhry and Li (2011) highlight the importance of trust and confidence in therapy, suggesting that longer-term approaches may be necessary for effective change in individuals or family systems.

In summary, the incongruence between Islāmic beliefs and SFBT stems from several key differences in theological perspectives, problem orientation, and the recognition of sin and evil. Islāmic teachings emphasise a holistic approach that integrates spiritual, moral, and present-focused elements, whereas SFBT adopts a secular, future-oriented framework. This difference can create a disconnect for Muslim clients who prioritize religious and spiritual considerations in addressing life's challenges.

9.2.3 Islāmic-Solution-Focused Brief Therapy (I-SFBT)

Islāmic-Solution-Focused Brief Therapy (I-SFBT) integrates principles from Islāmic teachings into the therapeutic approach, aligning it more closely with the Islāmic values and beliefs. This adaptation of the traditional SFBT model addresses the need for a therapy that resonates with the spiritual and cultural context of Muslim clients. By incorporating key elements from Islāmic teachings, I-SFBT offers a more holistic and relevant approach to therapy for these individuals. Islāmic monotheism—or *tawhîd*—should be the foundation of Islāmic-inspired SFBT. *Tawhîd* emphasises unity and coherence in all aspects of life, guiding clients to connect their faith with the therapeutic process. This approach focuses on seeking solutions while trusting in God's guidance. While traditional SFBT is future-oriented, an

Islāmic-inspired version also emphasises addressing present challenges in line with Islāmic teachings. The therapist helps Muslim clients resolve current problems within an Islāmic ethical framework, ensuring that their actions and choices are consistent with their faith. This integration empowers clients to draw on their religious beliefs for guidance and support in therapy.

I-SFBT integrates *tawakkul*—or reliance on God—into goal setting. Therapists encourage clients to trust in God's guidance while actively pursuing their goals in alignment with Islāmic principles. This approach recognises God's role in the therapeutic journey and taking personal responsibility for actions. Clients develop goals consistent with Islāmic teachings, seek God's guidance through prayer, and rely on patience. By promoting trust, inner peace, and reliance on God, I-SFBT enhances clients' perseverance, resilience, and overall well-being as they work towards their goals. I-SFBT incorporates Islāmic coping strategies, helping clients use their spiritual practices to overcome obstacles and maintain mental well-being. These strategies include prayer (*salah*), reflection (*tafakkur*), seeking refuge in God (*Istiaadhah*), trust in Allāh (*tawakkul*), reciting the Qur'ân, remembrance of God (*dhikr*), patience (*sabr*), gratitude (*shukr*), and acts of charity (*sadaqah*) (Rassool, 2025). Therapists can use Qur'ânic narratives to draw parallels with clients' situations, deriving insights and inspiration. For example, the story of Prophet Joseph (Yusuf) can help clients struggling with forgiveness, while Prophet Jacob (Ya'qub) exemplifies resilience. By discussing these narratives, therapists guide clients to embody these teachings and apply their principles to their own lives.

In an Islāmic-Solution-Focused Brief Therapy approach, therapists utilise questions that are sensitive to Islāmic beliefs and practices. These questions are structured to align with the client's faith and cultural background, enhancing the therapeutic process by integrating spiritual elements into problem-solving and goal-setting. The therapist acts as a facilitator, guiding the client to explore how their faith and community resources can contribute to overcoming challenges. Table 9.1 categorically organises the questions into family and significant others, religious teachings and faith, and support and strategies. Each category is designed to facilitate discussions and explorations that align with an I-SFBT approach, addressing familial support, religious guidance, and practical strategies for overcoming challenges.

An Islāmic-inspired approach to SFBT seeks to bridge the gap between conventional therapeutic techniques and Islāmic principles, making it particularly beneficial for Islāmic psychotherapists working with Muslim clients. This approach hinges on aligning the foundational assumptions of SFBT with Islāmic beliefs, ensuring that the therapeutic process respects and integrates religious and spiritual dimensions. For Islāmic psychotherapists, this alignment involves understanding the philosophical underpinnings and techniques of SFBT, which they can then adapt to incorporate Islāmic teachings and values. This adaptation allows therapists to address clients' psychological needs while also addressing their spiritual and moral dimensions, thereby making the therapy more culturally sensitive and relevant. Effective implementation of I-SFBT requires therapists to modify certain aspects of

Table 9.1 List of questions in Islāmic- SFBT for Muslims

Category	Questions
Family and significant others	Are there specific family members who have faced similar challenges and successfully navigated them?
	How did they solve it?
	What do your significant others or family members think about the problem?
	Can you think of a time when someone close to you provided valuable support or a solution to a problem?
	Who in your life, such as family members or friends, might have insights into your current situation or could offer support?
	What do others normally do in this situation?
	Reflect on a time when your family or religious community worked together effectively. How can you apply those strengths now?
	Imagine your ideal scenario where your significant others, extended family, and religious values are all contributing positively. What would that look like?
Religious teachings and faith	Are there teachings or principles from your Qur'ân or Sunnah that could guide you in approaching this challenge?
	How has your faith supported you in overcoming difficulties in the past, and how can it be a resource now?
	What Islāmic practices might bring comfort or clarity as you work towards a solution?
	What does the Imam or religious scholar say you should do about this?
	Would that work in this situation? Why or why not?
Support and strategies	Who could help with the barriers you have identified?
	What strategy could help make this change?
	What (or who) makes you feel better when this happens?

the traditional SFBT framework to better resonate with Islāmic beliefs and practices. By doing so, therapists can help Muslim clients navigate their challenges within a framework that is congruent with their faith, fostering a deeper connection between their spiritual life and psychological well-being. This approach not only enhances the therapeutic relationship but also empowers clients to draw strength from their faith traditions as they work towards positive change in their lives. In essence, an Islāmic-inspired approach to SFBT represents a culturally sensitive adaptation of psychotherapeutic techniques that acknowledges and incorporates Islāmic values.

9.3 Narrative Therapy: An Overview

Narrative therapy, based on post-modern social constructionist theories, challenges the notion of an objective reality, emphasising that reality is shaped through social interactions. White and Epston (1990) highlight key assumptions of narrative therapy, including the importance of respecting each client's perspective, separating the client from their problems, avoiding victim blaming, and viewing clients as the experts of their own lives. This approach asserts that clients have the capacity to address their own issues, with the therapist facilitating this process by focusing on the narratives clients construct about their lives. Parry and Doan (1994) further suggest that in narrative therapy, there is no singular truth, only various interpretations of reality shaped by social, cultural, and political contexts. Meaning is created through these narratives, and the therapy emphasises that individuals are not defined by their problems. Instead, problems are seen as separate entities, termed "problem stories." A significant aspect of narrative therapy is the avoidance of diagnostic labelling, promoting a view that individuals can reauthor their stories to reflect their strengths and capabilities.

Narrative therapy utilises techniques such as externalising conversations, mapping influences, and identifying unique outcomes to facilitate clients' exploration of alternative narratives. These interventions aim to uncover strengths, values, and resources that support the client's desired identity and aspirations. The approach has been applied effectively in individual, family, and community settings, addressing a wide range of psychological and relational challenges. Evidence supports narrative therapy's broad applicability and positive outcomes across various conditions, settings, and populations (Chow & Fung, 2021; Chimpén- López et al., 2021; Fatahi et al., 2021; Ghavibazou et al., 2020; Shakeri et al., 2020). However, ongoing research is needed to further validate its efficacy compared to other therapeutic approaches and to ensure cultural sensitivity in its application. Overall, narrative therapy offers a humanistic and empowering framework that encourages clients to reclaim authorship of their lives by rewriting stories that reflect their strengths and aspirations.

9.3.1 Narrative Therapy: Congruence with Islāmic Beliefs

Narrative therapy and Islāmic traditions both value storytelling as a significant means for understanding and shaping one's identity and worldview. In narrative therapy, the focus is on clients sharing their stories, reflecting on their experiences, and reinterpreting their meanings to construct new, empowering narratives. This therapeutic process aligns with the Islāmic tradition, where storytelling is integral, particularly through the narratives in the Qur'ân and the *Sunnah*, which serve to convey moral lessons and spiritual principles. For an Islāmic therapist, employing a narrative approach involves harmonising clients' personal stories with the Islāmic tradition. This includes guiding clients to reflect on their lives within the context of Qur'ānic teachings and the *Sunnah*, ensuring that their reconstructed narratives are consistent with Islāmic values.

Metaphors are a point of congruence between narrative therapy and Islāmic traditions. In narrative therapy, metaphors are used creatively to explore, challenge, and reshape narratives, helping clients construct more empowering self-stories. Sue et al. (2022) highlight the effectiveness of metaphoric statements and stories, which enable clients to form personal images and convey therapeutic plans of action. Witztum et al. (1988) suggest that "therapists telling client metaphoric stories implicitly convey therapeutic plans of action, which when carried out, may resolve clients' problems" (p. 2). This aligns with Islāmic traditions, where metaphors and storytelling are also integral to conveying moral lessons and guiding personal transformation. In Islāmic traditions, metaphors are prevalent in the Qur'ân, conveying profound spiritual and moral concepts. These metaphors capture complex ideas, making them more accessible and stimulating deeper contemplation (*tafakkur* and *tadabbur*). Armstrong and Munro (2018) suggest that "adherent Muslims have a natural metaphorical way of thinking that connects with some of the post-structural [post-modern] therapeutic skills and techniques and at the same time draw on past Qur'ânic solutions for contemporary problems" (p. 174). This natural inclination towards metaphorical thinking allows Islāmic psychotherapists to effectively use techniques like "metaphor therapy" (Ahammed, 2010) to address larger life questions, strengthen faith in God, and persuade disbelievers to believe in God.

Metaphors from the Qur'ân hold significant potential in psychotherapy within an Islāmic framework. They can encourage reflective cycles, contemplation, and insight, inspiring hope and resilience, facilitating emotional expression, and conveying profound spiritual truths. These metaphors bridge the gap between the therapist and the client, enabling clearer communication and understanding. They provide a symbolic framework for conceptualizing clients' experiences and challenges. Suhadi (2011) emphasises that an Islāmic psychotherapist using a narrative approach should be well-versed in the Qur'ân and its exegeses (*tafsir),* ensuring they operate within their competence and scope of practice. This grounding in Qur'ānic metaphors allows therapists to integrate spiritual wisdom with therapeutic techniques effectively.

9.3.2 Narrative Therapy: Dissonance with Islāmic Beliefs

Narrative therapy is inherently secular in its origin and methodology, focusing on the individual's stories and the meanings they derive from their experiences. This secular foundation does not inherently consider religious or spiritual dimensions, which are significant for many clients, including those from Islāmic backgrounds. However, there are some assumptions of narrative therapy and practices within this approach that may not align with Islāmic beliefs and practices. In narrative therapy, a significant divergence exists between the epistemological views of social constructionism and Islāmic doctrine. Narrative therapy—rooted in social constructionism—posits that knowledge is shaped by cultural and social factors (White & Epston, 1990). In contrast, Islāmic beliefs assert the existence of objective knowledge derived from divine revelation, emphasising absolute truth independent of social constructions. While Islāmic beliefs acknowledge the influence of social and cultural factors, they maintain that objective knowledge is grounded in divine revelation through the Qur'ân and the *Sunnah*, asserting that knowledge is inherently linked to divine guidance. Islāmic beliefs emphasise the Qur'ân as the ultimate truth and guide, shaping how Muslims interpret knowledge within their social and cultural contexts. Aligning beliefs and actions with Islāmic virtues and morality is integral, ensuring harmony with divine guidance and fostering spiritual well-being.

The philosophical misalignment between narrative therapy and the Islāmic worldview highlights the importance of understanding clients' unique perspectives shaped by religious, social, cultural, and historical contexts. Narrative therapy's focus on individual experiential narratives contrasts with Islāmic beliefs, which emphasise a comprehensive worldview encompassing both temporal and spiritual dimensions. Al-Attas (2001) emphasises that an Islāmic worldview constitutes a vision of reality and truth, impacting how individuals perceive and interpret their lives. For therapists, awareness of their own and their clients' worldviews is crucial for fostering empathy and effectively tailoring therapeutic interventions to align with Islāmic principles and values. The conflict between postmodern pluralism and moral relativism and the Islāmic worldview can lead to a disconnect for Muslim clients, emphasising a yearning for spiritual connection. Islām's core beliefs, including *tawhîd* (belief in one God), belief in angels, holy books, prophets, the Day of Judgement, and predestination, form the foundational narratives that unify Muslims and shape their understanding of reality. These beliefs provide Muslims with a framework to interpret their experiences, underlining the importance of spiritual and moral coherence in navigating life's challenges.

One significant difference between narrative therapy and Islāmic principles lies in their treatment of spirituality and religious practices. Narrative therapy—rooted in Western culture—typically does not explicitly address spirituality or religion unless they are individually significant to the client. In contrast, Islāmic traditions tightly intertwine spirituality and religion, viewing them as integral to a Muslim's life. In Islāmic contexts, spirituality encompasses adherence to specific doctrines, rituals, and practices, whereas Western notions of spirituality often emphasise personal beliefs and diverse spiritual experiences. This distinction highlights the challenge for narrative therapists in understanding how Islāmic beliefs shape clients' narratives, values, and identities without sufficient cultural competence or alignment with Islāmic worldviews. Islāmic psychotherapy emphasise integrating spiritual approaches into therapy, recognising the inseparability of spirituality and religious practices for Muslim clients. The therapy strives to incorporate Islāmic doctrines and practices into therapeutic interventions, ensuring sensitivity and alignment with the client's religious beliefs and cultural context. This approach contrasts with narrative therapy's potential limitations in addressing the holistic spiritual needs of Muslim clients due to its Eurocentric roots and focus on individualistic interpretations of spirituality.

The significant divergence between narrative therapy and Islāmic principles centres on their views regarding individual autonomy and the role of Divine will and decree (*al-qadaa' wa'l-qadar*). Narrative therapy emphasises the autonomy of individuals as authors of their own stories, responsible for their actions and capable of creating change in their lives through personal agency. In contrast, Islāmic principles recognise human free will and accountability for choices but assert that ultimate control rests with Divine will and decree, as expressed in the Qur'anic verse emphasising reliance on God's decree: Say, "Never will we be struck except by what God has decreed for us; He is our protector." And upon God let the believers rely." (At-Tawbah 9:51, interpretation of the meaning). This conflict highlights a fundamental difference between narrative therapy's emphasis on individual autonomy and Islāmic beliefs regarding the limits of human agency under Divine guidance.

The criticism of narrative therapy centres on its tendency to prioritise individual exploration of personal experiences, beliefs, and values, potentially neglecting the interconnectedness with family and community. This self-focused approach—while valuable for personal growth—can lead to conflicts within family dynamics, particularly when family roles and relationships are not adequately addressed. For Muslim clients, this critique is amplified by Islāmic traditions that emphasise the significance of family cohesion and support. Narrative therapy's focus on individual psychology—as highlighted by Minuchin (1998) and echoed by Hayward (2019)—may overlook the holistic role of family in therapy. In Islāmic therapy, the family is viewed as sacred and essential for social cohesion, playing a pivotal role in an individual's well-being. Therefore, Islāmic therapists advocate for integrating family into the therapeutic process, ensuring their participation in assessments, therapy sessions, and as a source of ongoing support.

9.3.3 *Islāmic Contemplative-Based Approach to Narrative Therapy*

Narrative therapy, originating from Western secular perspectives, began with a focus on exploring individual narratives and constructing meaning in a culturally sensitive manner. Over time, as therapeutic practices developed, there was a growing recognition of the importance of adapting these approaches to accommodate diverse cultural and religious frameworks, including Islāmic traditions. The adaptation of narrative therapy to align with Islāmic traditions involves the application of its principles, techniques, and interventions. This process ensures that the therapy remains culturally and religiously sensitive and relevant, promoting healing and growth while respecting the core tenets of both narrative therapy and Islāmic beliefs. Blanton (2007) advocates for a contemplative-based approach to narrative therapy that integrates contemplative skills, metaphors, modified interventions, and expansive views of reality and self. This approach is seen as fully congruent with Islāmic beliefs and practices, aligning with the concept of Islāmic contemplation (*tafakkur*) as described by Badri (2018). Badri highlights *tafakkur* as a cognitive spiritual practice that integrates rational thought, emotions, and spirit, emphasising its role in linking the mind with the heart and soul. The practice of *tafakkur* is viewed within

Islāmic traditions as a means to attain solace and healing for psychological disorders, often conceptualized as ailments of the soul (Henzell-Thomas, 2018).

Narrative therapy can be adapted to align with Islāmic healing practices, emphasising inner vision of God, contemplation of divine signs, and understanding one's mission in life. Adapted tools such as skills, values, and stories cards cater specifically to young Muslims, fostering cultural relevance in therapy. Additionally, the 'Life Certificate' serves as a narrative therapeutic document honouring deceased loved ones, reflecting Islāmic traditions of remembrance and respect. The use of written prayers, such as the collect, as interventions in narrative therapy shows adaptation to include spiritual practices meaningful to Muslim clients. Furthermore, attachment-focused narrative interventions are tailored for Muslim religious couples, addressing relationship dynamics within an Islāmic context (Dulwich Centre, 2022; Karris & Katarena, 2019; Rundio & Wong, 2021).

Sue and Sue (1999) emphasise the importance of understanding clients through their universal, group, and individual identities within psychotherapy, highlighting the significance of worldview. Research, such as Coleman et al. (1995), suggests that ethnic minority clients often prefer therapists who share their cultural background. For Muslim clients, narrative therapy adapted to an Islāmic worldview can be highly effective when approached with cultural/spiritual sensitivity, avoiding the imposition of individualistic or Eurocentric values. Therapists aiming to enhance efficacy and ethical sensitivity in working with Muslim clients should respect and integrate Islāmic beliefs into therapy without imposing conflicting ideologies. Models like cultural empathy (Ibrahim, 1991) can aid in establishing a shared understanding. Navigating the concepts of individual autonomy and Divine will and decree within Islāmic psychotherapy involves balancing respect for the client's beliefs with the integration of Islāmic principles into therapeutic practices. This approach requires acknowledging the limits of human control while fostering trust and reliance (*tawakkul*) in Allāh's plan. For non-Muslim narrative therapists, supporting clients' beliefs, showing curiosity about their worldview, and understanding practices based on the Qur'ân and *Sunnah* are crucial for effective therapy.

Narrative therapy can serve as a potent tool for Islāmic psychotherapists working with Muslim clients when there is harmony between the Islāmic worldview and the foundational principles of narrative therapy. Integrating the Qur'ân and *Sunnah* into the therapeutic process enables Muslim clients to find meaning and direction in their lives through narratives aligned with Islāmic teachings. Despite discrepancies between narrative therapy's social constructionist views and Islāmic beliefs, Islāmic psychotherapists can effectively utilise this approach by adapting its philosophical underpinnings. By recognising narrative therapy's potential to reflect divine healing, as highlighted by Hankle (2016), therapists can sanctify the practice to resonate with the Islāmic worldview, emphasising God's role as the ultimate source of healing. In summary, Blanton's contemplative-based narrative therapy approach and the Islāmic practice of *tafakkur* both highlight the integration of spiritual dimensions with psychological healing, offering a shared framework that resonates with both Western therapeutic practices and Islāmic spiritual traditions.

9.4 Hope Therapy: An Overview

Hope—as a fundamental aspect in Islāmic psychotherapy and mental health—is viewed as a pivotal force aiding in healing and resilience. In this context, hope encompasses both cognitive and emotional dimensions, fostering optimism and perseverance amidst challenges.

Snyder's hope theory (Snyder, 2000) emphasises internal sources and individual agency in cultivating hope. It suggests that individuals with high hope exhibit a proactive approach in navigating uncertainty and achieving their aspirations. The theory delineates hope into three components:

- Goals (the targets of mental action sequences).
- Pathways thinking (the perceived ability to devise routes to achieve goals).
- Agency thinking (confidence in one's capability to successfully utilise those pathways).

These components collaboratively contribute to motivation and readiness for change, facilitating goal attainment and personal growth (Cheavens & Stigen, 2012). Research over several decades supports the correlation between hope and positive outcomes, affirming its role in promoting effective goal setting and behavioural change (Cheavens & Whitted, 2023). Critically, Snyder's assumptions about hope, human nature, and the change process provide a foundational framework for hope therapy. Therapists operating within this model hold assumptions that individuals are capable of change, possess inherent strengths, and can actively engage in the pursuit of their goals. These assumptions guide therapeutic interventions aimed at nurturing hope, enhancing resilience, and empowering clients to navigate life's challenges with optimism and efficacy (Snyder, 2000).

Hope therapy, according to Lopez et al. (2000), involves two essential components: instilling hope and enhancing hope. The process begins with "hope finding," where therapists assist clients in identifying and exploring existing sources of hope through narrative exploration of past experiences. This phase aims to highlight instances of resilience and personal growth, emphasising the role of hope in overcoming challenges. Subsequently, "hope bonding" focuses on building and strengthening supportive relationships within the client's social network. These relationships provide emotional support and encouragement, fostering resilience and reinforcing the client's sense of hope and belonging.

In hope therapy, the stage of hope enhancing—as described by Lopez et al. (2000)—focuses on empowering clients to generate goal-oriented thoughts, develop actionable pathways toward achieving those goals, and maintain a sense of agency throughout the process. Therapists collaborate with clients to establish realistic goals, devise effective action plans, and employ various strategies such as visual imagery, affirmations, pathway checklists, and gratitude journals to bolster hope and perseverance. Additionally, hope reminding interventions, as suggested by Kirmani et al. (2016), serve to reinforce client commitment and focus on their goals, utilising personal hope stories, seeking support from a "hope buddy," reflecting on past successes, and addressing barrier thoughts through cognitive techniques. These approaches collectively aim to sustain and strengthen the client's hope as they progress toward their desired outcomes. Thus, integrating Snyder's hope theory into Islāmic psychotherapy underlines its potential to align with Islāmic principles while enhancing therapeutic outcomes through a culturally sensitive lens.

9.4.1 Islāmic-Based Hope Therapy

In Islāmic teachings, the concept of hope (*raja*) is deeply rooted in verses from the Qur'ân and prophetic traditions (*hadīth*), emphasising reliance on God's mercy, optimism, and trust in His guidance. While the term "hope" may not always be explicitly mentioned, these themes pervade the texts, urging believers to maintain hope in Allāh's benevolence even during challenges. Hope in Islām is intrinsically tied to seeking God's mercy and forgiveness, motivating individuals to strive for His approval and happiness. Muslims derive hope from their belief in Allāh's boundless kindness, compassion, and wisdom, finding solace in His ever-present guidance. They trust that challenges have a purpose, reinforcing hope during tough times. Contemplating Allāh's attributes, such as forgiveness and mercy, further strengthens their hope, acknowledging these qualities in all situations. Sincere supplication (*dua'h*) to Allāh also enhances hope as they seek divine guidance and assistance.

Despite worldly adversities, the belief in the eternal Hereafter provides hope, understanding that ultimate reward and happiness lie beyond this temporary life. Islām encourages trust in Allāh's benevolence (*tawakkul*), aligning with the principles of hope therapy. Islāmic beliefs emphasise patience (sabr) and positive thinking (*Husn al-zann*) during challenging times, aligning with hope therapy by fostering perseverance and optimism. Trust in Allāh's wisdom and the belief that His plan is beneficial promotes a positive mindset similar to hope therapy's focus on positivity. Islāmic teachings also emphasise compassion and forgiveness, encouraging kindness to oneself and others, and letting go of past grievances. These principles resonate with hope therapy, enhancing self-compassion, resilience, and positive relationships. Together, these aspects contribute to an Islāmic understanding of hope, bolstering spiritual strength and resilience in adversity. From an Islāmic perspective, hope therapy can be seen as a comprehensive approach that complements psychospiritual interventions by encouraging clients to integrate their spiritual beliefs, practices, and the principle of absolute trust in Allāh (*tawakkul*).

Islāmic hope therapy uniquely integrates Islāmic beliefs and spirituality into the hope-building process, aligning with teachings that promote hope, positive attitudes, and optimism during challenges. This approach, recognised for its potential to provide spiritual and psychological benefits (Farhoush et al., 2021), reflects the significant impact of spirituality on health outcomes. Hope prevents sadness, anxiety, and other mental illnesses (Wahyuna & Fitriana, 2020), and instilling it in clients during psychotherapy effectively increases motivation and willpower towards positive outcomes (Rassool & Khan, 2023). Hope therapy—both conventional and

Islāmic-based—aims to build hope and resilience. Conventional hope therapy uses psychological concepts and evidence-based strategies like positive thinking, goal-setting, problem-solving, and social support. In contrast, Islāmic-based hope therapy incorporates a theological framework, integrating Islāmic teachings to provide a greater sense of meaning and purpose. Both approaches offer practical techniques for navigating challenges, fostering optimism, and acknowledging psychological factors in creating hope.

Islāmic-based hope therapy integrates spiritual guidance and psychological interventions to foster hope and resilience. The spiritual component deepens one's connection with God, recognising Him as the ultimate source of hope and comfort, and emphasises reliance on Allāh, strengthening faith through prayer and remembrance. Psychological techniques, such as cognitive-behavioural approaches, solution-focused brief therapy, narrative therapy, resilience-building activities, and coping strategies, complement this spiritual dimension. This holistic approach addresses both psychological and spiritual well-being (Farhoush et al., 2021). In instilling hope, Islāmic therapists help clients find hope through faith, connecting personal experiences to Qur'ân and *hadīth* teachings that promote resilience and trust in Allāh's plan. Regular salah (prayer), tawakkul (reliance on Allāh), and *dhikr* (remembering Allāh) are emphasised to foster a direct connection with Allāh and enhance hope.

Islāmic-based hope therapy integrates constant reinforcement of set goals and challenges through hope reminding. This involves the use of Qur'ânic verses, *hadīths*, supplications, and reflections on Allāh's guidance to emphasise faith, patience, and trust in Allāh's plan. This approach provides continuous spiritual and mental support, helping individuals maintain hope despite life's difficulties. By consistently recalling these spiritual reminders, individuals can stay focused on their goals and find solace in their faith during challenging times. Hope enhancing in Islāmic-based therapy encourages individuals to reflect on the attributes of Allāh, fostering hope through understanding His mercy and compassion. It involves instilling hope by reinforcing the belief that Allāh is a constant guide and support through life's trials. This is achieved by seeking knowledge from Islāmic sources, particularly the Qur'ân and *Sunnah*, to align perspectives with Allāh's guidance and understand life's meaning and purpose. The therapy promotes positive thinking and gratitude, focusing on blessings and expressing thanks even in adversity. Additionally, it incorporates coping strategies such as positive affirmations, problem-solving, stress reduction, and Islāmic contemplation to enhance hope and resilience.

Islāmic-based hope therapy emphasises building and strengthening supportive relationships within the Muslim community (*ummah*), highlighting the importance of brotherhood and sisterhood among believers. These relationships provide comfort, guidance, and assistance during challenging times, fostering hope and emotional support. The principle of mutual assistance (*ta'awun*) is central, promoting the sharing of burdens among believers. By encouraging reciprocal support and establishing a self-help network grounded in moral and ethical ideals, this approach aligns with the example set by Prophet Muhammad (ﷺ), whose relationships with his companions exemplified hope bonding within an Islāmic context.

In summary, Islāmic-based hope therapy is a holistic approach integrating Islāmic teachings, spirituality, and psychological dimensions to promote hope and wellness. It encourages a profound connection with Allāh, complete faith in the Divine, and viewing life's challenges as opportunities for spiritual growth. The therapy emphasises Allāh's mercy, forgiveness, and assistance as sources of hope. It also highlights the importance of social support within the Muslim community (*ummah*), fostering a sense of belonging and encouragement. By addressing spiritual, emotional, and psychological components, Islāmic-based hope therapy empowers individuals to find hope and thrive on their spiritual path.

References

Ahammed, S. (2010). Applying Qur'ânic metaphors in counseling. *International Journal of Advanced Counselling, 32*, 248–255. https://doi.org/10.1007/s10447-010-9104-2

Al-Adab Al-Mufrad. *Al-Adab Al-Mufrad 258*. In-book reference: Book 13, Hadith 3.English translation: Book 13, Hadith 258. Sahih (Al-Albani). https://sunnah.com/adab:1183

Al-Attas, M. N. (2001). *Prolegomena to the metaphysics of Islām: An exposition of the fundamental elements of the worldview of Islām* (pp. 252–256). ISTAC.

Armstrong, A. M., & Munro, L. (2018). Insider/outsider: A Muslim woman's adventure practicing 'alongside' narrative therapy. *Australian and New Zealand Journal of Family Therapy, 39*(2), 174–185.

Badri, M. (2018). *Contemplation: An Islāmic Psychospiritual Study*. The International Institute of Islāmic Thought.

Bidwell, D. R. (1999). Hope and possibility, the theology of culture inherent to solution-focused brief therapy. *American Journal of Pastoral Counseling, 3*(1), 3–21.

Blanton, G. P. (2007). Adding silence to stories: Narrative therapy and contemplation. *Contemporary Family Therapy, 29*, 211–221.

Bond, C., Woods, K., Humphrey, N., Symes, W., & Green, L. (2013). The effectiveness of solution focused brief therapy with children and families: A systematic and critical evaluation of the literature from 1990–2010. *Journal of Child Psychology and Psychiatry, 54*(7), 707–723.

Cepeda, L. M., & Davenport, D. S. (2006). Person-centered therapy and solution-focused brief therapy: An integration of present and future awareness. *Psychotherapy: Theory, Research, Practice, Training, 43*(1), 1–12.

Chaudhry, S., & Li, C. (2011). Is solution-focused brief therapy culturally appropriate for Muslim American counselees? *Journal of Contemporary Psychotherapy, 41*, 109–113. https://doi.org/10.1007/s10879-010-9153-1

Cheavens, J. S., & Stigen, C. L. (2012). Hope theory and hope therapy. In N. M. Seel (Ed.), *Encyclopedia of the sciences of learning*. Springer. https://doi.org/10.1007/978-1-4419-1428-6_959

Cheavens, J. S., & Whitted, W. M. (2023). Hope therapy. *Current Opinion in Psychology, 49*, 101509. https://doi.org/10.1016/j.copsyc.2022.101509

Chimpén- López, C. A., Pacheco, M., Pretel-Luque, T., Bastón, R., & Chimpén- Sagrado, D. (2021). The couple's tree of life: Promoting and protecting relational identity. *Family Process, 00*, 1–14. https://doi.org/10.1111/famp.12727

Chow, E. O. W., & Fung, S.-F. (2021). *Narrative group intervention to rediscover life Wisdom among Hong Kong Chinese older adults: A single-blind randomized waitlist-controlled trial.*

Oxford University Press on behalf of The Gerontological Society of America. https://doi.org/10.1093/geroni/igab027

Coleman, H., Wampold, B. E., & Casali, S. L. (1995). Ethnic minorities' ratings of ethnically similar and European American counselors: A meta-analysis. *Journal of Counseling Psychology, 42*(1), 55–64. https://doi.org/10.1037/0022-0167.42.1.55

de Shazer, S. (1985). *Keys to solution in brief therapy*. W.W. Norton.

de Shazer, S., Berg, I. K., Lipchik, E., Nunnally, E., Molnar, A., Gingerich, W., & Weiner-Davis, M. (1986). Brief therapy: Focused solution development. *Family Process, 25*(2), 207–221.

Dulwich Centre. (2022). *Muslim contributions to narrative therapy and community work*. https://dulwichcentre.com.au/muslimcontributions-to-narrative-therapy-and-community-work/. Accessed 22 June 2024.

Farhoush, M., Jahangirzade, M., Ahmadi, M., Hafezi, M., & Abianeh Morteza, K. (2021). Development of hope therapy package based on the Islāmic approach in the face of the psychological consequences of coronary heart disease. *Journal of Clinical Psychology, 13*(2), 201–211. https://doi.org/10.22075/jcp.2021.21443.1977

Fatahi, N., Bardideh, M., Talebi Bahman Biglou, R., Gholami, Z., Akbarinejad, M., & Hoshyar, N. (2021). The effectiveness of narrative therapy on reducing behavior problems and improving self-perception in students. *Quarterly Journal of Child Mental Health, 7*(4), 297–312. https://doi.org/10.52547/jcmh.7.4.19

Ghavibazou, E., Hosseinian, S., & Abdollahi, A. (2020). Effectiveness of narrative therapy on communication patterns for women experiencing low marital satisfaction. *Australian & New Zealand Journal of Family Therapy, 41*(2), 195–207.

Hankle, D. D. (2016). Christian worldview and the use of narrative therapy in the Christian counseling setting. *Journal of Christian Healing, 32*(1), 5–24.

Hayward, M. (2019). *Critiques of narrative therapy: A personal response*. https://theint.co.uk/wpcontent/uploads/2019/02/critiques-of-narrative-therapy-a-personal-response.pdf. Accessed 22 June 2024.

Henzell-Thomas, J. (2018). Introduction. Cited in M. Badri, '*Contemplation: An Islāmic Psychospiritual Study.*' The International Institute of Islāmic Thought.

Ibrahim, F. A. (1991). Contribution of worldview to generic counseling and development. *Journal of Counseling and development, 70*, 13–19.

Ibn Majah. *Sunan Ibn Majah 4261*.In-book reference: Book 37, Hadith 162. English translation: Vol. 5, Book 37, Hadith 4261. Hasan (Darussalam). https://sunnah.com/ibnmajah:4261

Islām Q&A. (2012). Fatwa *177561*. Does the fact that Allāh answers the prayers of the disbelievers indicate that what they believe is true? http://Islāmqa.info/en/177561. Accessed 21 June 2024.

Karris, M., & Katarena, A. (2019). Religious couples re-storying after infidelity: Using narrative therapy interventions with a focus on attachment. *Counseling and Family Therapy Scholarship Review, 2*(1), 5.

Kim, J. S., Brook, J., & Akin, B. A. (2018). Solution-focused brief therapy with substance-using individuals: A randomized controlled trial study. *Research on Social Work Practice, 28*(4), 452–462.

Kirmani, M. N., Sharma, P., & Jahan, F. (2016). Hope therapy in depression: A case report. *International Journal of Public Health Mental Health and Neurosciences, 2*(3), 39–44.

Lala, I. (2023). The Qur'an and emotional well-being: Hope and fear in the Qur'an. *Pastoral Psychology, 72*, 245–275. https://doi.org/10.1007/s11089-023-01060-4

Lopez, S. J., Floyd, R. K., Ulven, J. C., & Snyder, C. (2000). Hope therapy: Helping clients build a house of hope. In C. R. Snyder (Ed.), *Handbook of hope: Theory, measures, and application* (pp. 123–150). Academic Press.

Maljanen, T., Paltta, P., Härkänen, T., Virtala, E., Lindfors, O., Laaksonen, M. A., Knekt, P., & Helsinki Psychotherapy Study Group. (2012). The cost-effectiveness of short-term psychodynamic psychotherapy and solution-focused therapy in the treatment of depressive and anxiety disorder during a one-year follow-up. *Journal of Mental Health Policy and Economics, 15*(1), 13–23.

Minuchin, S. (1998). Where is the family in narrative family therapy? *Journal of Marital and Family Therapy, 24*(4), 397–403.
Muhammad, H. (2012). *Muslim mental health: Considerations for psychotherapy and counseling: A literature review.* In partial fulfilment of the requirements for the Degree of Master of Arts in Adlerian Counseling and Psychotherapy, Adler Graduate School. www.alfredadler.edu/sites/default/files/Hadiyah%20Muhammad%20MP%202012.pdf. Accessed 21 June 2024.
Parry, A., & Doan, R. E. (1994). *Story re-visions: Narrative therapy in the postmodern world.* Guilford Press.
Rassool, G. H. (2016). *Islāmic counselling: From theory to practice*. Routledge.
Rassool, G. H. (2025). *Islāmic counselling & psychotherapy* (2nd ed.). Routledge.
Rassool, G. H., & Khan, W. N. A. (2023). Hope in Islāmic psychotherapy. *Journal of Spirituality in Mental Health*, 2–15. https://doi.org/10.1080/19349637.2023.2207751
Rundio, M. A., & Wong, A. G. (2021). Writing and praying collects as an intervention in narrative therapy. *Contemporary Family Therapy, 44*, 312–317. https://doi.org/10.1007/s10591-021-09586-6
Shakeri, J., Ahmadi, S. M., Maleki, F., Hesami, M. R., Parsa Moghadam, A., Ahmadzade, A., Shirzadi, M., & Elahi, A. (2020). Effectiveness of group narrative therapy on depression, quality of life, and anxiety in people with amphetamine addiction: A randomized clinical trial. *Iran Journal of Medical Science, 45*(2), 91–99.
Snyder, C. R. (2000). *Handbook of hope: Theory, measures and Applications*. Academic.
Sue, D. W., & Sue, D. (1999). *Counseling the culturally diverse: Theory and practice*. Wiley.
Sue, D. W., Sue, D., Neville, H. A., & Smith, L. (2022). *Counseling the Culturally Diverse: Theory and Practice*. Wiley.
Suhadi, J. (2011). Metaphor as a stylistic device of Islāmic teaching. *MIQOT: Jurnal Ilmu-ilmu KeIslāman, XXXV*(1), 187–202.
Valiante, W. C. (2003). Family therapy and Muslim families: A solution focused approach. *WIAMH – Newsletter, 2(4)*, 16. www.canadianIslāmiccongress.com/docs/family.php. Accessed 21 June 2024.
Wahyuna, A. H., & Fitriana, S. (2020). The concept of hope in the western and eastern perspective. *International Journal of Islāmic Educational Psychology (IJIEP), 1*(1). https://doi.org/10.18196/ijiep.1103
White, M., & Epston, D. (1990). *Narrative means to therapeutic ends*. WW. Norton.
Witztum, E., van der Hart, O., & Friedman, B. (1988). The use of metaphors in psychotherapy. *Journal of Contemporary Psychotherapy, 18*, 270–290.

Chapter 10
Islāmic Foundation on Emotional Health and Healing

10.1 Introduction

Islāmic psychologists increasingly acknowledge that their clients may prefer faith-based healing practices rooted in their Islāmic worldviews instead of relying on psychotropic medications or traditional psychotherapy for addressing mental health issues. This preference is grounded in the holistic approach to health that is deeply integrated into Islāmic teachings, as articulated in the Qur'ān and the *Sunnah*. In Islām, health is not merely the absence of illness but encompasses spiritual, psychological, and physical well-being. This holistic view is reflected in the concept of "*ash-shifa*," a term from the Qur'ān and specifically from Chapter *Al-Fātiĥah*, which means "that which heals" or "the restorer of health." This term underlines the belief that the Qur'ān itself has healing properties for the soul and the body. Healing within the Islāmic context is multifaceted. It is seen as a process, an intervention, and an outcome, and, at times, all three components (Levin, 2018). This chapter explores the rich tapestry of Qur'ânic verses and Prophetic traditions (*hadîths*) that provide profound insights into emotional well-being. It examines the spiritual foundations within Islām that support emotional healing and analyses specific Prophetic traditions offering psychological guidance.

10.2 Emotion and Mental Health

Emotion—a component of affect—is the experience of feeling. It plays a crucial role in everyday life, adding quality and meaning to our psychological and spiritual existence. The American Psychological Association defined emotion as "a complex reaction pattern, involving experiential, behavioural, and physiological elements, by which an individual attempt to deal with a personally significant matter or event"

G. H. Rassool, *Exploring the Intersection of Islāmic Spirituality and Psychotherapy*,
https://doi.org/10.1007/978-3-031-72724-5_10

(APA, 2024). This definition suggests that an emotion is a complex reaction pattern involving experiential, behavioural, and physiological elements, through which an individual attempts to deal with a personally significant matter or event. This comprehensive response helps the individual process and responds to important life experiences, influencing actions, thoughts, and physical states. Emotions are complex psychological states that include a subjective experience like (happiness, sadness, anger, and fear); physiological response that involves bodily reactions such as increased heart rate, sweating, or adrenaline rushes; and behavioural expression such as observable actions like smiling, crying, or shouting. Emotion and mood, though sometimes used interchangeably, refer to different concepts in psychology. An emotional state involves a conscious experience with clear intention, while a mood is a less intense, more prolonged affective state not directly tied to a specific experience (Beedie et al., 2005, 2011). In effect, emotional well-being in daily life is influenced by the balance of positive and negative emotions experienced during routine activities (Gärling et al., 2016).

Emotion and mental health are closely linked, as emotions significantly affect mental well-being. Emotional dysregulation—a symptom found across various mental health issues, such as anxiety, substance use disorders, eating disorders, and depression—can hinder efforts to engage in health-promoting behaviours (Menefee et al., 2022). Emotions play a pivotal role in mental health, influencing how individuals think, feel, and behave. Positive emotions—such as joy, gratitude, and contentment—enhance mental health by increasing resilience, improving coping strategies, and boosting overall life satisfaction. In contrast, persistent negative emotions like sadness, anxiety, and anger can harm mental health, potentially leading to depression, anxiety disorders, and stress-related issues. Growing evidence suggests that difficulties in effectively coping with challenging emotions are associated with various mental health conditions, including depression, borderline personality disorder, substance use disorders, eating disorders, somatoform disorders, and other psychopathological symptoms (Berking & Wupperman, 2012). There is evidence to suggest that positive emotions predicted increases in both resilience and life satisfaction (Cohn et al., 2009). There is also research evidence that positive evaluations of positive emotions are uniquely linked to better psychological health, while negative evaluations of negative emotions are uniquely linked to worse psychological health (Willroth et al., 2023). Emotional health and wellness—a key aspect of mental health—involves the ability to cope with and be aware of both positive and negative emotions.

According to the National Center for Emotional Wellness (2024), the term refers to an awareness, understanding, and acceptance of your emotions, and your ability to manage effectively through challenges and change. Emotionally healthy individuals have effective coping mechanisms for negative emotions and recognise when to seek professional help. Emotional health is also closely linked to physical health (Hernandez et al., 2018), as excessive stress and negative emotions can indirectly cause health issues through behaviours influenced by emotional regulation. Emotion regulation strategies such as cognitive reappraisal showed a significant positive correlation with indicators of good mental health (Hu et al., 2014). Earlier research indicates a connection between positive emotions and health but does not fully explain the underlying mechanisms involved in this relationship (Ricard et al., 2014). Further investigation is needed to understand how positive emotions influence health outcomes and the specific pathways through which they operate. This could involve exploring psychological, physiological, and behavioural factors that mediate or moderate the impact of positive emotions on health. Understanding and managing emotions through effective strategies can significantly enhance emotional health and wellness, reduce the risk of mental health issues, and improve overall quality of life. Recognising the importance of emotions in mental health highlights the need for comprehensive approaches to mental health care that address emotional, psychological, and social factors.

10.3 The Qur'ân, *Hadīth,* and Emotional Behaviours

From an Islāmic perspective, the Qur'ân expresses human emotion in the most detailed way. Allāh says in the Qur'ân:

وَأَنَّهُۥ هُوَ أَضْحَكَ وَأَبْكَىٰ

- *And that it is He who makes [one] laugh and weep.* (An-Najm 53: 43, interpretation of the meaning):

This means that Allāh has endowed humans with the capacity for both positive and negative emotions, including the ability to experience laughter and tears along with their respective triggers. While the Qur'ân is not an encyclopaedia of psychology, but it offers guidance that supports good spiritual and emotional health. This implies that spiritual and emotional well-being are intertwined. From a psychological perspective, the idea that Allāh is the one who induces laughter and tears reflects a recognition of the profound influence of emotions on human experiences. Psychologically, these emotions play crucial roles in regulating mood, relieving stress, and fostering social connections. The acknowledgment that Allāh is the source of these emotions highlights the spiritual dimension of human psychology.

Love is generally seen as a drive that can evoke positive or negative feelings. Among the five forms of love identified by ancient Greek philosophers is divine love for God, known as Agape or Eros in Christian theology. Nygren (1930) noted that Eros represents an upward movement, an attempt to ascend from humanity toward God, while Agape signifies God's love for humans. In contrast, in Islāmic theology, the love of Allāh and His Prophet (ﷺ) should always exceed the love for another human being. The demand for the love of Allāh and His Messenger (ﷺ), for instance, is stated in the following verse from the Qur'ân. Allāh says:

قُلْ إِن كَانَ ءَابَآؤُكُمْ وَأَبْنَآؤُكُمْ وَإِخْوَٰنُكُمْ وَأَزْوَٰجُكُمْ وَعَشِيرَتُكُمْ وَأَمْوَٰلٌ ٱقْتَرَفْتُمُوهَا وَتِجَٰرَةٌ تَخْشَوْنَ كَسَادَهَا
وَمَسَٰكِنُ تَرْضَوْنَهَآ أَحَبَّ إِلَيْكُم مِّنَ ٱللَّهِ وَرَسُولِهِۦ وَجِهَادٍ فِى سَبِيلِهِۦ فَتَرَبَّصُوا۟ حَتَّىٰ يَأْتِىَ ٱللَّهُ بِأَمْرِهِۦ ۗ وَٱللَّهُ لَا يَهْدِى
ٱلْقَوْمَ ٱلْفَٰسِقِينَ

- *Say, [O Muhammad], If your fathers, your sons, your brothers, your wives, your relatives, wealth which you have obtained, commerce wherein you fear decline, and dwellings with which you are pleased are more beloved to you than Allāh and His Messenger and jihad in His cause, then wait until Allāh executes His command. And Allāh does not guide the defiantly disobedient people* (At-Tawbah 9: 24, interpretation of the meaning).

This verse is supported by a *hadīth* which is narrated by 'Abdullah bin Hisham: "We were with the Prophet (ﷺ) and he was holding the hand of 'Umar bin Al-Khattab." 'Umar said to Him, "O Allāh's Messenger (ﷺ)! You are dearer to me than everything except my own self." The Prophet (ﷺ) said, "No, by Him in Whose Hand my soul is, (you will not have complete faith) till I am dearer to you than your own self." Then 'Umar said to him, "However, now, by Allāh, you are dearer to me than my own self." The Prophet (ﷺ) said, "Now, O 'Umar, (now you are a believer)." (Bukhârî (a)). In this context, the love and obedience of Allāh, the Almighty, and His Messenger is a sign of true piety and devotion. It is narrated by Anas, that the Prophet (ﷺ) said, "Whoever possesses the following three qualities will taste the sweetness of faith: The one to whom Allāh and His Apostle become dearer than anything else; Who loves a person and he loves him only for Allāh's sake; Who hates to revert to disbelief (Atheism) after Allāh has brought (saved) him out from it, as he hates to be thrown in fire." (Bukhârî (b)).

The Qur'ânic verse and *hadīths* imply that believers who love Allāh should obey His commandments, fulfil obligations, and avoid disobedience. To love the Messenger of Allāh (ﷺ) entails following his path without religious deviations or innovations, in order to worship Allāh in the way that He commanded. The Prophet's (ﷺ) *Sunnah* should be implemented in our daily routine. Abu Hurayrah (may Allāh be pleased with him) narrated that: The Prophet (ﷺ) said: "Whoever obeys me, obeys Allāh; and whoever disobeys me, disobeys Allāh." (Bukhârî (c)). Allāh describes the characteristics of those who truly love Him:

يَـٰٓأَيُّهَا ٱلَّذِينَ ءَامَنُوا۟ مَن يَرْتَدَّ مِنكُمْ عَن دِينِهِۦ فَسَوْفَ يَأْتِى ٱللَّهُ بِقَوْمٍ يُحِبُّهُمْ وَيُحِبُّونَهُۥٓ أَذِلَّةٍ عَلَى ٱلْمُؤْمِنِينَ
أَعِزَّةٍ عَلَى ٱلْكَـٰفِرِينَ يُجَـٰهِدُونَ فِى سَبِيلِ ٱللَّهِ وَلَا يَخَافُونَ لَوْمَةَ لَآئِمٍ ۚ ذَٰلِكَ فَضْلُ ٱللَّهِ يُؤْتِيهِ مَن يَشَآءُ ۚ وَٱللَّهُ
وَٰسِعٌ عَلِيمٌ

- *O you who have believed, whoever of you should revert from his religion - Allāh will bring forth [in place of them] a people He will love and who will love Him [who are] humble toward the believers, powerful against the disbelievers; they strive in the cause of Allāh and do not fear the blame of a critic. That is the favour of Allāh; He bestows it upon whom He wills. And Allāh is all-Encompassing and Knowing.* (Al-Ma'idah 5: 54, interpretation of the meaning).

This verse highlights Allāh's sovereignty and the special relationship between Allāh and His devoted followers. It addresses believers, warning that those who abandon their faith will be replaced by people whom Allāh loves and who love Him. These people are characterised by their humility towards fellow believers, strength against disbelievers, dedication to striving in Allāh's cause, and resilience against criticism. The verse highlights that such traits are a favour from Allāh, granted according to His will, underlining His all-encompassing knowledge and authority.

Utz (2011) stipulates the characteristics of those who love Allāh. They are those who "strive in the path of Allāh against His enemies with one's heart, soul, hand, tongue, and wealth; and not fearing the reproach of anyone, as there is contentment in doing what is pleasing to Allāh, unconcerned about receiving criticism or praise from other people." (p. 158).

Hope (*raja*) is an important virtue for Muslims—characterised by reliance on Almighty God in all circumstances. The concept of *raja* in Islām is deeply intertwined with faith and trust in Allāh's mercy, forgiveness, and ultimate wisdom. It encourages believers to remain optimistic and maintain a positive outlook, even in challenging circumstances, by relying on Allāh's benevolence and guidance. Hope is an emotional expectation, with Allāh providing limitless resources of hope. Despite trials and tribulations, believers are encouraged to avoid despair and maintain hope in Allāh. With reference to the verse "For indeed, with hardship [will be] ease" (Inshirah 94:5, interpretation of the meaning), there is *hadīth* that is relevant here. Abu Hurayrah (may Allāh be pleased with him) relates a story, "A man and his wife from an earlier generation were poor. Once when the man came back from a journey, he went to his wife saying to her, while feeling hunger and fatigued, 'Do you have anything to eat' She said, 'Yes, receive the good news of Allāh's provisions.' He again said to her, 'If you have anything to eat, bring it to me.' She said, 'Wait a little longer.' She was awaiting Allāh's mercy. When the matter was prolonged, he said to her, 'Get up and bring me whatever you have to eat, because I am really hungry and fatigued.' She said, 'I will. Soon I will open the oven's cover, so do not be hasty.' When he was busy and refrained from insisting for a while, she said to herself, 'I should look in my oven.' So, she got up and looked in her oven and found it full of the meat of a lamb, and her mortar and pestle were full of seed grains; it was crushing the seeds on its own. So, she took out what was in the mortar and pestle, after shaking it to remove everything from inside, and took the meat out that she found in the oven." (Ahmad). There is a link between hope and mercy. In the following verse of the Qur'ân, Allāh says:

قُلْ يَٰعِبَادِىَ ٱلَّذِينَ أَسْرَفُوا۟ عَلَىٰٓ أَنفُسِهِمْ لَا تَقْنَطُوا۟ مِن رَّحْمَةِ ٱللَّهِ ۚ إِنَّ ٱللَّهَ يَغْفِرُ ٱلذُّنُوبَ جَمِيعًا ۚ إِنَّهُۥ هُوَ ٱلْغَفُورُ ٱلرَّحِيمُ

- *Say, "O My servants who have transgressed against themselves [by sinning], do not despair of the mercy of Allāh. Indeed, Allāh forgives all sins. Indeed, it is He who is the Forgiving, the Merciful."* (Az-Zumar 39:53, interpretation of the meaning).

This verse is supplemented by *hadīth* which is narrated by Asma bint Yazid. I heard the Messenger of Allāh (ﷺ) reciting: Say: "O My slaves who have transgressed against themselves! Despair not of the mercy of Allāh, verily, Allāh forgives all sins and I do not mind (referring to Qur'ân 39:53)."(Tirmidhî). From a psychological perspective, the verse can be seen as a profound message of hope, forgiveness, and psychological resilience. It encourages individuals not to despair, which can counteract feelings of hopelessness and depression. Recognising that one has sinned or made mistakes can lead to guilt and self-condemnation. The verse suggests that forgiveness is always possible, promoting self-forgiveness. Knowing that sins can be forgiven may encourage individuals to strive for better behaviour and self-improvement. The emphasis on mercy can foster a sense of compassion and empathy towards oneself and others. The name *al-Rahîm*—derived from the Arabic word *rahmah* (mercy)—signifies specific mercy for believers. It assures them that they should not lose hope, regardless of the number of sins committed, as Allāh forgives all sins except for associating partners with Him.

10.4 The Qur'ân and Emotional Regulation

The Qur'an provides solace and comfort to individuals facing inner turmoil, promotes emotional resilience, and stability, and offers guidance for ethical behaviour and interpersonal relationships. Allāh says in the following two verses of the Qur'ân:

يَٰٓأَيُّهَا ٱلنَّاسُ قَدْ جَآءَتْكُم مَّوْعِظَةٌ مِّن رَّبِّكُمْ وَشِفَآءٌ لِّمَا فِى ٱلصُّدُورِ وَهُدًى وَرَحْمَةٌ لِّلْمُؤْمِنِينَ

- *O mankind, there has to come to you instruction from your Lord and healing for what is in the breasts and guidance and mercy for the believers.* (Yunus 10:57, interpretation of the meaning).

وَنُنَزِّلُ مِنَ ٱلْقُرْءَانِ مَا هُوَ شِفَآءٌ وَرَحْمَةٌ لِّلْمُؤْمِنِينَ ۙ وَلَا يَزِيدُ ٱلظَّٰلِمِينَ إِلَّا خَسَارًا

- *And We send down of the Qur'ân that which is healing and mercy for the believers, but it does not increase the wrongdoers except in loss.* (Al-Isra 17:82, interpretation of the meaning).

These verses highlight the belief that the Qur'ân serves as a source of guidance, healing, and mercy for believers. From an Islāmic psychological perspective, the verses emphasise that the Qur'ân addresses not only spiritual needs, but also emotional and behavioural aspects of human psychology. Additionally, it emphasises that the Qur'ânic healing and mercy are accessible to those who believe in its message. Furthermore, the verses suggest that those who reject or disregard the guidance of the Qur'ân will experience increased loss, implying that neglecting its teachings can result in spiritual and emotional deprivation. Thus, the Qur'ân is a healing for the body, spirit, and the soul. There is evidence to suggest that the Qur'ânic recitation have a positive effect on the mental health (Mahjoob et al., 2016), reduction in depression (Ansari et al., 2005), and effective as a non-pharmacological treatment in the management of psychological problems such as anxiety (Ghiasi & Keramat, 2018). A scoping review by Owens et al. (2023) identified *Salah* [prayer] and supplicant praying, recitation, reading, memorising, and listening to the Qur'ân in reducing anxiety, depression, and stress and increasing quality of life and coping.

Numerous Qur'ânic verses highlight the importance of hope, urging believers to stay hopeful even in the most challenging times, trusting that Allāh will ease their difficulties. Allāh says in the Qur'ân.

فَإِنَّ مَعَ ٱلْعُسْرِ يُسْرًا
إِنَّ مَعَ ٱلْعُسْرِ يُسْرًا

- *For indeed, with hardship [will be] ease.*

- *For indeed, with hardship [will be] ease.* (Inshirah 94:4–5, interpretation of the meaning).

سَيَجْعَلُ ٱللَّهُ بَعْدَ عُسْرٍ يُسْرًا

- *Allāh will bring about, after hardship, ease.* (At-Talaq 65:7, interpretation of the meaning).

From a psychological perspective, these verses provide a profound sense of reassurance and hope, which are crucial for mental well-being. The repeated assurance that ease follows hardship (Inshirah 94:4–5) reinforces the concept of resilience, helping individuals maintain a positive outlook even during difficult times. This belief can reduce stress and anxiety by fostering an expectation of relief and improvement. The verse from At-Talaq 65:7 further emphasises that Allāh will bring ease after hardship, encouraging patience and perseverance. This perspective aligns with the psychological understanding that maintaining hope and a forward-looking mindset can significantly enhance one's ability to cope with adversity. Believers who internalise these messages are likely to experience greater emotional stability and resilience, as they trust that their struggles will ultimately lead to better circumstances.

10.5 Islāmic Foundation of Healing

From an Islāmic perspective, healing originates from a divine source and occurs through a connection with the sacred. The Islāmic foundation of healing is deeply rooted in the spiritual, psychological, and physical aspects of human well-being. It integrates faith, practices, and principles derived from the Qur'ân and *hadīth* to promote holistic health. Belief in the Oneness of God (*tawhîd*) offers a profound sense of purpose and meaning, which is important for mental health. *Tawhîd* emphasises that life is governed by the will of a single, all-powerful God. This belief provides Muslims with a clear purpose: to worship and obey God, and to live according to His guidance. This sense of purpose can bring direction and clarity to one's life, reducing feelings of aimlessness or existential anxiety. It also offers a moral framework and ethical guidelines derived from the Qur'ân and *hadīth*. Following these guidelines helps individuals make meaningful choices aligned with their faith, which reinforces a sense of purpose and coherence in their actions.

Islāmic healing is perceived as an ongoing process that involves continuous engagement with one's faith. This process includes regular prayer, meditation, adherence to dietary laws, and other forms of worship, which collectively contribute to maintaining overall well-being and preventing illness. Healing practices, such as prayer, recitation of the Qur'ān, and adherence to Prophetic traditions (*Sunnah*), are actively used to intervene in times of mental and physical distress. These practices provide immediate relief and comfort, serving as a form of direct treatment. The ultimate goal of these practices is to restore health and well-being. Healing is seen as the desired outcome of engaging with one's faith and spiritual practices. This outcome is not limited to physical recovery but includes spiritual and emotional healing.

Healing is also obtained through individual processes and natural substances, such as herbs and medicines. It was narrated by Aisha (may Allāh be pleased with her) that Allāh's Messenger (ﷺ) used to treat with *ruqyah* [prayers for healing or protective purposes] saying, "O the Lord of the people! Remove the trouble The cure is in Your Hands, and there is none except You who can remove it (the disease)." (Bukhârî (d)). It is believed that Allāh, known as *As-Shafi* (The Healer), is the true source of healing, not the psychologist or healthcare practitioner. In this context, the Islāmic psychologist or health care practitioner is the facilitator and not the healer. It is Almighty Allāh that know the diseases of the soul, heart, body, and mind and their cures. Surely Allāh has testified this in the Qur'ān.

وَإِن يَمْسَسْكَ ٱللَّهُ بِضُرٍّ فَلَا كَاشِفَ لَهُۥٓ إِلَّا هُوَ

- *And if Allāh should touch you with adversity, there is no remover of it except him.* (Al-'An'ām 6:17, interpretation of meaning).

This verse emphasises the Islāmic belief that Allāh is the ultimate source of relief from adversity. It signifies that when facing difficulties, only Allāh has the power to remove them, highlighting the reliance on divine intervention and the acknowledgment of Allāh's supreme control over all aspects of life. This belief reinforces the idea that true healing and resolution of problems are ultimately in the hands of Allāh. From an Islāmic perspective, healing involves the purification of multiple dimensions – mind, body, and soul.

Islāmic teachings encompass a rich tapestry of spiritual practices aimed at fostering personal growth, emotional resilience, and communal harmony. *Salah* (prayer) provides a structured daily routine that not only connects individuals with Allah but also imbues life with discipline and spiritual contemplation. *Tawakkul* (trust in God) encourages believers to relinquish anxieties by placing faith in Allah's wisdom and support during challenging times, thereby promoting resilience and a sense of peace. *Istighfar* (seeking forgiveness) and *tawbah* (repentance) offer pathways to emotional healing and spiritual purification, acknowledging mistakes, fostering remorse, and committing to positive change. Seeking forgiveness and pardon is also a critical component of psychospiritual well-being in Islām. Ibn 'Abbas (may Allāh be pleased with him) said: The Messenger of Allāh (ﷺ) said, "If anyone constantly seeks pardon (from Allāh), Allāh will appoint for him a way out of every distress and a relief from every anxiety and will provide sustenance for him from where he expects not." (Abū Dāwūd). Forgiving others is also a critical component of emotional well-being. Abud Darda' 'Abbas (may Allāh be pleased with him) told that he heard God's Messenger (ﷺ) say, "No one will suffer any bodily injury and forgive it* without God raising him a degree for it and removing a sin from him." *Literally "give it as sadaqah." (Tirmidhî & Ibn Majah). Forgiving others can liberate individuals from the burdens of anger and resentment, promoting inner peace. *Tawbah*– or repentance–is the act of seeking forgiveness from Allāh for one's sins and mistakes. It is a fundamental aspect of Islāmic spirituality, emphasising the merciful nature of God and the possibility of redemption. The process of *tawbah* involves self-reflection, remorse, and a commitment to personal change. This introspective journey can be deeply therapeutic, allowing individuals to release guilt and shame. Moreover, Islām' s emphasis on God's infinite mercy and forgiveness provides comfort and hope, facilitating emotional healing.

Dhikr–or the remembrance of Allāh–involves the repeated recitation of specific phrases glorifying God, such as "*Subhan Allāh*" (Glory be to God), "*Alhamdulillah*" (All praise is due to God), and "*Allāhu Akbar*" (God is the Greatest). This practice is central to Islāmic spirituality and has profound implications for mental health and emotional well-being. Engaging in *dhikr* fosters contemplation and a focused state of mind, which can help alleviate stress and anxiety. The repetitive nature of *dhikr* can induce a reflective state, promoting relaxation and mental clarity. By continuously redirecting thoughts towards the divine, individuals can cultivate a sense of peace and spiritual fulfilment. Supplications (*dua'hs*) serve as a means to strengthen one's faith and seek divine guidance in decision-making, while practices like *ruqyah* (spiritual healing) provide comfort and relief from physical and spiritual ailments, reinforcing spiritual well-being. Charity (*sadaqah*) not only purifies wealth and soul but also fosters altruism and empathy towards the less fortunate, promoting social justice and reducing materialism.

Patience–or *sabr*–is a highly esteemed virtue in Islām, frequently mentioned in the Qur'ân and *hadīth*. It involves enduring hardships and adversities with a steadfast and calm manner, trusting in Allāh's wisdom and timing. The practice of *sabr* is important in the healing process, as it encourages individuals to cope with difficulties without succumbing to despair. It helps maintain emotional equilibrium and fosters resilience. The Qur'ân often associates *sabr* with divine reward, providing spiritual motivation for individuals to persevere through challenges. Gratitude (*shukr*) is presented as a means to enhance emotional well-being and attract further blessings, fostering a positive and contented mindset. Surah Ibrahim (14:7) reminds, "If you are grateful, I will surely increase you [in favour]; but if you deny, indeed, My punishment is severe." (interpretation of the meaning). These practices collectively promote and cultivate a holistic approach to spiritual and emotional development that enhances individual well-being and contributes to a harmonious society rooted in Islāmīc principles. Table 10.1 outlines the key Islāmic healing concepts and their respective benefits and applications.

10.6 Conclusion

The Islāmic foundation of healing and emotional health offers a rich and comprehensive framework for understanding and enhancing well-being. Rooted in the teachings of the Qur'ân and the Prophetic traditions (*hadīths*), this framework emphasises the interconnectedness of the physical, mental, and spiritual aspects of health. Practices such as regular prayer, remembrance of Allāh, supplications, and recitation of the Qur'ân are not only spiritual obligations but also potent tools for fostering emotional resilience, self-discipline, and inner peace. By encouraging

Table 10.1 Key Islāmic healing concepts and their respective benefits and applications

Islāmīc concept	Benefits	Applications
Qur'ân recitation	Increased spiritual connection	Daily recitation, and at special occasions like *Ramadan*
	Inner peace and tranquillity	Listening to recitations during stress, anxiety, or before sleep
	Strengthening faith and understanding	Regular study and reflection on verses (*tafsir*)
	Earning divine rewards (*hasanat*)	Reading and memorising Qur'ân regularly, especially in original Arabic
	Emotional stability and resilience	Reflecting on the meanings and messages of the Qur'ân in difficult times
	Comfort and solace	Reciting or listening to specific chapters known for providing comfort, including Surah *Al-Fatiha*
	Healing and recovery	Performing incantations (*ruqyah*)
	Coping mechanism in trauma	Turning to the Qur'ân for strength and guidance during traumatic experiences
Dhikr (remembrance of Allāh)	Stress reduction	Engage in repeated recitations and contemplations
	Emotional stability	Constantly reconnect with divine presence
Salah (prayer)	Routine and structure	Daily structured prayers provide stability and discipline
	Islāmic contemplation and reflection	Engage in physical, mental, and spiritual aspects of *salah*
Tawakkul (trust in Allāh)	Resilience and coping	Trust in divine wisdom and support during hardships
	Letting go of worries	Release excessive worries through trust in Allāh
Istighfar (seeking forgiveness)	Guilt and self-forgiveness	Regularly seek forgiveness for emotional healing
		Acknowledge mistakes and seek divine pardon
Tawbah (repentance)	Spiritual purification: Cleanses the heart and soul from sins. Restores one's relationship with Allāh.	Acknowledging mistakes: Recognising and admitting sins. Feeling remorse: Sincere regret and remorse for wrongdoing.
	Psychological benefits: Relieves guilt and promotes peace of mind. Provides a sense of relief and emotional healing	Seeking forgiveness: Making a commitment to avoid repeat offenses. Praying for forgiveness: Supplicating to Allāh for pardon
	Behavioural improvement: Encourages positive changes in behaviour Motivates to refrain from sinful acts in the future	Making amends: Rectifying harm caused to others. Change in conduct: Striving towards righteous behaviour.

(continued)

Table 10.1 (continued)

Islāmīc concept	Benefits	Applications
Supplications (*dua'hs*)	Strengthens faith and spirituality	Seeking guidance in decision-making
	Provides comfort and solace	Asking for forgiveness and mercy
	Increases gratitude	Seeking protection from harm and evil
	Fosters humility	Praying for health and well-being
	Establishes connection with Allāh	Making requests for success in endeavours
Ruqyah	Spiritual healing and purification	Healing from physical and spiritual ailments
	Protection from evil eye and harm	Warding off negative influences
	Strengthening faith and spirituality	Offering comfort and reassurance
	Psychological relief	Addressing anxiety and fear
	Connection to religious practice	Rituals during illness or distress
Charity (*sadaqah*)	Purifies wealth and soul	Helping the needy and less fortunate
	Increases blessings and rewards	Providing for essential needs (food, clothing)
	Altruism and empathy	Engage in acts of charity (*sadaqah* and *zakat*)
	Reducing materialism	Help others to enhance personal well-being and purpose
Patience and perseverance (*sabr*)	Endurance	Cultivate resilience and manage stress calmly
	Hope and positivity	Develop a positive outlook towards challenges
Compassion (*rahmah*)	Promotes emotional well-being	Supporting those in distress
	Fosters empathy and understanding	Resolving conflicts peacefully
	Reflects spiritual growth	Practicing forgiveness and tolerance
Gratitude (*shukr*)	Increases blessings and abundance	Thanking Allāh for blessings and favours
	Fosters contentment and happiness	Expressing gratitude towards others
	Strengthens relationships	Maintaining positive attitudes in adversity
	Improves mental and emotional well-being	Cultivating humility and patience
	Deepens faith and spirituality	Encouraging charitable acts as a form of gratitude
	Positive outlook	Practice gratitude to improve happiness and reduce negativity
		Acknowledge and appreciate blessings
Justice and fairness (*'adl*)	Equity and balance	Promote fairness in relationships and reduce conflicts
		Maintain mental peace through balanced interactions
Community and support (*ummah*)	Social support	Be part of the Muslim community for emotional and psychospiritual well-being

compassion, patience, gratitude, and contemplation, Islāmic teachings provide practical strategies for managing stress, anxiety, and other emotional challenges, promoting a balanced and fulfilling life.

Integrating these principles into modern therapeutic practices—particularly within the context of Islāmic psychotherapy—offers significant potential for improving mental and emotional health among Muslim individuals and communities. This approach respects and utilises the cultural and religious values of clients, providing them with relevant and resonant support. By blending traditional therapeutic techniques with the spiritual wisdom of Islāmic, clinicians can address psychological issues more holistically, fostering not just the alleviation of symptoms but also the nurturing of the soul. This dual focus on psychological and spiritual well-being ensures a more profound and lasting impact on the overall health and quality of life of those seeking help. This holistic approach not only treats symptoms but also nurtures the soul, fostering a sense of inner peace and balance that is essential for long-term health and welfare.

References

Abū Dāwūd. *Riyad as-Salihin 1873*. In-book reference: Book 19, Hadith 5. https://sunnah.com/riyadussalihin/19

Ahmad. Cited in Tafsir Ibn Kathir- Surah 65. At-Talaq, Ayaat 6 To 7. http://www.alim.org/library/quran/AlQuran-tafsir/TIK/65/6, (26 May 2024).

American Psychological Association. (2024). *Emotion*. https://dictionary.apa.org/emotion. Accessed 25 May 2024.

Ansari, J. A., Negahban, B. T., Sayyadi, A. A. R., & Aghamohamad, H. P. (2005). The effect of the Koran reciting on the depressed patients in psychiatry department of Moradi hospital in Rafsanjan. *Scientific Journal of Kurdistan University of Medical Sciences, 10*(2 (Serial number 36)), 42–48. SID. https://sid.ir/paper/76394/en.

Beedie, C. J., Terry, P. C., & Lane, A. M. (2005). Distinctions between emotion and mood. *Cognition and Emotion, 19*(6), 847–887.

Beedie, C. J., Terry, P. C., Lane, A. M., & Devonport, T. J. (2011). Differential assessment of emotions and moods: Development and validation of the emotion and mood components of anxiety questionnaire. *Personality and Individual Differences, 50*(2), 228–233.

Berking, M., & Wupperman, P. (2012). Emotion regulation and mental health: Recent findings, current challenges, and future directions. *Current Opinion in Psychiatry, 25*(2), 128–134. https://doi.org/10.1097/YCO.0b013e3283503669

Bukhârî (al). *Sahih al-Bukhârî 6632*.In-book reference: Book 83, Hadith 12. USC-MSA web (English) reference: Vol. 8, Book 78, Hadith 628. https://sunnah.com/bukhârî:6632

Bukhârî (b)l. *Sahih al-Bukhârî 21*.In-book reference: Book 2, Hadith 14. USC-MSA web (English) reference: Vol. 1, Book 2, Hadith 21. https://sunnah.com/bukhârî:21

Bukhârî (c)l. Sahih al-Bukhârî 7137. In-book reference: Book 93, Hadith 1. USC-MSA web (English) reference: Vol. 9, Book 89, Hadith 251. https://sunnah.com/bukhârî:7137

Bukhârî (d). *Sahih al-Bukhârî 5744*. In-book reference: Book 76, Hadith 59. USC-MSA web (English) reference: Vol. 7, Book 71, Hadith 640. https://sunnah.com/bukhârî:5744

Cohn, M. A., Fredrickson, B. L., Brown, S. L., Mikels, J. A., & Conway, A. M. (2009). Happiness unpacked: Positive emotions increase life satisfaction by building resilience. *Emotion, 9*(3), 361–368. https://doi.org/10.1037/a0015952

Gärling, T., Gamble, A., Fors, F., & Hjerm, M. (2016). Emotional well-being related to time pressure, impediment to goal progress, and stress-related symptoms. *Journal of Happiness Studies: An Interdisciplinary Forum on Subjective Well-Being, 17*(5), 1789–1799. https://doi.org/10.1007/s10902-015-9670-4

Ghiasi, A., & Keramat, A. (2018). The effect of listening to Holy Quran recitation on anxiety: A systematic review. *Iranian Journal of Nursing and Midwifery Research, 23(6)*, 411–420. https://doi.org/10.4103/ijnmr.ijnmr_173_17

Hernandez, R., Bassett, S. M., Boughton, S. W., Schuette, S. A., Shiu, E. W., & Moskowitz, J. T. (2018). Psychological Well-being and Physical Health: Associations, Mechanisms, and Future Directions. *Emotion Review: Journal of the International Society for Research on Emotion, 10*(1), 18–29. https://doi.org/10.1177/1754073917697824

Hu, T., Zhang, D., Wang, J., Mistry, R., Ran, G., & Wang, X. (2014). Relation between emotion regulation and mental health: A meta-analysis review. *Psychological Reports, 114*(2), 341–362. https://doi.org/https://doi.org/10.2466/03.20.PR0.114k22w4

Ibn Majah. *Sunan Ibn Majah, The Book of the Sunnah*. Arabic/English book reference: Vol. 1, Book 1, Hadith 3.

Levin, J. (2018). Scientists and healers: Toward collaborative research partnerships. *Explore, 4*(5), 302–310.

Mahjoob, M., Nejati, J., Hosseini, A., & Bakhshani, N. M. (2016). The effect of Holy Quran voice on mental health. *Journal of Religion and Health, 55*(1), 38–42.

Menefee, D. S., Ledoux, T., & Johnston, C. A. (2022). The importance of emotional regulation in mental health. *American Journal of Lifestyle Medicine, 16*(1), 28–31. https://doi.org/10.1177/15598276211049771

Nygren, A. (1930). Cited in Agape and Eros – Summary, eNotes Publishing Ed. eNotes Editorial. eNotes.com, Inc. eNotes.com. http://www.enotes.com/topics/agape-eros#summary-summary-839443. Accessed 25 May 2024.

Owens, J., Rassool, G. H., Bernstein, J., Latif, S., & Aboul-Enein, B. (2023). Interventions using the Qur'ân to promote mental health: A systematic scoping review. *Journal of Mental Health, 32*(4), 842–862. https://doi.org/10.1080/09638237.2023.2232449

Ricard, M., Lutz, A., & Davidson, R. J. (2014). Mind of the meditator. *Scientific American, 311*(5), 38–45. https://doi.org/10.1038/scientificamerican1114-38

The National Center for Emotional Wellness. (2024). *Definition of emotional wellness*. https://www.nationalcenterforemotionalwellness.org/about-the-national-center. Accessed 25 May 2024.

Tirmidhî. *Jami' at-Tirmidhî, Chapters on Tafsir*. English reference: Vol. 5, Book 44, Hadith 3237. Arabic reference: Book 47, Hadith 3545.

Tirmidhî, & Ibn Majah. *Mishkat al-Masabih 3480*. In-book reference: Book 16, Hadith 30. https://sunnah.com/mishkat:3480

Utz, A. (2011). *Psychology from an Islāmīc perspective*. International Islāmīc Publication House.

Willroth, E. C., Young, G., Tamir, M., & Mauss, I. B. (2023). Judging emotions as good or bad: Individual differences and associations with psychological health. *Emotion, 23*(7), 1876–1890. https://doi.org/10.1037/emo0001220

Chapter 11
The Healing Power of Compassion (*Rahmah*) Forgiveness (*Istighfar*), Gratitude (*Shukr*), Hope (*Raja*), and Patience (*Sabr*)

11.1 Introduction

Islāmic teachings place a profound emphasis on the virtues of compassion (*rahmah*), forgiveness (*istighfar*), gratitude (*shukr*), hope (*raja*), and patience (*sabr*) as cornerstones of emotional and spiritual well-being. These virtues are not merely abstract concepts but are deeply embedded in the daily practices and beliefs of Muslims, guiding them towards a balanced and fulfilling life. In Islāmic psychotherapy, the virtues of compassion (*rahmah*), forgiveness (*istighfar*), gratitude (*shukr*), hope (*raja*), and patience (*sabr*) are integral to the healing process. These virtues, deeply rooted in the Qur'ân and Prophetic traditions (*hadīths*), provide a comprehensive framework for addressing emotional and psychological challenges. Compassion fosters empathy and understanding, creating a supportive and safe therapeutic environment. Forgiveness helps clients release resentment and achieve serenity (*sakinah*)—emotional peace—while gratitude cultivates a positive attitude and resilience. Hope instils optimism and motivation for recovery, and patience equips individuals with the strength to endure and overcome adversities.

Together, these virtues form a comprehensive framework for emotional and spiritual health, offering practical tools for managing stress, anxiety, and other psychological and spiritual challenges. By integrating these principles into therapeutic practices, we can develop more effective strategies for supporting the mental and emotional health of Muslim individuals and communities. Thus, this approach not only addresses symptoms but also nurtures the soul, promoting holistic and sustainable well-being. This chapter aims to explore the healing power of these virtues and their practical applications in fostering emotional resilience and holistic health.

G. H. Rassool, *Exploring the Intersection of Islāmic Spirituality and Psychotherapy*,
https://doi.org/10.1007/978-3-031-72724-5_11

11.2 Compassion (*Rahmah*)

Rahmah (compassion) is a core concept in Islāmic teachings, emphasising its significance as a fundamental attribute of Allāh and a virtue for believers. *Rahmah* is presented as a cornerstone of Islāmic ethics, promoting social justice, kindness, and empathy. By embedding *rahmah* into everyday interactions and community life, Muslims are encouraged to create a just and compassionate society. By fostering compassion, individuals can reduce stress, build positive relationships, and improve overall emotional well-being. Compassion directed toward others and self-compassion have consistently shown associations with positive outcomes in various studies. Research by Pace et al. (2009) and Breines et al. (2014) indicates that compassion reduces stress levels. Additionally, studies such as those by MacBeth and Gumley (2012), Muris and Petrocchi (2017), Homan and Sirois (2017), Matos et al. (2017), and Wilson et al. (2019) demonstrate that both forms of compassion are linked to lower levels of mental ill-health. Moreover, research by Zessin et al. (2015) has highlighted that compassion—whether directed outwardly or inwardly—is associated with increased overall well-being. Research findings emphasise that compassion—especially self-compassion and compassion received from others—played a crucial protective role during the COVID-19 pandemic (Matos et al., 2022). These forms of compassion act as buffers, mitigating the adverse impacts on mental health and promoting social well-being. These findings highlight the dual benefits of compassion in enhancing mental health, reducing stress, and fostering well-being.

To effectively use *rahmah* (compassion) in Islāmic psychotherapy, therapists need to understand its profound significance within Islāmic teachings. By grounding therapeutic practices in the concept of *rahmah*, therapists can create a compassionate and empathetic environment that aligns with the clients' spiritual values. This involves recognising the inherent worth of every individual and approaching them with kindness, patience, and understanding. Table 11.1 outlines the techniques for integrating rahmah into Islāmic psychotherapy, their application, benefits, and a case study example with a client called Ahmad.

11.3 Healing the Past Through Forgiveness (*Istighfar*)

The concept of *Istighfar* (act of seeking forgiveness) within Islāmic teachings highlights its significance as both a divine attribute and a virtue for believers—the broader implications of forgiveness in the life of a Muslim—highlighting its essential role in both spiritual and personal growth. True forgiveness—it is claimed (Enrigh, 2017)—goes further by offering something positive such as empathy, compassion, and understanding towards the person who wronged you. This additional element makes forgiveness both a virtue and a powerful concept in positive psychology.

Table 11.1 Integrating *rahmah* into Islāmic psychotherapy

Technique	Benefit	Application	Case Study: Ahmad's journey to emotional resilience
Active listening and empathetic communication	Makes clients feel heard and valued Fosters a trusting therapeutic relationship Encourages open dialogue	Train therapists in active listening and empathetic communication techniques. Fully concentrate, understand, and respond thoughtfully to clients' concerns	Ahmad's therapist practices active listening, ensuring Ahmad feels understood and valued. Strengthens the therapeutic relationship, making Ahmad more comfortable sharing his feelings
Contemplation	Reduces stress. Promotes emotional resilience. Enhances overall well-being by fostering a compassionate mindset	Guide clients through Islāmic contemplation and loving-kindness reflective practices. Focus on the present moment and Hereafter (akhirah) and cultivate feelings of compassion towards oneself and others	Ahmad practices daily Islāmic contemplation and reflective practices and loving-kindness using Qur'ânic verses. Helps him focus on positive thoughts and reduce anxiety
Service and acts of kindness	Enhances clients' sense of purpose. Strengthens community connection Increases overall happiness Reinforces the practice of *rahmah*	Encourage clients to engage in acts of kindness and service to others (e.g., volunteering, helping someone in need)	Ahmad volunteers at a local charity. Engages in compassionate actions, enhancing his sense of purpose, community connection, and overall happiness
Self-compassion exercises	Reduces self-criticism. Builds self-esteem. Develops a healthier relationship with oneself, crucial for emotional healing	Encourage clients to engage in self-compassion exercises (e.g., writing self-compassionate letters, practicing self-affirmation)	Ahmad writes letters to himself, acknowledging his struggles and offering kindness and support Helps him combat negative self-talk and build self-esteem

Forgiveness has been extensively studied for its profound effects on both mental and physical health. Various research findings highlight how forgiving others—as well as oneself—can lead to significant improvements in overall physical and mental health. A meta-analysis by Wade et al. (2014) found that forgiveness interventions significantly reduced symptoms of depression and anxiety. Participants who engaged in forgiveness practices reported lower levels of these mental health issues compared to control groups. A study by Lawler-Row et al. (2008) showed that forgiveness was associated with lower levels of stress, depression, and anxiety, suggesting that forgiving can alleviate the burden of negative emotions and psychological distress. Research highlights the interactive effects of cumulative stress severity and forgiveness on health. It suggests that adopting a forgiving coping style can significantly mitigate stress-related disorders. By reducing the negative impact of accumulated stress, forgiveness serves as a protective factor that enhances overall health and well-being (Toussaint et al., 2016a). There is longitudinal evidence demonstrating that higher levels of forgiveness are linked to reduced stress and, consequently, improved mental health. Strategies to cultivate forgiveness could therefore have positive effects on managing stress and enhancing overall health (Toussaint et al., 2016b).

From Christian traditions, Enright's forgiveness therapy process model (Enright, 2001) employs a 20-step system to guide individuals through four phases: uncovering negative feelings about the offense, deciding to forgive, working towards understanding the offender, and developing empathy and compassion for them. This model has proven effective in one-on-one interventions in demonstrating significant reductions in depression, anxiety, and post traumatic stress disorder (PTSD) among women who experienced partner's emotional abuse (Reed & Enright, 2006). By engaging in these cognitive exercises, participants begin to view the offender as a wounded human being rather than merely defining them by their hurtful actions.

Prayer plays a significant role in enhancing forgiveness by fostering a deeper sense of empathy, compassion, and understanding. Through prayer, individuals often seek divine assistance in overcoming resentment and anger, which helps to soften their hearts and open them up to the possibility of forgiving others. Prayer can provide a sense of peace and spiritual guidance, making it easier to let go of grudges and view those who have wronged them with compassion. This spiritual practice encourages self-reflection, humility, and a connection to Allāh, all of which contribute to a more forgiving attitude. The findings of a study (Toussaint et al., 2015) indicate that a brief prayer can significantly enhance forgiveness, a change observed consistently across American and Indian cultures and among three different religious groups in India. This suggests that brief prayers for others may be beneficial for individuals in close relationships, certain counselling settings, and various other life contexts.

11.3.1 The Islāmic Process Model of Forgiveness

The Islāmic Process Model of Forgiveness encompasses six stages that guide believers through a transformative journey towards spiritual purification and reconciliation. The model is presented in Fig. 11.1.

Acknowledgment (*itiraf*): This stage involves recognising and admitting one's mistakes and sins before Allāh. It requires sincere introspection and acknowledging the wrongs committed, whether they involve others or oneself. Qur'ânic teachings emphasise the importance of acknowledging one's faults as a prerequisite for seeking forgiveness and spiritual growth (Ali 'Imran 3:135, interpretation of the meaning). Grudges (*al-'ada'*): Holding grudges or resentment towards others is antithetical to Islāmic teachings on forgiveness. The Qur'ân encourages believers to

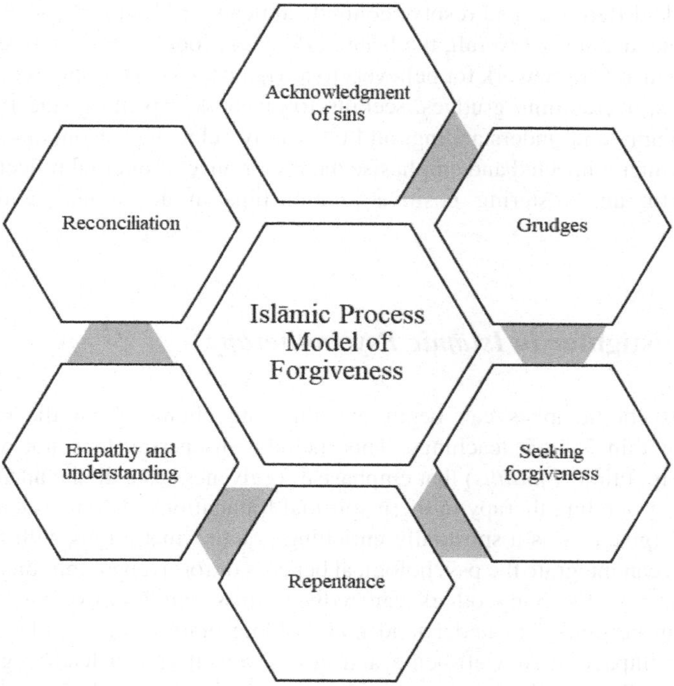

Fig. 11.1 Islāmic process model of forgiveness

pardon and overlook offenses committed against them (An-Nur, 24:22, interpretation of the meaning). This stage involves actively working towards letting go of negative feelings and replacing them with empathy and compassion, aligning one's heart with the principles of forgiveness. *Istighfar* is the act of seeking forgiveness from Allāh for sins and wrongdoings committed, including harbouring grudges. It involves humbly acknowledging faults and shortcomings before Allāh and seeking His mercy and forgiveness (Ash-Shura, 42:40, interpretation of the meaning).

Tawbah is the sincere repentance and turning back to Allāh after acknowledging sins. It includes feeling remorse for past actions, resolving to change one's behaviour, and seeking Allāh's forgiveness. The Qur'ân describes repentance as turning towards Allāh with sincerity and a desire for spiritual renewal (At-Tahrim 66:8, interpretation of the meaning). Developing empathy (*at-ta'āṭuf*) and understanding (*al-fahm*) towards others is crucial in the forgiveness process. It involves recognising the perspectives and feelings of others, which helps in fostering compassion and reconciliation. The Prophet Muhammad (ﷺ) exemplified empathy and understanding in his interactions with people from different backgrounds and situations. The final stage of the Islāmic Process Model of Forgiveness is reconciliation (*al-muṣāliḥah*). It entails making efforts to mend relationships, restore trust, and promote harmony within oneself and with others. The Qur'ân encourages believers to reconcile differences and resolve conflicts amicably (Al-Hujurāt, 49:9, interpretation of the meaning). Overall, the Islāmic Process Model of Forgiveness provides a comprehensive framework for believers to navigate through the stages of acknowledging sins, overcoming grudges, seeking forgiveness, repenting sincerely, developing empathy and understanding, and ultimately achieving reconciliation. These stages are interconnected and emphasise the importance of internal reflection, spiritual growth, and fostering positive relationships in accordance with Islāmic teachings.

11.3.2 **Istighfar** *in Islāmic Psychotherapy*

Islāmic psychotherapists can begin by educating clients about the concept of *Istighfar* within Islāmic teachings. This includes discussing Qur'ânic verses and Prophetic traditions (*hadīths*) that emphasise forgiveness as a divine attribute and a virtue. By grounding therapy in these spiritual foundations, therapists can help clients see forgiveness as a spiritually enriching practice that aligns with their faith. Therapists can integrate the psychological benefits of forgiveness into their practice, explaining how forgiving others can reduce stress and improve mental health. Clients can be guided to understand how holding onto grudges and resentments negatively impacts their well-being and how forgiveness can lead to greater life satisfaction. This can be supported with psychological research findings, helping clients appreciate the dual benefits of forgiveness for both their spiritual and emotional health.

Table 11.2 outlines the Islāmic process model of forgiveness in relation to its stages, Qur'ânic verses and Islāmic spiritual interventions.

Table 11.3 presents practical strategies and exercises for integrating *istighfar* (forgiveness) into Islāmic psychotherapy, highlighting their application through case studies. These strategies are essential in therapeutic settings as they guide individuals through the process of forgiveness, addressing both interpersonal conflicts and self-blame. By navigating the journey of forgiveness step-by-step, acknowledging pain, and empathising with others, therapists facilitate emotional healing and liberation, as seen in Sarah's case study. Techniques like self-forgiveness and active listening promote self-compassion and empathy, crucial for fostering a supportive therapeutic environment, exemplified by Ahmed and Leyla's experiences. Encouraging acts of kindness and reconciliation—as shown in Umar and Fatimah's cases—integrates forgiveness into daily life and familial relationships, enhancing well-being. Moreover, addressing resistance to forgiveness—as in Ibrahim's case—equips therapists with strategies to overcome barriers and facilitate emotional growth. Overall, these strategies demonstrate how *istighfar* can be effectively integrated into Islāmic psychotherapy to promote healing, resilience, and interpersonal harmony.

Table 11.2 Islāmic process model of forgiveness: Stages Qur'ânic verses and Islāmic spiritual interventions

Stages	Qur'ânic verses	Islāmic spiritual interventions
Acknowledgment of sins (itiraf bi-dhunub)	And those who, when they commit an immorality or wrong themselves [by transgression], remember Allah and seek forgiveness for their sins (Ali 'Imran 3:135, interpretation of the meaning)	Reflection on one's actions, acknowledging the harm caused
Grudges (*al-'ada*)	And let them pardon and overlook. Would you not like that Allah should forgive you? (An-Nur, 24:22, interpretation of the meaning)	Seeking forgiveness from Allāh for harbouring grudges, letting go of resentment
Seeking forgiveness (*istighfar*)	And the retribution for an evil act is an evil one like it, but whoever pardons and makes reconciliation, his reward is [due] from Allāh (Ash-Shura, 42:40, interpretation of the meaning).	Seeking forgiveness (*istighfar*) specifically for holding grudges and repenting from feelings of hatred
Repentance (*tawbah*)	The repentance accepted by Allāh is only for those who do wrong in ignorance [or carelessness] and then repent soon after. It is those to whom Allāh will turn in forgiveness, and Allāh is ever Knowing and Wise (An-Nisa 4:17, interpretation of the meaning) O you who have believed, repent to Allāh with sincere repentance. Perhaps your Lord will remove from you your misdeeds and admit you into gardens beneath which rivers flow [in Paradise]. (At-Tahrim 66:8, interpretation of the meaning)	Repenting (*tawbah*) for nurturing grudges, turning back to Allāh in sincere repentance
Empathy and understanding (*at-ta'āṭuf wal-fahm*)	"And We have not sent you, [O Muhammad], except as a mercy to the worlds." (Al-Anbiya, 21:107, interpretation of the meaning)	Compassionate actions, following the Prophet's example (*Sunnah*)
Reconciliation (*al-muṣāliḥah*)	And if two factions among the believers should fight, then make settlement between the two (Al-Hujurāt, 49:9, interpretation of the meaning)	Arbitration, seeking mutual understanding and peace

11.4 Gratitude (*Shukr*): Fostering Positive Emotions

Gratitude (*shukr*) is both an act of worship and a moral virtue, integral to Islāmic teachings. This section also discusses relevant Qur'ânic verses and Prophetic traditions (*hadīths*) that emphasise the importance of gratitude, underlining its significance in fostering a positive mindset and spiritual growth. In the Qur'ân, Allāh repeatedly calls upon believers to express gratitude for His blessings, emphasising that gratitude leads to increased blessings and spiritual growth. For instance, in Surah Ibrahim (14:7, interpretation of the meaning), Allāh says, "And [remember]

Table 11.3 Practical strategies and exercises for embracing forgiveness (*istighfar*) with case study

Strategy/exercise	Description	Case study application
The process of forgiveness	Step-by-step guidance on how to navigate the journey of forgiveness, including acknowledging pain, empathising with others, and letting go of grudges.	Sarah's healing journey. Sarah—who struggled with resentment towards her in-laws—is guided to acknowledge her pain and empathise with her in-laws' perspective. She gradually learns to let go of the grudge, feeling a sense of relief and emotional liberation.
Self-forgiveness	Techniques for individuals to practice self-forgiveness and release self-blame and guilt.	Ahmed's self-forgiveness. Ahmed—who felt intense guilt over past mistakes—is encouraged to write self-compassionate letters, forgiving himself for his errors. This practice helps Ahmed to release self-blame and build self-esteem.
Active listening and empathetic communication	Providing guidance on engaging in empathetic conversations and therapeutic interactions that reflect the principles of *rahmah*	Leyla's therapeutic sessions. Leyla's therapist practices active listening and empathetic communication, making Leiya feel understood and valued. This fosters a trusting relationship, enabling Leyla to open up about her feelings and work through her issues.
Service and acts of kindness	Encouraging individuals to engage in acts of kindness and service to others as a way of embodying *rahmah* in daily life.	Umar's community engagement. Umar—struggling with loneliness—is encouraged to volunteer at a local charity. His involvement in acts of kindness not only helps others but also enhances his sense of purpose and community connection.
Reconciliation	Insights into the process of reconciling with others after forgiveness, when appropriate and safe to do so	Fatimah and her family. Fatimah works on reconciling with her estranged sister. Through guided sessions, she learns to approach reconciliation with empathy and understanding, ultimately restoring their relationship
Coping with resistance	Strategies for dealing with resistance and challenges that may arise when attempting to forgive	Ibrahim's resistance to forgiveness. Ibrahim finds it difficult to forgive a colleague. His therapist helps him explore and address his resistance, gradually enabling him to overcome barriers to forgiveness and find peace.

when your Lord proclaimed, 'If you are grateful, I will surely increase you [in favour]; but if you deny, indeed, My punishment is severe.'" Islāmic teachings encourage believers to be grateful not only for material blessings but also for spiritual gifts such as faith, health, and guidance. The Prophet Muhammad (ﷺ) exemplified gratitude in his daily life and interactions, teaching that expressing thanks to Allāh strengthens faith and attracts divine blessings. One of his well-known sayings draws attention to this principle: "He who does not thank the people is not thankful to Allāh (Abū Dāwūd)." This *hadīth* emphasises the holistic nature of gratitude in

Islām, extending beyond personal blessings to include recognition and appreciation of others' kindness and support. Practically, Islāmic teachings recommend various acts of gratitude, such as saying "*Alhamdulillah*" (All praise is due to Allāh) in all circumstances, performing acts of charity (*sadaqah*) as a form of thanks, and reflecting on Allāh's blessings through personal supplications (*dua'h*). Gratitude in Islāmic teachings thus serves as a cornerstone of faith, fostering humility, contentment, and a deeper spiritual connection with Allāh. Prophet Muhammad (ﷺ) encourages believers to seek virtues like patience, gratitude, and hope amidst challenges. Suhaib reported that Allāh's Messenger (ﷺ) said: "Strange are the ways of a believer for there is good in every affair of his and this is not the case with anyone else except in the case of a believer for if he has an occasion to feel delight, he thanks (God), thus there is a good for him in it, and if he gets into trouble and shows resignation (and endures it patiently), there is a good for him in it." (Muslim).

Emmons and McCullough (2003) suggested that gratitude involves two steps: acknowledging a positive outcome and recognising an external source for this positive outcome. The authors pointed out that people can feel gratitude towards various sources, including God, animals, fate, coincidence, nature, the weather, and even for avoiding mistakes. Studies have found that gratitude is positively associated with various religious attributes, such as frequent engagement in religious practices, valuing religion, having a personal relationship with God, experiencing spiritual transcendence (Emmons & Kneezel, 2005) and expressing religious commitment (Rosmarin et al., 2011). The findings of a study showed that religious efficacy (experiencing answers to prayers or miracles) and having religious friends were linked to increased feelings of gratitude (Kraus et al., 2015).

Multiple studies have found that people with higher levels of dispositional gratitude exhibit better psychological health, including higher perceived social support and lower levels of stress, depression, and anxiety (Disabato et al., 2017; Froh et al., 2011; Petrocchi & Couyoumdjian, 2016). Several studies have tested whether gratitude practices can improve mental health. Activities such as the Three Good Things exercise [This activity involves not only writing down three things that went well but also identifying the causes of those good things] (Seligman et al., 2005), keeping a gratitude journal (Kerr et al., 2014), and writing gratitude letters (Wong et al., 2016). Gratitude interventions—involving brief activities to cultivate gratefulness—are among the most effective positive psychological interventions (Allen, 2018). The interventions include guidance on gratitude journaling, expressing gratitude to others, mindful gratitude practices, and incorporating gratitude rituals into daily routines. These strategies are designed to help individuals build emotional resilience and foster a deeper sense of appreciation and connectedness in their lives. The findings of a meta-analysis on the effects of gratitude interventions (Diniz et al., 2023) showed that patients who underwent gratitude interventions experienced increased feelings of gratitude, improved mental health, fewer symptoms of anxiety and depression, and a more positive mood and emotions.

*11.4.1 Integrating Gratitude (*Shukr*) into Islāmic Psychotherapy*

The integration of gratitude (*shukr*) into Islāmic psychotherapy involves practical strategies such as gratitude journaling, expressing gratitude, awareness gratitude practices, gratitude rituals, and community support. Clients can maintain a gratitude journal, starting or ending entries with "*Alhamdulillah*" and reflecting on blessings with relevant Qur'anic verses or *hadīths*. Expressing gratitude to others through phrases like "*JazakAllāhu Khairan*" and engaging in thoughtful gratitude exercises after prayers can deepen spiritual connections. Additionally, creating daily gratitude rituals, such as incorporating gratitude into morning and evening *adhkar* (remembrances), helps clients develop a consistent practice. For example, starting the day with the *dua'h* (supplication) of waking up: "*Alhamdulillah alladhi ahyana ba'da ma amatana wa ilayhin nushur*" (All praise is due to Allāh, who gave us life after He caused us to die, and unto Him is the resurrection) and ending the day with the *dua'h* before sleeping, expressing thanks for the day's blessings. Encouraging participation in community activities and support groups focused on Qur'ânic study fosters a supportive environment where gratitude is shared and emphasised. These strategies not only enhance emotional resilience but also strengthen clients' spiritual connections and overall well-being. Table 11.4 outlines the practical strategies for integrating gratitude (*shukr*) into Islāmic psychotherapy, along with case studies to illustrate the effectiveness of each strategy in real-life scenarios.

11.5 The Healing Power of Hope (*Raja*)

Hope (*raja*) in Islāmic teachings holds profound significance, permeating various aspects of faith, spirituality, and daily life. Islāmic teachings emphasise Allāh's infinite mercy and guidance. Believers are encouraged to maintain hope in Allāh's benevolence, forgiveness, and support during times of difficulty and adversity. Qur'ânic verses such as "So indeed, with hardship there is ease. Indeed, with hardship there is ease" (Surah Ash-Sharh, 94:5–6, interpretation of the meaning) remind believers of the cyclical nature of challenges and reassurance. This highlights the importance of maintaining hope and trust in Allāh's divine plan, even in the face of adversity. Central to Islāmic belief is the concept of *qadr* (Divine decree), which encompasses both predestination and free will. Believers are taught to have hope in Allāh's wisdom and plan, trusting that everything occurs according to His knowledge and decree. This belief fosters resilience and acceptance, reinforcing the notion that trials are tests of faith and opportunities for spiritual growth.

Furthermore, Islām teaches that hope is intertwined with acts of worship, such as patience (*sabr*) and gratitude (*shukr*). Patience in enduring hardships and gratitude for blessings are seen as acts of worship that strengthen one's faith and resilience. Islām encourages believers to continuously seek forgiveness (*istighfar*) and

Table 11.4 Practical strategies for integrating gratitude (*shukr*) into Islāmic psychotherapy

Strategy	Guidance	Islamic integration	Case studies
Gratitude journaling	Encourage clients to write down three things they are thankful for each day	Start or end entries with "*Alhamdulillah*" and relate blessings to Qur'ânic verses or *hadīths*	A client struggling with depression began journaling daily, integrating "*Alhamdulillah*" for each entry. Over time, their mood improved as they recognised daily blessings
Expressing gratitude	Advise clients to regularly express gratitude to others through verbal affirmations, notes, or acts	Use phrases like "*JazakAllahu Khairan*" when thanking others, invoking blessings for the recipient	A client with strained family relationships started expressing gratitude using "*JazakAllahu Khairan*," leading to improved family dynamics and emotional healing
Contemplative gratitude practices	Introduce contemplative exercises focusing on gratitude, such as breathing exercises and mental listings	Perform after prayers (*salah*), thanking Allāh for specific blessings, anchoring it in routine	A client with anxiety incorporated gratitude into their supplications, which helped them feel more grounded and less anxious, appreciating Allāh's ongoing support
Gratitude rituals	Help clients create daily rituals that incorporate gratitude, making it habitual	Integrate into morning and evening *adhkar*, using *dua'hs* to start and end the day with thanks to Allāh	A client adopted gratitude rituals in their *adhkar*, leading to a more positive outlook on life and consistent feelings of spiritual and emotional contentment
Community and spiritual support	Encourage participation in community activities and support groups focused on gratitude	Join Qur'ânic study groups to share experiences of gratitude and reflect on *shukr* in the Qur'ân and *Sunnah*	A client with social isolation joined a Qur'ânic study group, where sharing gratitude experiences fostered a sense of community and enhanced emotional resilience

repentance (*tawbah*), fostering hope in Allāh's mercy and the opportunity for spiritual renewal. The act of repentance is viewed as a means to rectify mistakes and strive towards spiritual growth. Islāmic teachings provide a comprehensive framework that extends hope beyond this worldly life to the Hereafter (*akhirah*). Believers are motivated by the promise of eternal reward in Paradise for their perseverance and good deeds, reinforcing hope and optimism in their spiritual journey. Muslims are encouraged to supplicate to Allāh in times of need and gratitude, believing in the efficacy of prayer and Allāh's responsiveness. This practice strengthens the bond between the believer and their Creator, nurturing hope and trust in divine intervention. The Islāmic teachings provide a robust foundation for believers to cultivate and sustain hope in all aspects of life, guiding them towards spiritual fulfilment and resilience.

Hope has been extensively studied in relation to mental health, with numerous studies highlighting its profound impact on psychological well-being and resilience. Hope has been identified as a powerful promoter of overall mental health and has shown potential in aiding the healing process for various conditions, including severe mental illness, suicidal ideation, depression, anxiety, and trauma-related disorders. Studies by Huen et al. (2015), Gallagher et al. (2020), Tomasulo (2020), and Sari et al. (2021) have highlighted the significant role of hope in facilitating emotional resilience and recovery from psychological challenges. Research indicates that hope contributes more positively to well-being compared to optimism or self-efficacy, as highlighted by findings from Krafft et al. (2021). Moreover, hope is associated with several psychosocial processes and outcomes that contribute to overall life satisfaction and quality of life. Studies such as those by Corn et al. (2020) and Long et al. (2020) demonstrate that individuals with higher levels of hope experience greater positive affect, emotional adjustment, illness-related coping skills, and perceptions of life as meaningful. Hope also enhances a sense of purpose in life and fosters stronger social support networks, further enriching individuals' psychological resilience and ability to navigate life's challenges effectively. These findings collectively illustrate the broad-reaching benefits of cultivating hope as a fundamental component of mental health and well-being. Research consistently shows that individuals who possess optimism and hope tend to adapt more effectively to adversity (Laranjeira & Querido, 2022). They are less prone to developing mental disorders and demonstrate behaviours that promote better health outcomes and greater life satisfaction.

11.5.1 Integrating Hope in Islāmic Psychotherapy

In the context of Islāmic psychotherapy, understanding and implementing the concept of hope (*raja*) draws upon both Islāmic teachings and psychological principles to enhance therapeutic outcomes. First, integrating hope involves recognising its deep-rooted significance in Islāmic tradition, as reflected in Qur'ânic verses and Prophetic traditions that emphasise hope as a fundamental aspect of faith and resilience in the face of adversity. From a practical standpoint, Islāmic psychotherapy can incorporate hope by guiding clients to align their goals and aspirations with Islāmic values and teachings. Therapists may encourage clients to set realistic and motivating goals that reflect their spiritual journey and personal growth, thereby nurturing a hopeful mindset. Techniques such as positive affirmations and visualisation exercises—rooted in Islāmic principles of gratitude and contemplative and reflective practices—can help clients sustain hope and motivation during therapy.

Furthermore, fostering social support and community engagement plays an important role in Islāmic psychotherapy's approach to nurturing hope. Encouraging clients to connect with supportive networks within their religious community can provide emotional reinforcement and encouragement, reinforcing the therapeutic journey toward resilience and well-being. Case studies and personal narratives within Islāmic psychotherapy serve as practical illustrations of how individuals have transformed their lives through cultivating hope. These examples demonstrate how therapeutic interventions grounded in Islāmic principles can effectively enhance resilience, emotional well-being, and spiritual growth. By integrating the concept of hope (raja) into therapeutic strategies, Islāmic psychotherapy not only addresses psychological challenges but also strengthens clients' spiritual connections and overall sense of purpose and fulfilment.

In Table 11.5, each case study title provides a brief description of the client's situation, followed by specific Islāmic interventions. The Islāmic interventions include references to Qur'ânic verses, *dua'hs* (supplication) practices, gratitude journaling, positive affirmations, contemplation, and community support through Islāmic networks. The outcomes highlight how these interventions contributed to fostering hope, resilience, and spiritual growth within each client's therapeutic journey. This structured approach demonstrates practical applications of Islāmic psychotherapy in addressing real-life challenges while integrating Islāmic principles of hope and faith.

11.6 The Wisdom of Patience (*Sabr*)

The Islāmic concept of *sabr* differs from the Christian, and possibly Western, concept of patience in its theoretical definitions. Both acknowledge patience in relation to human suffering, but the Islāmic notion of sabr plays a much more active role than its semantic Christian counterpart (Aoude, 2024). *Sabr* is a central virtue and form of worship in Islām, drawing upon Qur'ânic verses and Prophetic traditions that emphasise its significance in maintaining faith and resilience during challenges. *Sabr* has dual role as a spiritual practice and a psychological coping mechanism, aligning with contemporary research on emotional regulation, stress reduction, and overall mental well-being. Al-Ghazālī (1982) sums up the importance of patience in relation to faith in his famous work on spiritual purification. He stated that most virtues of faith are acquired through practicing patience. He compared *sabr* to a symbolic tree: *ŵaʿāifa* (the stem), *âl* (the branches), and *raja* (the fruits).

Al-Ghazālī (2003) suggested that we cannot predict when God will provide sustenance. Therefore, we must prepare ourselves by clearing our hearts, just as one prepares soil by removing weeds and planting seeds. However, all our efforts will be futile without the arrival of divine mercy, similar to how rain is essential for the growth of crops. According to Al-Ghazālī, patience is integral to faith because trials may signify Allāh's benevolent intentions for humanity. Through adversity, sins are purged, and individuals are presented with opportunities to perform good deeds. Moreover, patience entails awaiting mercy, which can manifest as temporal relief in worldly matters or as eternal blessings in the afterlife.

Patience is echoed in several verses of the Qur'ân, including "O you who have believed, seek help through patience and prayer. Indeed, Allāh is with the patient."

Table 11.5 Case studies and Islāmic interventions for instilling hope in Islāmic psychotherapy

Case study title	Description	Islamic interventions	Outcome
Overcoming loss	A client struggling with grief and loss after the death of a loved one	Guided Qur'ânic reflections, *dua'h* sessions focusing on Allāh's mercy and plan (Qur'ânic verses: 2:155–157)	Found solace and renewed hope, accepting Allāh's plan and finding spiritual peace
Addiction recovery	A client struggling with addiction and seeking spiritual and emotional healing	Incorporation of repentance (*tawbah*) and seeking forgiveness (*istighfar*), community support from Islāmic self-help groups	Achieved sobriety, found strength in faith, and maintained recovery through Islāmic spiritual practices
Loss of Faith	A client struggling with doubts and a crisis of faith, feeling disconnected from their religious beliefs	Personalised spiritual guidance sessions, exploration of Qur'ânic verses on faith (e.g., 2:286), d*ua'h* for guidance	Rediscovered faith, strengthened spiritual connection, and regained confidence in Islamic teachings
Marital discord	A couple facing communication breakdown and unresolved conflicts in their marriage	Couples therapy integrating Islāmic principles of respect and mutual understanding. Arbitration (Qur'ânic verse: 4:36)	Restored marital harmony, enhanced communication, and renewed commitment to Islāmic values in their marriage
Family conflict	A client experiencing strained relationships within the family, leading to emotional distress	Positive affirmations (using phrases like "*Insha'Allah*"), contemplative exercises during *salah* (prayer)	Improved family communication, found inner peace through spiritual reflection and forgiveness
Anxiety and depression	A client experiencing severe anxiety and depression symptoms, impacting daily functioning and well-being	Contemplation and reflective exercises after salah (prayer), recitation of Qur'ânic verses (e.g., 94:5–6), dua'h for peace and ease	Reduced anxiety and depression symptoms, found peace and emotional stability through spiritual practices
Academic struggles	A student experiencing academic setbacks and stress due to failing grades and pressure to succeed	Seeking knowledge and guidance from Qur'ânic verses (e.g., 20:114, 2:286), *dua'h* for academic success	Developed resilience, improved study habits, and achieved academic improvement through spiritual guidance
Chronic illness	A client coping with a chronic illness and its impact on daily life and spiritual well-being	Goal-setting aligned with personal values (*dua'h* for healing), community support (Islāmic support groups)	Enhanced coping strategies, strengthened faith, found support and encouragement in Islāmic community
Career transition	A client facing uncertainty and anxiety due to a career change and financial instability	Daily *dua'h* routines (*dua'h* before seeking livelihood), gratitude journaling (reflecting on blessings)	Developed resilience, pursued new opportunities confidently, trusting in Allāh's provision

(Surah Al-Baqarah 2:153, interpretation of the meaning); "And indeed, he who is patient and forgives – indeed, that is of the matters [requiring] determination." (Surah Ash-Shura 42:43**,** interpretation of the meaning); "Say, 'O My servants who have believed, fear your Lord. For those who do good in this world is good, and the earth of Allāh is spacious. Indeed, the patient will be given their reward without account.'" (Surah Az-Zumar 39:10, interpretation of the meaning).

On the virtue of patience—it is narrated by Abu Sa'id Al-Khudri (may Allāh be pleased with him)—the Prophet Muhammad (ﷺ) said: "No fatigue, nor disease, nor sorrow, nor sadness, nor hurt, nor distress befalls a Muslim, even if it were the prick he receives from a thorn, but that Allāh expiates some of his sins for that." (Bukhârî). It was narrated that Abu Hurayrah (may Allāh be pleased with him), said: "The Messenger of Allāh (ﷺ) said: 'The strong believer is better and more beloved to Allah than the weak believer, although both are good. Strive for that which will benefit you, seek the help of Allah, and do not feel helpless. If anything befalls you, do not say, "if only I had done such and such" rather say "Qaddara Allahu wa ma sha'a fa'ala (Allah has decreed and whatever he wills, He does)." For (saying) 'If' opens (the door) to the deeds of Satan." (Ibn Majah). These references from the Qur'ân and *hadīths* illustrate the Islāmic perspective on sabr as a virtue that encompasses perseverance, steadfastness, and acceptance of Allāh's decree. *Sabr* is not merely passive endurance but an active virtue that involves maintaining faith, resilience, and trust in Allāh during times of difficulty and adversity. It is seen as a means of spiritual growth and a path to earning rewards and blessings from Allāh.

Patience—in its essence—is deeply intertwined with resilience, which refers to the capacity to bounce back from adversity, challenges, or setbacks. When someone exhibits patience, they demonstrate a willingness to endure hardship with a calm disposition and steadfast resolve. This attitude fosters resilience by enabling individuals to maintain their composure and focus on finding solutions rather than succumbing to despair or frustration. The findings of a study (Schnitker, 2012) showed that patience enhances goal pursuit and satisfaction, particularly when facing obstacles. In a training programme aimed at increasing trait patience. This programme resulted in greater patience, reduced depression, and increased positive affect compared to a control group, indicating that patience can be developed (Schnitker, 2012). Patience has a significantly positive impact on stress tolerance (Al-Arja, 2023). Patience is important in organisational settings, where individuals can improve their patience through emotional self-regulation (Comer & Sekerka, 2014). Emotional self-regulation helps individuals to remain calm under pressure, avoid impulsive reactions, and sustain a positive work environment, ultimately contributing to the organization's success.

*11.6.1 Integrating Patience (*Sabr*) in Islāmic Psychotherapy*

Integrating patience (*sabr*) into Islāmic psychotherapy involves leveraging Islāmic teachings and practices to help clients develop and maintain patience as a key component of their emotional and mental health. To implement patience (*sabr*) in

Table 11.6 Case studies and Islāmic intervention

Case study	Islāmic intervention	Description
Ahmed's journey to self-awareness:	Muhasabah (Self-reflection)	Ahmed, a young professional, uses muhasabah to reflect on his actions and emotions daily. This practice helps him identify moments of impatience and develop strategies to improve his responses, enhancing his patience over time
Fatimah's academic challenges:	Reinterpreting challenges	Fatima faces academic pressure and learns to reinterpret her struggles as opportunities for growth. Inspired by Qur'ân 94:6, she manages her stress better and builds patience, leading to improved academic performance
Sarah's workplace gratitude:	Gratitude Journaling	Sarah maintains a gratitude journal, noting daily blessings and expressing "*Alhamdulillah*." this practice shifts her focus from workplace challenges to positives, making her more patient and content
Ali's contemplation:	Contemplation and supplication	Ali incorporates contemplation, supplication, and remembrance of Allāh (*dhikr*) These practices help him manage family stress more effectively, enhancing his patience and overall emotional balance
Yasir's community support:	Joining support groups	Yasir joins a Qur'ân study group after losing his job. Sharing his struggles and receiving community support helps him develop patience and resilience, aiding in his job search and emotional recovery

Islāmic psychotherapy, therapists should start with an initial assessment to evaluate the client's current level of patience and identify problematic areas. They should develop personalised therapeutic plans that incorporate Islāmic teachings and practices and conduct regular check-ins to monitor progress and adjust approaches as needed. Encouraging community engagement and participation in support groups provides additional reinforcement, while offering educational resources such as relevant Qur'ânic verses and *hadīths* emphasises the importance of patience. This integrated approach helps enhance clients' emotional and mental well-being, enabling them to navigate life's challenges with greater resilience and faith. Table 11.6 outlines case studies and Islāmic interventions.

11.7 Conclusion

This chapter on this comprehensive exploration into Islāmic teachings and psychology highlights the profound intersections of *rahmah* (compassion), *raja* (hope), *istighfar* (forgiveness), *shukr* (gratitude), and *sabr* (patience) with emotional resilience, well-being, and psychospiritual health. Each concept, rooted deeply in Islāmic tradition, resonates with contemporary psychological frameworks, illustrating their universal relevance and transformative potential. By providing practical strategies for nurturing these virtues, the chapter empowers readers to integrate them into their daily lives and therapeutic interactions.

In essence, the contents of the chapter not only bridge the gap between Islāmic teachings and modern psychology but also equip clinicians with invaluable tools to enhance their professional practice in Islāmic psychotherapy.

References

Abū Dāwūd. Sunan Abi Dāwūd 4811. In-book reference: Book 43, Hadith 39. English translation: Book 42, Hadith 4793. Sahih (Al-Albani). https://sunnah.com/abudawud:4811

Al-Arja, N. S. (2023). Patience and its relationship to stress tolerance in relation to demographic factors of the medical system in Bethlehem Governorate during the COVID-19 pandemic. *Frontiers in Psychology, 14*, 1059589. https://doi.org/10.3389/fpsyg.2023.1059589

Al-Ghazālī, A. H. M. (1982). *Ihya Ulum -id-Din* (M. F. Karim, Trans.) (Vol. 1–IV). Kitab Bhavan.

Al-Ghazālī, A. H. M. (2003). *On Patience and Gratitude* (L. Bakhtiar, Trans.). Kazi Publications.

Allen, S. (2018). *The science of gratitude*. A white paper prepared for the John Templeton Foundation by the Greater Good Science Center at UC Berkeley. https://ggsc.berkeley.edu/images/uploads/GGSC-JTF_White_Paper-GratitudeFINAL.pdf?_ga=2.82610261.2142947331.1637096170-1362583773.163459086. Accessed 25 June 2024.

Aoude, S. (2024). *The concept of sabr in Islāmic spiritual care – Definitions and contextual adaptions*. https://www.academia.edu/25631939/The_concept_of_sabr_in_Islāmic_spiritual_care_definitions_and_contextual_adaptions. Accessed 26 June 2024.

Breines, J. G., Thoma, M. V., Gianferante, D., Hanlin, L., Chen, X., & Rohleder, N. (2014). Self-compassion as a predictor of interleukin-6 response to acute psychosocial stress. *Brain, Behavior, and Immunity, 37*, 109–114. https://doi.org/10.1016/j.bbi.2013.11.006

Bukhârî. Sahih al- Bukhârî 5641, 5642. In-book reference: Book 75, Hadith 2. USC-MSA web (English) reference: Vol. 7, Book 70, Hadith 545. https://sunnah.com/bukhari:5641

Comer, D. R., & Sekerka, E. L. (2014). Taking time for patience in organizations. *Journal of Management Development, 33*(1), 6–23. https://doi.org/10.1108/JMD-11-2013-0132

Corn, B. W., Feldman, D. B., & Wexler, I. (2020). The science of hope. *The Lancet. Oncology, 21*(9), e452–e459. https://doi.org/10.1016/S1470-2045(20)30210-2

Diniz, G., Korkes, L., Tristão, L. S., Pelegrini, R., Bellodi, P. L., & Bernardo, W. M. (2023). The effects of gratitude interventions: A systematic review and meta-analysis. *Einstein (Sao Paulo, Brazil), 21*, eRW0371. https://doi.org/10.31744/einstein_journal/2023RW0371

Disabato, D. J., Kashdan, T. B., Short, J. L., & Jarden, A. (2017). What predicts positive life events that influence the course of depression? A longitudinal examination of gratitude and meaning in life. *Cognitive Therapy and Research, 41*(3), 444–458. https://doi.org/10.1007/s10608-016-9785-x

Emmons, R. A., & Kneezel, T. T. (2005). Giving thanks: Spiritual and religious correlates of gratitude. *Journal of Psychology and Christianity, 24*(2), 140–148.

Emmons, R. A., & McCullough, M. E. (2003). Counting blessings versus burdens: An experimental investigation of gratitude and subjective well-being in daily life. *Journal of Personality and Social Psychology, 84*(2), 377–389. https://doi.org/10.1037/0022-3514.84.2.377

Enrigh, B. (2017). Cited in K. Weir. Forgiveness can improve mental and physical health. American Psychological Association, 48,1,30. https://www.apa.org/monitor/2017/01/cecorner#:~:text=Research%20has%20shown%20that%20forgiveness%20is%20linked%20to,fewer%20physical%20health%20symptoms%20and%20lower%20mortality%20rates. Accessed 25 June 2024.

Enright, R. D. (2001). *Forgiveness is a choice: A step-by-step process for resolving anger and restoring hope*. American Psychological Association.

Froh, J. J., Emmons, R. A., Card, N. A., Bono, G., & Wilson, J. A. (2011). Gratitude and the reduced costs of materialism in adolescents. *Journal of Happiness Studies, 12*(2), 289–302. https://doi.org/10.1007/s10902-010-9195-9

Gallagher, M. W., Long, L. J., & Phillips, C. A. (2020). Hope, optimism, self-efficacy, and posttraumatic stress disorder: A meta-analytic review of the protective effects of positive expectancies. *Journal of Clinical Psychology, 76*(3), 329–355. https://doi.org/10.1002/jclp.22882

Homan, K. J., & Sirois, F. M. (2017). Self-compassion and physical health: Exploring the roles of perceived stress and health-promoting behaviors. *Health Psychology Open, 4*(2), 2055102917729542. https://doi.org/10.1177/2055102917729542

Huen, J. M., Ip, B. Y., Ho, S. M., & Yip, P. S. (2015). Hope and hopelessness: The role of hope in buffering the impact of hopelessness on suicidal ideation. *PloS One, 10*(6), e0130073. https://doi.org/10.1371/journal.pone.0130073

Ibn Majah. Sunan Ibn Majah 79. In-book reference: Introduction, Hadith 79. English translation: Vol. 1, Book 1, Hadith 79. Sahih (Darussalam). https://sunnah.com/ibnmajah:79

Kerr, S. L., O'Donovan, A., & Pepping, C. A. (2014). Can gratitude and kindness interventions enhance well-being in a clinical sample? *Journal of Happiness Studies, 16*(1), 17–36. https://doi.org/10.1007/s10902-013-9492-1

Krafft, A. M., Guse, T., & Maree, D. (2021). Distinguishing perceived hope and dispositional optimism: Theoretical foundations and empirical findings beyond future expectancies and cognition. *Journal of Well-Being Assessment, 2021*(2021), 1–21. https://doi.org/10.1007/s41543-020-00030-4

Kraus, R., Desmond, S. A., & Palmer, Z. D. (2015). Being thankful: Examining the relationship between young adult religiosity and gratitude. *Journal of Religion and Health, 54*(4), 1331–1344. https://doi.org/10.1007/s10943-014-9923-2

Laranjeira, C., & Querido, A. (2022). Hope and optimism as an opportunity to improve the "positive mental health" demand. *Frontiers in Psychology, 13*, 827320. https://doi.org/10.3389/fpsyg.2022.827320

Lawler-Row, K. A., Karremans, J. C., Scott, C., Edlis-Matityahou, M., & Edwards, L. (2008). Forgiveness, physiological reactivity and health: The role of anger. *International Journal of Psychophysiology: Official Journal of The International Organization of Psychophysiology, 68*(1), 51–58. https://doi.org/10.1016/j.ijpsycho.2008.01.001

Long, K. N., Kim, E. S., Chen, Y., Wilson, M. F., Worthington, E., Jr., & VanderWeele, T. J. (2020). The role of hope in subsequent health and well-being for older adults: An outcome-wide longitudinal approach. *Global Epidemiology, 2*, 100018. https://doi.org/10.1016/j.gloepi.2020.100018

MacBeth, A., & Gumley, A. (2012). Exploring compassion: A meta-analysis of the association between self-compassion and psychopathology. *Clinical Psychology Review, 32*(6), 545–552. https://doi.org/10.1016/j.cpr.2012.06.003

Matos, M., Duarte, C., Duarte, J., Pinto-Gouveia, J., Petrocchi, N., Basran, J., et al. (2017). Psychological and physiological effects of compassionate mind training: A pilot randomized controlled study. *Mindfulness, 8*, 1699–1712. https://doi.org/10.1007/s12671-017-0745-7

Matos, M., McEwan, K., Kanovský, M., et al. (2022). Compassion protects mental health and social safeness during the COVID-19 pandemic across 21 countries. *Mindfulness, 13*, 863–880. https://doi.org/10.1007/s12671-021-01822-2

Muris, P., & Petrocchi, N. (2017). Protection or vulnerability? A meta-analysis of the relations between the positive and negative components of self-compassion and psychopathology. *Clinical Psychology & Psychotherapy, 24*(2), 373–383. https://doi.org/10.1002/cpp.2005

Muslim. Sahih Muslim 2999. In-book reference: Book 55, Hadith 82. USC-MSA web (English) reference: Book 42, Hadith 7138. https://sunnah.com/muslim:2999

Pace, T. W., Negi, L. T., Adame, D. D., Cole, S. P., Sivilli, T. I., Brown, T. D., Issa, M. J., & Raison, C. L. (2009). Effect of compassion meditation on neuroendocrine, innate immune and behavioral responses to psychosocial stress. *Psychoneuroendocrinology, 34*(1), 87–98. https://doi.org/10.1016/j.psyneuen.2008.08.011

Petrocchi, N., & Couyoumdjian, A. (2016). The impact of gratitude on depression and anxiety: The mediating role of criticizing, attacking, and reassuring the self. *Self and Identity, 15*(2), 191–205. https://doi.org/10.1080/15298868.2015.1095794

Reed, G. L., & Enright, R. D. (2006). The effects of forgiveness therapy on depression, anxiety, and posttraumatic stress for women after spousal emotional abuse. *Journal of Consulting and Clinical Psychology, 74*(5), 920–929. https://doi.org/10.1037/0022-006X.74.5.920

Rosmarin, D. H., Pirutinsky, S., Cohen, A. B., Galler, Y., & Krumrei, E. J. (2011). Grateful to God or just plain grateful? A comparison of religious and general gratitude. *The Journal of Positive Psychology, 6*(5), 389–396. https://doi.org/10.1080/17439760.2011.596557

Sari, S. P., Agustin, M., Wijayanti, D. Y., Sarjana, W., Afrikhah, U., & Choe, K. (2021). Mediating effect of hope on the relationship between depression and recovery in persons with Schizophrenia. *Frontiers in Psychiatry, 12*, 627588. https://doi.org/10.3389/fpsyt.2021.627588

Schnitker, S. A. (2012). An examination of patience and well-being. *The Journal of Positive Psychology, 7*(4), 263–280. https://doi.org/10.1080/17439760.2012.697185

Seligman, M. E. P., Steen, T. A., Park, N., & Peterson, C. (2005). Positive psychology progress: Empirical validation of interventions. *American Psychologist, 60*(5), 410–421. https://doi.org/10.1037/0003-066X.60.5.410

Tirmidhî. Jami' at-Tirmidhî 2024. In-book reference: Book 27, Hadith 130. English translation: Vol. 4, Book 1, Hadith 2024. Sahih (Darussalam). https://sunnah.com/tirmidhi:2024

Tomasulo, D. (2020). *Learned hopefulness: The power of positivity to overcome depression*. New Harbinger Publications.

Toussaint, L. M., Kamble, S., Marschall, J. C., & Duggi, D. B. (2015). The effects of brief prayer on the experience of forgiveness: An American and Indian comparison. *International Journal of Psychology, 51*(4), 288–295. https://doi.org/10.1002/ijop.12139

Toussaint, L., Shields, G. S., Dorn, G., & Slavich, G. M. (2016a). Effects of lifetime stress exposure on mental and physical health in young adulthood: How stress degrades and forgiveness protects health. *Journal of Health Psychology, 21*(6), 1004–1014. https://doi.org/10.1177/1359105314544132

Toussaint, L. L., Shields, G. S., & Slavich, G. M. (2016b). Forgiveness, stress, and health: A 5-week dynamic parallel process study. *Annals of Behavioral Medicine: A Publication of the Society of Behavioral Medicine, 50*(5), 727–735. https://doi.org/10.1007/s12160-016-9796-6

Wade, N. G., Hoyt, W. T., Kidwell, J. E. M., & Worthington, E. L., Jr. (2014). Efficacy of psychotherapeutic interventions to promote forgiveness: A meta-analysis. *Journal of Consulting and Clinical Psychology, 82*(1), 154–170. https://doi.org/10.1037/a0035268

Wilson, C. A., Mackintosh, K., Power, K., & Chan, W. Y. S. (2019). Effectiveness of self-compassion related therapies: A systematic review and meta-analysis. *Mindfulness, 10*, 979–995. https://doi.org/10.1007/s12671-018-1037-6

Wong, J., Owen, J., Gabana, N. T., Brown, J. W., Mcinnis, S., Toth, P., & Gilman, L. (2016). Does gratitude writing improve the mental health of psychotherapy clients? Evidence from a randomized controlled trial. *Psychotherapy Research, 28*(2), 192–202. https://doi.org/10.1080/10503307.2016.116933

Zessin, U., Dickhäuser, O., & Garbade, S. (2015). The relationship between self-compassion and well-being: A meta-analysis. *Applied Psychology. Health and Well-Being, 7*(3), 340–364. https://doi.org/10.1111/aphw.12051

Chapter 12
Synthesis and Consolidation of Spirituality and Islāmic Psychotherapy

12.1 Introduction

The integration of spirituality and psychotherapy is increasingly recognised as a significant component of holistic mental health care, addressing not only the psychological needs of individuals but also their spiritual health. Islāmic psychotherapy is rooted in the teachings of Islāmic spirituality, which emphasise the importance of balance and harmony between the mind, body, and soul. This integration offers a comprehensive approach to mental health that encompasses spiritual practices and beliefs. This holistic approach is evident in the Qur'ânic verse, "Indeed, the soul is a persistent enjoiner of evil, except those upon which my Lord has mercy. Indeed, my Lord is Forgiving and Merciful" (Yusuf 12:53, interpretation of the meaning). This verse highlights the struggle within the human soul and the need for divine mercy and forgiveness, underlining the significance of spiritual guidance in achieving psychological health. The aim of this chapter is to consolidate the various aspects of spirituality and Islāmic psychotherapy explored throughout the book, providing a comprehensive synthesis and consolidation of the key principles. This chapter serves as a culmination of these insights, offering a roadmap for individuals seeking to integrate these principles into their professional and clinical practices and to effectively address the mental health needs of Muslim clients, acknowledging and respecting their spiritual beliefs and practices.

12.2 A Synthesis on Integrating Islāmic Spirituality in Psychotherapy

In exploring the intersection of Islāmic spirituality and psychotherapy, this comprehensive synthesis delves into fundamental principles aimed at fostering holistic healing and growth. The journey begins by acknowledging spirituality's important

G. H. Rassool, *Exploring the Intersection of Islāmic Spirituality and Psychotherapy*,
https://doi.org/10.1007/978-3-031-72724-5_12

role in enhancing mental health outcomes, contrasting with critiques of a "soulless psychology" that neglects spiritual dimensions. Emphasising a culturally sensitive approach, the integration of Islāmic perspectives underlines the importance of *tawhīd* (monotheism) as foundational to Islāmic psychotherapy, aligning therapeutic practices with core beliefs articulated in the six articles of faith. Decolonising psychology knowledge emerges as a critical theme, advocating for a globalised understanding that incorporates diverse cultural and religious perspectives. This paradigm shift aims to challenge Western dominance in psychological theory and practice, promoting inclusivity and respect for Islāmic spirituality. The anatomy of Islāmic psychotherapy is then explored, delineating its epistemological, ontological, and axiological underpinnings. This spiritually integrated therapy framework ensures that therapeutic interventions resonate authentically with Islāmic principles, addressing the holistic needs of individuals within the frsework of an Islāmic worldview.

Central to this synthesis is the concept of *fitrah*, which explains the innate spiritual nature of human behaviour as articulated in Qur'ânic verses and *hadīths*. Understanding and realigning the *fitrah* is crucial for therapists seeking to address spiritual dimensions in their clients' psychological health. The psychology of the self deepens this exploration, examining the multifaceted components of *nafs* (self), *rûh* (spirit), *qalb* (heart), and *'aql* (intellect). These discussions highlight the interplay between spiritual and psychological aspects of human identity, providing insights into therapeutic strategies that honour and integrate these dimensions. Further insights are collected from evaluating psychological approaches vis-à-vis Islāmic spirituality. Analysing psychoanalytic, client-centred, and cognitive-behavioural therapies reveals both congruences and tensions with Islāmic beliefs. Post-modern therapies such as solution-focused brief therapy and narrative therapy offer alternative frameworks that can be adapted to align more closely with Islāmic teachings, emphasising solutions rooted in faith and narrative healing. The healing power of Islāmic principle, compassion (*rahmah*), forgiveness (*istighfar*), gratitude (*shukr*), hope (*raja*), and patience (*sabr*) is a focal point of integration within Islāmic psychotherapy. Each principle is explored for its psychological and spiritual benefits, offering practical guidance on their implementation in therapeutic settings. This holistic approach emphasises resilience, emotional well-being, and personal growth through embracing these foundational virtues.

In conclusion, this synthesis stresses the transformative potential of integrating Islāmic spirituality into psychotherapeutic practice. By knitting together these diverse threads, from theological foundations to psychological application, the synthesis provides a roadmap for practitioners to navigate the complexities of human experience with sensitivity to spiritual dimensions. Embracing Islāmic principles within psychotherapy not only enriches therapeutic outcomes but also nurtures a deeper understanding of faith-based approaches to healing and growth in contemporary contexts.

12.3 Integrating Faith and Psychological Insights

Integrating faith with psychological insights fosters a dynamic interaction that enhances both personal and professional growth and healing. This holistic approach acknowledges that faith provides a spiritual foundation rich with beliefs, values, and practices that offer support and guidance through life's challenges. These faith-based elements can be incorporated into the practice of Islāmic psychotherapy, offering a spiritual compass that aligns with psychological care. Equally, psychological insights bring valuable tools and frameworks that help individuals understand human behaviour, emotions, and mental processes. These insights facilitate the identification and management of psychological issues, providing evidence-based practices for mental health care. Religion-adapted cognitive behavioural therapy, for example, has been shown to be effective in treating a variety of mental health disorders (de Abreu Costa & Moreira-Almeida, 2022; Rajaei, 2010), and its principles can be integrated with Islāmic teachings to enhance therapeutic outcomes. This approach uses a combination of behavioural activation, contemplation, or prayer to facilitate cognitive restructuring, using religious values and coping strategies to support therapeutic outcomes.

When faith and psychological insights are combined, they create a comprehensive and balanced strategy for addressing both internal struggles, such as anxiety, depression, and emotional turmoil, and external challenges, such as relationship issues and stressors from the environment. This integrated approach not only aims at symptom relief but also fosters deeper personal growth, resilience, and a sense of purpose and meaning in life. In the context of Islāmic psychotherapy, this synergy enables practitioners to offer a more complete and culturally sensitive form of care, ultimately leading to more effective and enduring outcomes for clients. For example, research by Azhar and Varma (1995) demonstrated that integrating Islāmic principles with psychotherapy improved treatment outcomes for Muslim patients with depression. Islāmic psychotherapy integrates both faith and psychological insights to synthesise their respective strengths in promoting holistic healing and growth. This approach ensures that clients receive comprehensive care that integrate their spiritual beliefs alongside addressing their psychological needs. At its core, integrating faith and psychology involves recognising the interplay between spiritual beliefs and psychological well-being. Faith provides a lens or worldview through which individuals interpret their experiences and find meaning in trials and tribulations. For instance, beliefs about divine mercy during times of hardship can offer solace and resilience. Psychological insights, such as cognitive-behavioural techniques or contemplative practices, complement these beliefs by providing practical methods to manage stress, regulate emotions, and cultivate stress regulation and management.

Practically, this integration can manifest in various ways. For example, someone experiencing anxiety may draw strength from prayers or spiritual rituals while also employing relaxation techniques recommended by psychology. Similarly, individuals navigating grief may find comfort in religious rituals and community support, alongside psychological strategies for processing loss and adjusting to new realities. These examples illustrate how Islāmic spiritual interventions, including modified cognitive behaviour therapy (CBT) and client-centred therapy (CCT), can be effectively integrated with various psychological therapies to support mental, emotional, and spiritual well-being. Integrating Islāmic psychotherapy and spiritual interventions can provide a holistic approach to mental health, incorporating religious beliefs and practices with psychological techniques. Table 12.1 illustrates practical examples of spiritual interventions in Islāmic psychotherapy,

Table 12.1 Integrating spiritual interventions in Islāmic psychotherapy

Area	Description	Example
Islāmic -Modified Cognitive Behaviour Therapy (I-CBT)	Adapting I-CBT techniques to include Islāmic principles and practices	Using CBT to challenge negative thoughts, behavioural activation, contemplation, or prayer to facilitate cognitive restructuring and reframing
Islāmic -Modified CCT	Client-Cantered Therapy that integrates Islāmic principles and practices	Encouraging self-discovery and personal growth through a non-judgmental, empathetic approach, while aligning with Islāmic teachings on compassion and understanding.
Narrative therapy	Using stories from the Qur'ân and *hadīths* to facilitate personal growth and healing	Narrative therapy sessions that focus on the stories of Prophets to draw parallels and find solutions to personal struggles
Hope therapy	Encouraging hope and optimism through Islāmic teachings and practices	Hope therapy that involves reading and reflecting on hopeful verses from the Qur'ân and *hadīths* and practicing regular supplications for guidance and support
Islāmically oriented family therapy	Integrating Islāmic values and practices within family therapy sessions	Family therapy that includes discussions on Islāmic values, regular family prayers, and stories from the Qur'ân to improve family dynamics
Salat (prayer)	Incorporating the act of regular prayer as a means of connecting with Allāh and finding peace	Encouraging clients to perform *salat* five times a day as a form of meditation and stress relief
Dua'h (supplications)	Using personal prayers and supplications to seek help and comfort	Teaching clients to make dua'h after formal prayers and into daily routines Extra supplications during difficult times, focusing on seeking Allāh's support and guidance
Dhikr (remembrance of Allāh)	Repeating phrases that remind one of Allāh's presence and mercy	Integrating *dhikr* into daily routines to maintain mindfulness and reduce anxiety
Recitation of the Qur'ân	Reading and reflecting on the Qur'ân for guidance and comfort	Encouraging clients to recite and contemplate the Qur'ân daily as a form of spiritual nourishment and psychological support

(continued)

Table 12.1 (continued)

Area	Description	Example
Fasting (*sawm-nawafil*)	Using voluntary fasting as a means of spiritual discipline and mental clarity	Encouraging clients to fast regularly (beyond Ramadan) to develop self-control and spiritual focus
Ruqyah (Incantations)	Reciting specific verses from the Qur'ân for protection and healing	Including *ruqyah* in therapy for clients experiencing spiritual distress or evil eye, Jinn possession of black magic
Islāmic contemplation practices (*tafakkur*)	Reflective practices to enhance spiritual connection and mindfulness	Practicing Tafakkur (deep thinking) by reflecting on the signs of Allah in nature and personal experiences to gain spiritual insights and emotional clarity
Pastoral care (*ruhani* care)	Spiritual support provided by religious/faith (*Imams*) leaders with psychological training	*Imâms* trained in therapy or counselling who use Qur'ânic stories and metaphors to help individuals understand and overcome their challenges
Crisis intervention	Providing immediate psychological and spiritual support in times of crisis.	An *Imâm* offering crisis intervention that includes calming techniques and guided *dua'h* for comfort and support.
Ummah support	Islāmic organisations offering comprehensive mental health programmes with spiritual elements	A mosque providing a mental health clinic that includes counselling, group therapy, and ruqyah sessions for healing
Retreats	Organising retreats that combine spiritual and psychological healing practices	A weekend retreat for trauma survivors that includes spiritual reflection, *ruqyah*, and therapeutic workshops on hope and resilience

Key spiritual interventions and spirituality in Islāmic psychotherapy

Key elements	**Description**	**Benefits**	**Applications**
Tawakkul (reliance on Allah)	Developing trust in Allah's wisdom and accepting His decree with contentment	Reduces anxiety, fosters peace of mind, and increases resilience	Incorporate supplications, discussions on divine trust, and reflections on stories of the Prophets
Dhikr (remembrance of Allah)	Engaging in regular remembrance and meditation on Allah's names and attributes	Promotes mindfulness, emotional stability, and spiritual growth	Practice daily adhkar, guided meditations, and integration of dhikr in daily routines
Istighfar (seeking forgiveness)	Regularly seeking Allah's forgiveness for one's sins and shortcomings	Facilitates emotional cleansing, reduces guilt, and enhances spiritual well-being	Encourage daily recitations of istighfar, reflective practices on past actions, and setting intentions for self-improvement
Salah (prayer)	Performing the five daily prayers with mindfulness and sincerity	Provides structure, spiritual connection, and emotional relief	Ensure regular and timely prayers, focusing on mindfulness and presence during salah, and incorporating supplications

Quranic reflection	Reflecting on the meanings and teachings of the Quran to find guidance and solace	Provides spiritual guidance, emotional comfort, and moral direction	Facilitate Quranic study sessions, personal reflections on verses, and applying Quranic teachings to personal life
Supplications (dua)	Engaging in personal prayers to seek Allah's guidance and help in times of need	Enhances spiritual connection, emotional relief, and hope	Encourage clients to regularly make personal supplications, especially during times of distress. Facilitate learning specific supplications for different situations
Ruqyah (spiritual healing)	Using Quranic recitations and prayers for spiritual healing and protection from harm	Provides emotional comfort, spiritual protection, and mental peace	Teach clients specific verses and prayers for Ruqyah, encouraging its use for personal and family well-being. Facilitate Ruqyah sessions when needed
Islamic contemplation (tafakkur)	Deep reflection on the signs of Allah in creation and one's own experiences	Enhances spiritual awareness, emotional resilience, and inner peace	Guide clients through contemplative practices, encouraging reflection on nature, life events, and personal growth in light of Islamic teachings
Sadaqah (charity)	Giving charity to help those in need, whether through money, time, or effort	Increases feelings of purpose, empathy, and spiritual satisfaction	Encourage clients to engage in regular acts of charity, helping them find opportunities to give back to their community, fostering a sense of fulfilment and gratitude.

Implementation in Therapy

1. **Initial Assessment**: Evaluate the client's current spiritual practices and areas where integration can be beneficial.
2. **Personalised Plans**: Develop individualised therapeutic plans that incorporate specific Islāmic teachings and practices.
3. **Regular Check-ins**: Conduct regular sessions to monitor progress, provide support, and adjust practices as needed.
4. **Community Engagement**: Encourage clients to participate in community activities and support groups for reinforcement.
5. **Educational Resources**: Provide clients with resources such as Qur'ânic verses, Hadiths, and literature that emphasise the importance of these principles.

By following these guidelines, Islamic psychotherapy can effectively enhance clients' emotional and mental well-being, helping them navigate life's challenges with greater resilience and faith.

12.4 Toolbox on Strategies for Integrating Spirituality and Psychotherapy

This section of this chapter provides a comprehensive toolbox for integrating spirituality and psychotherapy for Islāmic psychotherapists, emphasising a holistic approach to therapy. The toolbox includes strategies such as self-reflection exercises, where therapists engage in guided journaling and reflective prayer to explore their beliefs and emotions, enhancing self-awareness and alignment with spiritual values. Professional and continuing development plans are developed, incorporating faith-based principles and actionable steps to achieve professional and personal goals. Islāmic meditation and contemplation practices, like *dhikr*-based meditation and breath awareness, are taught to promote emotional balance and self-care. Supervisors guide therapists in setting goals, creating vision boards, and establishing accountability partners to support goal attainment. Building a supportive professional community through peer support groups and mentorship programs is encouraged. Additionally, ethical and professional development will be emphasised, with discussions on case studies and ethical dilemmas informed by both professional standards and Islāmic values. This toolbox aims to provide Islāmic psychotherapists with the resources and strategies needed to offer spiritually and psychologically integrated care. Table 12.2 presents a toolbox on strategies for integrating spirituality and psychological health for Islāmic psychotherapist.

12.5 Reflecting on the Transformative Journey

This section invites readers to reflect on their professional transformative journey at the intersection of spirituality and psychotherapy. It encourages them to revisit the key insights, practices, and experiences they have encountered throughout the book and consider how they can apply this knowledge and these insights to their clinical practice. By engaging in this reflective process, readers can gain a deeper understanding of their growth and the impact of integrating spirituality into psychotherapeutic practices. Table 12.3 outlines the reflective activities on the transformation journey related to integrating spirituality with psychotherapy.

These reflective activities guide Islāmic psychotherapists in integrating spirituality into their professional practice. Activities such as spiritual self-assessment and personal spiritual practices encourage therapists to examine and enhance their own spiritual beliefs and practices, considering their influence on their professional work. By reflecting on personal spiritual practices like regular prayer, reading the Qur'ân, and engaging in community service, therapists can understand how maintaining their spiritual well-being supports their ability to help clients and model these practices in therapy. Other activities like case study analysis and exploring Qur'ânic verses in a therapeutic context help therapists apply spiritual insights to their practice. Through detailed case analysis, therapists can observe the impact of

Table 12.2 Toolbox on strategies for integrating spirituality and psychological health for Islāmic psychotherapist

Tool	Description	Example
Islāmic Practices	Incorporating traditional Islāmic spiritual practices for psychological and spiritual health	*Salat* (Prayer), d*ua'h* (supplications), *dhikr* (remembrance of Allāh), Fasting (*nawafil, sawm*), ruqyah (incantations), recitation of the Qur'ân
Professional development	Strategies for creating personalised growth plans and professional development that incorporate faith-based principles and psychological health strategies.	Faith-based goal setting. Continuing professional education in Islāmic studies. Action steps, progress tracking
Islāmic contemplation and reflective practices	Reflective practices to enhance spiritual connection and guided exercises for self-reflection and introspection, emotions, and aspirations	Practicing tafakkur (deep thinking), muraqabah (spiritual watchfulness) dhikr-based meditation, guided visualisation to promote spiritual insights and emotional regulation.
Therapeutic techniques	Integrating psychological techniques with Islāmic principles	Islāmic-modified CBT, Islāmic-modified CCT, Hope Therapy, Narrative Therapy, Islāmic modified Solution Focus Brief Therapy, and Islāmic modified Family Therapy
Clinical supervision	Guided exercises for self-reflection and introspection for therapists during supervision sessions	Supervisors guiding therapists in reflective journaling about their beliefs, emotions, and professional aspirations to enhance self-awareness and align their practice with their spiritual values
Ethical and professional development	Fostering a deep understanding of ethical guidelines and professional development within an Islāmic framework	Discussing case studies and ethical dilemmas during supervision sessions, considering both professional standards and Islāmic values to ensure therapists provide ethically sound and spiritually congruent care
Community and support	Insights into the importance of building a supportive community and seeking guidance from mentors, therapists, or spiritual leaders.	Peer support groups, mentorship programmes and therapy.

spiritual integration on the therapeutic process and outcomes. Additionally, creating client-centred spiritual exploration exercises and reflecting on ethical considerations unique to Islāmic psychotherapy ensures that therapeutic interventions are culturally sensitive and ethically sound. These activities collectively enhance therapists' understanding of the interplay between spirituality and psychotherapy, enriching their professional identity and practice.

Table 12.3 Reflective activities on the transformation journey related to integrating spirituality with psychotherapy

Reflective activity	Description
Spiritual self-assessment	Conduct a self-assessment of your spiritual beliefs and practices. Reflect on how these personal elements influence your professional work. Write a summary of your spiritual journey, highlighting key moments of growth and their alignment with your therapeutic practice. This helps understand the interplay between personal spirituality and professional identity.
Personal spiritual practices	Reflect on your own spiritual practices as an Islāmic psychotherapist. Consider how activities such as regular prayer, reading Qur'ân, and engaging in community service influence your professional life. Write about how maintaining your spiritual well-being enhances your ability to support clients and how you can model these practices in a therapeutic setting.
Client-centred spiritual exploration	Develop a reflective exercise focused on exploring clients' personal spiritual beliefs and practices within an Islāmic context. Create open-ended questions that encourage clients to share their spiritual experiences, challenges, and aspirations. Reflect on how understanding clients' spiritual lives can inform and enrich your therapeutic interventions, ensuring they are culturally and spiritually sensitive.
Qur'ânic verses and therapeutic application	Select a few Qur'ânic verses that resonate with themes or challenges in your therapeutic practice. Reflect on how these verses can be interpreted and applied within a psychotherapeutic context. Write a brief account on how these spiritual insights can guide your therapeutic approach, offering specific examples of integrating these teachings into client sessions.
Ethical considerations in Islamic psychotherapy	Reflect on the ethical considerations unique to integrating Islāmic principles into psychotherapy. Consider issues such as maintaining professional boundaries, respecting clients' autonomy, and navigating potential conflicts between religious teachings and psychological practice. Write a reflective piece on upholding ethical standards while incorporating Islamic values into therapy sessions and identify strategies for addressing any dilemmas that may arise.
Case study analysis	Review a recent case where you consciously incorporated spiritual practices or perspectives. Write a detailed analysis of the case, focusing on how spiritual integration impacted the therapeutic process and outcomes. Consider the client's response, your reactions, and any noticeable shifts in the therapeutic relationship. This exercise enhances awareness of the practical effects of merging spirituality with psychotherapy.
Interdisciplinary learning	Reflect on the potential benefits of interdisciplinary learning by engaging with Islāmic scholars, religious leaders, and other professionals who work at the intersection of spirituality and mental health. Consider how collaborating with these individuals can enhance your understanding of Islamic teachings and their application in psychotherapy. Write about the insights gained from these interactions and how they can inform and improve your therapeutic practice
Journaling personal insights	Set aside time each week to journal your thoughts and feelings about integrating spirituality into your psychotherapy practice. Reflect on specific instances where spirituality played a role in your sessions, noting any challenges, breakthroughs, or insights. This practice can help you track your progress, identify patterns, and gain a deeper understanding of how spiritual elements influence your therapeutic work

(continued)

Table 12.3 (continued)

Reflective activity	Description
Peer discussion groups	Organise or join a discussion group with fellow practitioners who are also exploring the integration of spirituality and psychotherapy. Share experiences, challenges, and successes with each other. This collaborative reflection can provide new perspectives, support, and ideas for incorporating spirituality into your clinical practice more effectively.
Client feedback collection	Seek feedback from clients regarding their experiences with the spiritual aspects of your therapy sessions. Prepare a set of questions that explore their perceptions of how spirituality was integrated into their therapy and its impact on their healing process. Reflect on this feedback to gain insights into the effectiveness of your approach and identify areas for improvement.

12.6 Conclusion

Integrating Islāmic spirituality into psychotherapy represents a holistic approach that enables the interconnectedness of spiritual and psychological well-being. Throughout this exploration, we have examined various strategies and reflections, emphasising the profound impact of merging these two domains. By synthesising Islāmic spiritual principles with therapeutic practices, Islāmic psychotherapists can offer a more culturally and spiritually attuned approach to their clients. This integration not only enhances the therapeutic relationship but also fosters a deeper sense of healing and personal growth for both the therapist and the client. As we conclude this journey, it is essential to recognise the transformative potential of reflecting on and incorporating spirituality into psychotherapy. The reflective activities outlined provide a comprehensive framework for continuous self-assessment, personal spiritual practice, and ethical consideration, ensuring that therapists remain grounded and effective in their practice. By embracing this integrated approach, Islāmic psychotherapists can better support their clients in achieving holistic health, ultimately enriching their professional identity and the therapeutic process. This ongoing commitment to integrating spirituality with psychotherapy is a testimony to the dynamic and evolving nature of the field, promising a more profound and impactful practice for the future. The future is bright!

References

Azhar, M. Z., & Varma, S. L. (1995). Religious psychotherapy in depressive patients. *Psychotherapy and Psychosomatics, 63*(3–4), 165–168. https://doi.org/10.1159/000288954

de Abreu Costa, M., & Moreira-Almeida, A. (2022). Religion-adapted cognitive behavioral therapy: A review and description of techniques. *Journal of Religion and Health, 61*(1), 443–466. https://doi.org/10.1007/s10943-021-01345-z

Rajaei, A. R. (2010). Religious cognitive-emotional therapy: A new form of psychotherapy. *Iranian Journal of Psychiatry, 5*(3), 81–87.

Index

A

B

C

D

E

F

G

H

G. H. Rassool, *Exploring the Intersection of Islamic Spirituality and Psychotherapy*,
https://doi.org/10.1007/978-3-031-72724-5

S

T

SPRINGER NATURE

GPSR Compliance

The European Union's (EU) General Product Safety Regulation (GPSR) is a set of rules that requires consumer products to be safe and our obligations to ensure this.

If you have any concerns about our products, you can contact us on ProductSafety@springernature.com

In case Publisher is established outside the EU, the EU authorized representative is:

Springer Nature Customer Service Center GmbH
Europaplatz 3
69115 Heidelberg, Germany

The manufacturer's authorised representative in the EU is Springer Nature Customer Service Centre GmbH, Europaplatz 3, 69115 Heidelberg, Germany. If you have any concerns regarding our products, please contact ProductSafety@springernature.com

Printed and bound by CPI Group (UK) Ltd, Croydon, CR0 4YY
30/09/2026
02225589-0001